ANTONIA FRASER

CHARLES II

—— HIS LIFE AND TIMES ——

ANTONIA FRASER
CHARLES II
HIS LIFE AND TIMES

Picture Research by Julia Brown

Weidenfeld & Nicolson
London

Captions:
Page 1: Charles II carved limewood mirror, the frame showing
the royal arms and motto, among the decorations of foliage,
fruit, crab, lobster and sea serpents.
Page 3: A wooden panel painted with Charles II's coat of
arms, celebrating the Restoration.
Page 6: An elaborate design, gilt and coloured paper, shows
Charles and his bride Catharine of Braganza.

First published in 1979
by George Weidenfeld & Nicolson Ltd
Orion House, 5 Upper St Martin's Lane
London WC2H 9EA

First published in this abridged, illustrated format 1993.

British Library Cataloguing-in-Publication Data
A Catalogue record for this book is available from the
British Library.

ISBN 0-297-83221-2

Editorial Services and Design by Toucan Books Ltd
Printed and bound in Italy

Dedicated to Christopher Falkus

In gratitude for all his encouragement over the years,
including the publication of the original version of
this book in 1979, and his editorial work in
shaping it for this new, shortened, illustrated edition

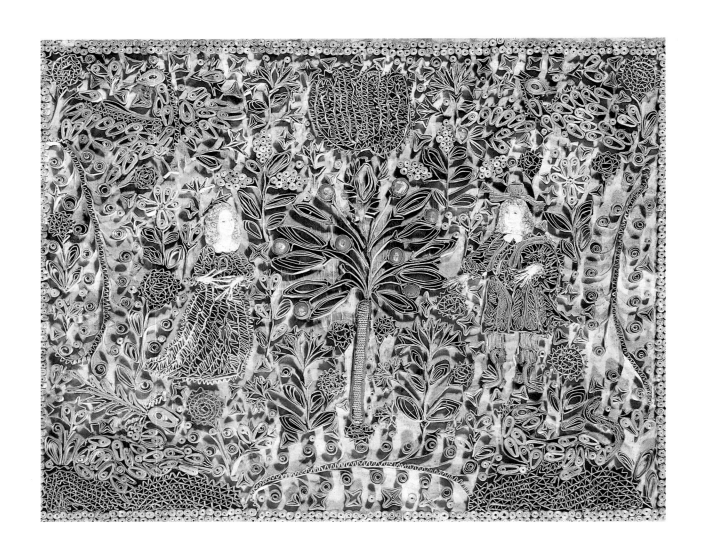

CONTENTS

CHAPTER ONE
SON AND HEIR

On 29 May 1630, at noon, with Venus the star of love and fortune shining high over the horizon, a healthy son was born to the King and Queen of England. Henrietta Maria, wife of Charles I, had presented him with an heir. King Charles was twenty-nine years old, his French wife twenty. He loved her passionately. At the time it seemed like the end of a fairy tale.

The marriage of the baby's parents in May 1625 had brought together a disparate pair – at any rate in terms of religion. The King was not only the supreme governor of the Protestant Church in his own country, but was emotionally committed to Anglicanism. He eschewed equally the Roman Catholic tenets which lay, as it were, beyond the right wing of Anglicanism, and the Puritan practices which increasingly permeated its left. Henrietta Maria on the other hand had been brought up as a pious Roman Catholic, and never abandoned her religion. Her father, the magnificent, dominating Henri Quatre, had deserted the Protestantism of his youth in order to attain the French crown, with the observation, 'Paris is worth a Mass': the French royal family was in future ostentatiously Catholic.

In addition to this mixed religious heritage Charles, the first child in our history to be born heir to all three kingdoms, also enjoyed an appropriately mixed heritage of blood. Through his father he descended from Scottish James, son of that ill-fated enchanter Mary Queen of Scots and the degenerate Darnley. James had married a Danish princess, Anne, daughter of Frederick II and Sophie of

Prince Charles, aged twelve, pictured arming himself at the Battle of Edgehill where he had a narrow escape at the opening engagement of the Civil War. Painting by William Dobson.

Marie de Medici greeted by her daughter Henrietta Maria on her arrival on a visit to St James's Palace. It was through Marie, wife of the great Henry IV of France, that her grandson Charles was to inherit his dark 'Italian' looks.

William Laud, the 'High Church' cleric who became the target of the growing Puritan opposition to both the bishops and the 'Catholic' tendencies of Charles I's Court. Painting by Van Dyck, 1635.

Mecklenbergh-Schwerin. The blood which Charles inherited through his mother was half French and half Italian. So Charles was one-quarter Scots, one-quarter Danish, one-quarter French and one-quarter Italian. His striking physical appearance was even more foreign than his blood. First, he had an Italianate darkness of complexion. His mother wrote to a friend in France that 'he was so dark that she was ashamed of him', and later the sobriquet 'the Black Boy' would be used, still commemorated in English inn signs. Then there was his height. He may have been as much as six feet three inches tall. The effect may be imagined in an age when the average male height, owing to diet and disease, was so much less than today.

It would seem therefore that Charles' individual appearance was a combination of those two bloods least associated with him in the popular imagination – Danish and Italian. The result, attractive as it may be by modern standards, was not much admired at the time. Charles was considered rather peculiar-looking, as he himself was the first to admit, with typical self-deprecation: 'Odd's fish, I am an ugly fellow,' he observed to the painter Lely after inspecting his own portrait.

Those days lay far in the future when, at St James's Palace, Queen Henrietta Maria reached that 'happy hour for herself and us', as one contemporary put it. Her labour began at about four o'clock in the morning. The baby was born shortly before noon. Almost immediately, according to the custom of the time, he was taken from his mother and given to a wet-nurse to be fed. Rockers, all Protestant, stepped forward to the royal cradle: it had been part of Henrietta Maria's marriage contract, carefully laid down, that her children should not be nursed by Catholics.

The baptism, which took place on 27 June, was also according to the rite of the English Church. The ceremony was performed by the Bishop of London, the King's friend and future Archbishop of Canterbury, William Laud. It was a significant choice, for already Laud's name was synonymous with the repression of Puritanism within the English Church. And in 1631, young Charles was handed over to the impeccably Anglican Countess of Dorset, his official governess.

The nursery of King Charles and Queen Henrietta Maria, once established, was soon filled with healthy and charming children. The Queen bore a total of nine children in fourteen years, of whom six survived infancy, a high proportion by the standards of the time. There was Mary, the Princess Royal, born in November 1631. James Duke of York followed in October 1633, and Elizabeth in 1635. Henry

Charles I, Henrietta Maria and their eldest child Prince Charles by Hendrick Pot. The happy family was to be overtaken by events leading to execution, exile and the collapse of monarchy.

Duke of Gloucester was born in 1639, and Henriette-Anne in 1644.

For Charles it was a loving childhood and he enjoyed a great deal of uncritical affection. But as the children moved on their cheerful round, winters at St James's Palace, happy summers at any one of a number of royal palaces such as Greenwich, Hampton Court and Oatlands, their father was playing out his part in a very different kind of drama. For if there was one bad fairy at Charles' christening it was

A painting after Van Dyck, 1637, shows Charles as part of the 'cheerful nursery'. On the left is Mary, the Princess Royal, standing next to James Duke of York. On Charles' left is Princess Elizabeth nursing the baby Princess Anne.

a Puritan sprite. The Puritans were hostile both to the Catholicism of the Queen and to the 'High Church' Anglicanism of the King. And they were increasingly vocal and demanding in the forum of Parliament which had acquired, in the eyes of Parliamentarians, the sole right to grant 'extraordinary' taxation (as opposed to customary revenues from customs duties and legal fines) for the King's policies.

It is difficult to date precisely that moment at which the King's troubles began in

Charles I, Henrietta Maria,
Prince Charles and the Court
at Greenwich Park – one of
the royal residences among the
idyllic round of castles, palaces
and parks which comprised the
Prince's early childhood.
By Adriaen van Staelbent.

earnest. His first great Parliamentary defeat, ending in the acceptance of the Petition of Right, had taken place in June 1628, two years before Charles' birth. In August the King suffered a personal as well as a political blow when his favourite, the Duke of Buckingham – already under pressure from Parliament – was assassinated. The King had accepted the Petition with reluctance, and only because the acute financial demands of his foreign policy left him no choice but to conciliate Parliament. But at the same time he was extremely careful to make it clear that his personal prerogative, that vexed but vital attribute of a British monarch, had been left intact.

The exact nature of the royal prerogative was a subject of running debate throughout the seventeenth century. But in 1628 no one denied its actual existence. In practice the King was generally allowed the sole right to direct foreign policy. More vaguely, he claimed other prerogative rights which would not be clearly established by the time of his death, nor that of his eldest son. It was more to the point that the King had the power to prorogue or to dissolve Parliament without the agreement of the Commons. Prorogation was a form of suspension. Dissolution implied an election and with it the possibility of a differently constituted House of Commons. But neither bound the King to recall Parliament within a specified period.

In the spring of 1629 King Charles I dissolved Parliament after a series of unruly scenes and, as he saw it, 'seditious' speeches from the MPs calling attention to 'unlawful' taxation. Parliament did not sit again until 1640. In the meantime the King governed, or attempted to do so, by use of his prerogative powers without the assent of the Commons. Charles was therefore born into the second year of what was afterwards termed the Eleven Years' Tyranny.

With Parliament in abeyance, there was still no closed season for religious differences. The Puritans can be roughly divided into the Independents (such as Oliver Cromwell), who believed in the privacy of conscience and a general tolerance of sects, and the Presbyterians (including many leading Scottish nobles), who believed in the authority of the elders, and thus the need for conformity. Both factions, while disagreeing with each other fiercely on matters of Church organization, were united against any High Church tendencies in the Church of England. Their particular fear was 'Popery', but since Roman Catholicism was in fact proscribed by the law in England, and the numbers of Catholics were diminishing, their precise target was the right wing of the English Church. The Puritan argument suggested that those guilty of High Church practices might turn into Catholics at any moment.

Political and religious issues were interwoven. For example, it was relevant that those Anglicans who supported the secular authority of the bishops tended to be more favourable to the King. This in turn persuaded the King that Puritanism was to be identified with attacks upon the monarchy as well as upon the Church.

In Scotland, the ritual of the English Church had always been dourly regarded. At least old King James had known, none better, how to deal with that country. King Charles I had been born there, but that was all. Fatally the King and his bishops imposed a new High Church prayer book in Scotland in 1637 which received an ominous response early in the following year when the Scots formed the National Covenant. Those who took its Oath pledged their lives to resist by force the recent innovations in the Church, which they declared to be contrary to the Word of God – and to the spirit of the Reformation. It was a document which in one form or another (for it was extended five years later) would haunt the King's son for the next twenty years.

In the spring of 1638, as the Scottish horizons grew dark with the clouds of approaching war, the young Charles was made a Knight of the Garter and Prince of Wales. The medal struck for the occasion – presciently – showed 'the Royal Oak' under a Prince's Coronet. He was also granted his own household, according to the serene routine of the time, and was established with both a governor, the Earl of Newcastle, and a tutor, Dr Brian Duppa. Newcastle combined a love of sport (he was an expert horseman) with a passion for the arts. His most famous piece of advice was to avoid being too devout, since one can be a good man and a bad king. Like another tip he gave Charles, 'Above all be civil to women', it cannot have had an unwelcome sound to his pupil's ears. Dr Duppa, a protégé of Laud, was a distinguished divine who was by nature both learned and devout. The values which Charles carried into his adult life were those of Newcastle, not Duppa.

It was important for Charles' future that his little world also included the orphaned Duke of Buckingham and his brother Lord Francis Villiers. Indeed, it is impossible to understand the deep bond which existed between Charles and Buckingham in later years – despite the most reckless behaviour on Buckingham's part – unless one remembers this shared childhood and its memories.

By the summer of 1639 the chapter of happiness was nearing its end. The King was taking the high road to Scotland, armed on this occasion not with the Prayer Book but with the sword. The confrontation which ensued was subsequently known as 'the first Bishops' War', and, as the drama unfolded, the King increasingly took his eldest son into his own care and company, associating him with his own decisions. This was partly from the natural habit of the time to take aristocratic boys out of female-dominated society. But in Charles' case the situation was aggravated by the need to prove to the world at large that the Prince of Wales was in no way over-influenced by the Roman Catholic Queen. And in the turbulent times at hand it meant that a secure childhood gave way to a youth marked by a series of traumatic incidents.

The first of these occurred when Charles was ten years old. It concerned the trial of the King's servant Strafford. Thomas Wentworth, later Earl of Strafford,

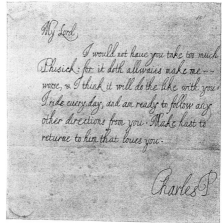

Lord Newcastle, engraved as a warrior. He was an affable gentleman, courteous to both sexes, sports loving and affectionate.

One of Charles' letters to his tutor Lord Newcastle.

A map of Charles I's camp during the first Bishop's War.

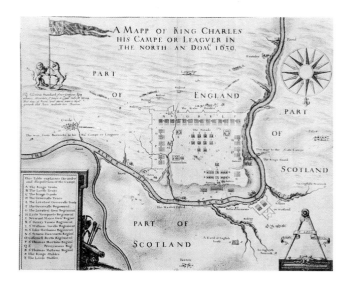

had been sent to Ireland as Lord Deputy in 1633, to try to introduce a semblance of order into those Augean Stables. Now, as the military proceedings of 1639 against the Scots ground into stalemate, Strafford, who had returned from Ireland at the King's request, was moving into the position of the King's chief counsellor. When the King, hobbled by lack of money and lack of political support against the Scots, finally called Parliament in the spring of 1640, it was Strafford who advised him to do so. And when the King dissolved this assembly again in May – hence its historical name of the Short Parliament – it was with the aid of Strafford's practical management. And so, when a further military action in the summer of 1640 resulted in the humiliation of the English forces by the Scots at Newburn, near Newcastle, and a new Parliament became necessary, the King's chief counsellor was a natural target for the Parliamentary opposition.

Thomas Wentworth, later Earl of Strafford, the former critic of Charles I who rose to be his chief minister and thus an object of hatred to the King's Parliamentary opponents. By Van Dyck, 1636.

On 3 November that body to be known as the Long Parliament met for the first time. The intention of the opposition under the great Parliamentary leader John Pym was to demand the resolution of their manifold grievances against the Crown. One of the first of these grievances was embodied in the person of 'Black Tom Tyrant', as Strafford was bitterly designated. It was the Irish association which was fatal. The Irish troops which Strafford was discovered to be offering the King as aid against the Scots became in the minds of the excitable Commons a fearful force of Papist invaders. Strafford was to be the scapegoat for the whole body of the King's unsatisfactory policies, and in March 1641 the Parliamentarians succeeded in bringing him to trial.

Taking place in Westminster Hall, the trial would seem afterwards like an awful dress rehearsal for the ordeal of the King, set on the same stage eight years later. Young Charles attended the seven weeks of proceedings daily. By virtue of his title as Prince of Wales, he sat to the right of his father's throne, wearing the full robes of his rank. The trial itself failed, but immediately afterwards the old lion of Parliament, John Pym, with his young lions at his heels, called for an Act of Attainder. The House of

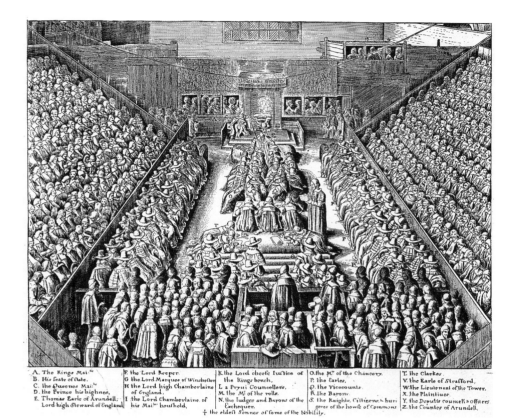

A. The Kings Mai.^{tie}
B. His seate of state.
C. the Queenes Mai.^{tie}
D. the Prince his highnes.
E. Thomas Earle of Arundell, Lord high Steward of England

F. the Lord Keeper.
G. the Lord Marques of Winchester
H. the Lord high Chamberlaine of England.
I. the Lord Chamberlaine of his Mai.^{ties} houshold,

K. the Lord cheefe Iustice of the Kinge bench,
L. 2 Pryui Councellors.
M. the M.^{rs} of the rolls.
N. the Iudges and Barons of the Exchequer.
† the eldest Sonnes of some of the Nobility.

O. the M.^{rs} of the Chancery.
P. the Earles.
Q. the Vicecounts.
R. the Barons.
S. the Knights, Cittizens & burgesses of the howse of Commons

T. the Clarkes.
V. the Earle of Strafford,
W.the Lieutenant of the Tower.
X. the Plaintiuer.
Y. the Deputis councell & officers
Z. the Countes of Arundell.

The celebrated trial of Strafford, engraved by Hollar, 1641. The King sent his son to intercede for his minister's life and proved too weak to prevent the execution of his most able servant.

Commons voted it through. All Strafford's 'sinewy' arguments that he had not committed treason were in vain. The penalty for High Treason was death.

On 2 May the King married off Charles' nine-year-old sister Mary to the twelve-year-old Prince of Orange, son of the Stadtholder of the Netherlands. It was hoped that Parliament would be appeased by this Protestant but otherwise unremarkable match. Parliament was not appeased. Nor was the anti-Papist mob thronging Whitehall. By 10 May the King could hesitate no longer. The royal assent to Strafford's execution was given.

The next day the King decided to send Charles down to the House of Lords with a desperate yet somehow embarrassed message. Could not Strafford 'fulfil the natural course of his life in a close imprisonment'? Even the postscript after the King's signature had a rather shabby sound to it: 'and if Strafford must die, it were charity to reprieve him until Saturday'. Armed with this paper, the ten-year-old Prince of Wales failed to persuade Parliament to stay its hand. Strafford was executed the next day.

Charles' sister Mary, aged nine, married Prince William of Orange of the Netherlands, aged twelve. This Protestant match of 2 May 1642 was partly to appease the Parliamentary opposition to Strafford, but in this it failed. The marriage produced a son who became William III of Great Britain. Van Dyck's wedding portrait.

Events now moved swiftly. Parliament put a series of humiliating political and religious propositions to the King, including provisions for control of the army and, of course, safeguards for the Protestant upbringing of Charles and the young royal family. In October 1641 there were squabbles with the Commons about Charles' education: one faction demanded that only 'safe' people (religiously safe, that is, not Popish) should be allowed near him. The arguments were still going on in January 1642. That was the month in which the King, failing in his attempt to arrest five Members of the Commons, was humiliatingly rebuffed by the Speaker of the House himself. So finally he left the capital.

The following six months of the year were spent by both sides, King and Parliament, in preparations for war. The King reacted to the Commons' threats concerning his son by keeping Charles more closely with him. In fact, Charles would remain at his father's side for the next three years, and, together with his brother James, was with his father on that ominous day, 22 August 1642, when the standard of war was raised at Nottingham Castle. The King's glittering entourage included their Palatine cousin, the twenty-two-year-old Prince Rupert, a spirited young fellow with theories about warfare which would shortly be tested. The whole scene must have recalled the days of ritual chivalry.

At Edgehill in the following October came the reality of Charles' first battle, the opening contest of the Civil War. On the morning of the battle he and his brother were left in the charge of Dr William Harvey, the famous physician, and told in effect to keep out of mischief. Gradually the traditional ennui of war became too much for Dr Harvey, who surreptitiously took a book out of his pocket. He was only restored to a sense of his surroundings by the impact of a cannon ball grazing the ground beside him. Then and only then did Dr Harvey hastily move his royal charges away to safety.

The evening's well-known incident is recounted in various different versions, but there is general

agreement that the Prince of Wales and the Duke of York came within an ace of being captured. A body of Parliamentary horses was seen riding down on them, but unaware of their identity, the little royal party moved towards this body as if towards saviours. Suddenly the Parliamentarians were recognized for what they were. 'I fear them not!' shouted Charles, whipping his pistol out of his holster. Suddenly one Parliamentary trooper broke ranks and rode towards them. Fortunately, at this dramatic moment the Prince was rescued from the consequences of his own hardihood, and of his aides' folly, by the appearance of a Royalist on a good mount; he proceeded to pole-axe the trooper.

For all this drama, Edgehill was generally regarded as a draw. Both sides recoiled to regroup their existing forces and recruit the vital new men needed for a more decisive outcome. The King headed with his sons for Oxford. The loyalty of Oxford was as carefully preserved as that of Cambridge was fractured. The famous

Prince Rupert, Charles' cousin and the dashing soldier whose exploits seemed at first to be winning the war for the Royalist side.
By Gerrit van Honthorst.

A miniature of the Prince aged thirteen by David des Granges. A year later he would be sent to the West Country in nominal command of the King's forces and never see his father again.

dreaming spires of the University dreamt, if anything, of a monarchical victory. The King was quickly able to set up a Parliament of his own. Its acts would subsequently be castigated as illegal by that other, so-called true Parliament of Westminster. Nevertheless, at the time, there were many Royalists who considered the Oxford Parliament, enjoying the King's backing, as the valid assembly.

Charles remained at his father's side during his various wartime peregrinations until a violent attack of measles laid him low. The disease also went to his eyes: he suffered from conjunctivitis for some time afterwards. But he had recovered sufficiently to attend the inconclusive Battle of Copredy Bridge in June 1644. After this the King learnt of the battle at Marston Moor in distant Yorkshire, a Parliamentary victory. Charles was also present at the second Battle of Newbury in October. Newbury was one of the few engagements of the Civil War in which the great Parliamentary soldier Oliver Cromwell took part that did not result in an outstanding victory for Parliament. The reason was a divided Parliamentary command and the growing struggle between the political and military arms of the party – a struggle which would last until the formation of the New Model Army the following spring. At the time the action was botched, and the King allowed to escape back to Oxford. Here he resided, more or less secure, for over a year.

In recognition of his growing stature, the Prince of Wales was now given his own Council of advisers. The other royal children were not faring so well. Mary, the child bride of William of Orange, was not happy in her adopted country. Elizabeth, because she was delicate, and Henry, because he was a baby, remained in the royal nurseries in London. Here the little captives – as they quickly became, cut off from both father and mother – suffered at first from the general lack of funds. At times there was hardly enough to eat. Later they were encumbered with alien Presbyterian attendants at the orders of Parliament.

Even marking time in Oxford, Charles, the eldest brother, was infinitely luckier. Now his freedom was to be extended. As the war news reaching Oxford worsened, the King began to feel that the moment to separate himself physically from his heir had arrived. Besides, an experience of responsibility would 'unboy' Charles. Early in 1645 he was made nominal General of the Western Association – a conglomerate of the four most western counties. Here the royal cause was in unnecessary disarray owing to internal disputes. Charles was given a new Council by the King. It included Sir Edward Hyde and John (created Lord) Colepepper. On 4 March 1645, Charles left Oxford, in the pouring rain, for the West. His younger brother James, at

Charles' armour, to be seen at the Tower of London. Charles is not best known as a warrior but in the Civil Wars, and most particularly at the Battle of Worcester, he proved a valiant fighter.

eleven, was considered too young to go with him and remained cooped up in Oxford. Charles would never see his father again. But of that, as of the other griefs which lay ahead, the new General of the Western Association was fortunately unaware.

It was the King's intention, which seemed feasible from Oxford, that Charles should remain in safety in Bristol. Having been set up as a puppet commander, he should continue to act as such. The puppet master was to be Sir Edward Hyde.

Hyde, later Earl of Clarendon, is a central figure in the story of Charles, in youth, early manhood and the first years of his restored kingship. Originally a lawyer, in 1640 Hyde was to be found attacking prerogative courts, royal judges and Laudian bishops. He even voted for Strafford's attainder. Later he became an advocate for a new kind of Royalism, based on an Anglican Church, both liberated and strengthened, and as such was transformed into not only a defender but also a firm friend of Charles I. The relationship with the King's son would draw to a close nearly twenty-five years after this western foray. It ended with Clarendon telling a middle-aged monarch 'twenty times a day' that he was lazy and not fit to govern. It ended with an ageing statesman dismissed by an apparently ungrateful king.

Hyde, at the beginning of their close association, viewed himself as one deputed to supervise – and, where necessary, restrain – the young Prince of Wales. He was a man of extreme gravity of character even in his younger years, the sort of gravity which is quickly taken for pomposity by the young. Charles on the other hand was being encouraged to see himself as having a useful and expanding role to play. Hyde liked to guide by disapproval: Charles liked to learn by encouragement; it was never an ideal combination.

Some of Hyde's disapproval was certainly incurred by another fairly natural piece of youthful folly. In Bridgwater Charles encountered once more his former nurse, Mrs Christabella Wyndham, wife of the governor of the town. To her should probably be accorded the honour of having first seduced the young Prince of Wales. By the sexual standards of the time, to play such a gracious role in the life of a young prince was more of a privilege than an offence. But where Mrs Wyndham did overstep the mark, according to contemporary mores, was by showing gross familiarity to the Prince of Wales in public. In doing so, she greatly shocked and annoyed Hyde. Furthermore Mrs Wyndham, in Hyde's view, distracted Charles from the conduct of his own business. Yet Charles did apply himself, as even Hyde admitted, 'with great ingenuity' to the affairs of the Council.

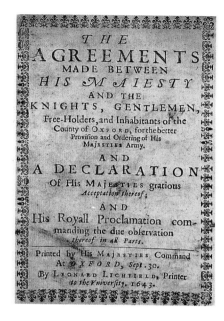

The proclamation formalizing Charles I's decision to establish his headquarters at Oxford. The town was fiercely 'Royalist' and figures again as such in the reign of Charles II.

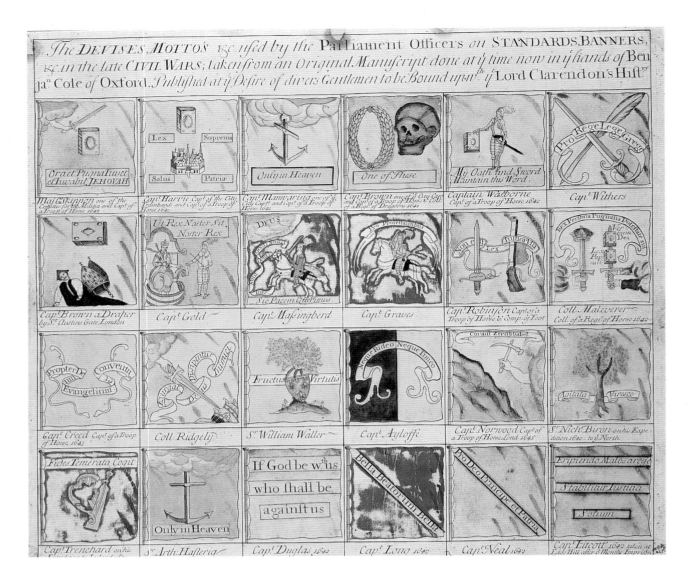

Standards and banners of some of the Parliamentary officers ranged against the King, 1642. The Parliamentary forces included members of the nobility as well as prosperous gentry and in fact their economic resources outweighed those of the King.

The leading Parliamentary commanders. Sir Thomas Fairfax was the supreme commander but he could not reconcile himself to the King's execution.

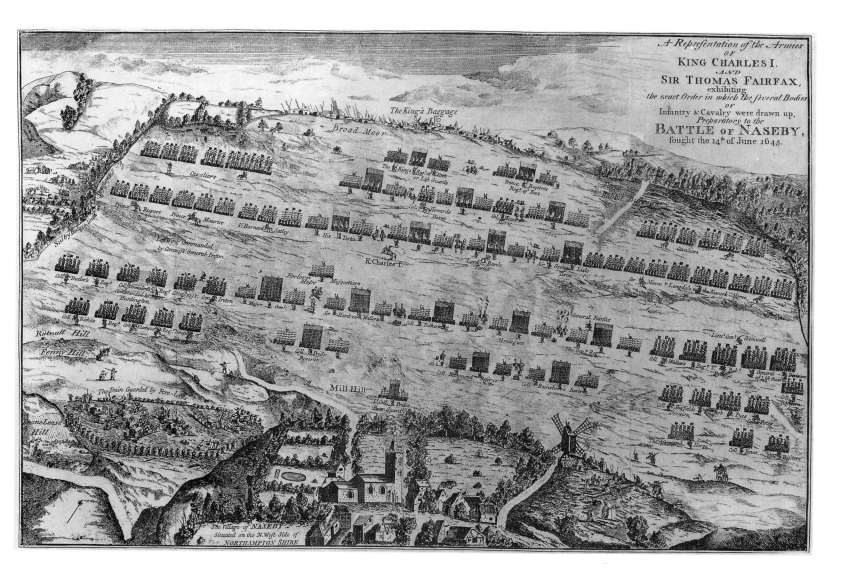

A Reprefentation of the Armies
OF
KING CHARLES I.
AND
SIR THOMAS FAIRFAX,
exhibiting
the exact Order in which the feveral Bodies
OF
Infantry & Cavalry were drawn up,
Preparatory to the
BATTLE OF NASEBY,
fought the 14th of June 1645.

But petty feuds among the Royalists continued to proliferate, while elsewhere in England a revolutionary war machine, the New Model Army, was being assembled by the King's enemies. On 14 June the New Model Army clashed with the King at Naseby, in Northamptonshire: this, their paramount victory, extinguished his military hopes. Not only that, but the King's secret papers, revealing his 'treacherous' Irish dealings, were discovered. The Royalist cause in England was virtually lost. A month later, to complete the pattern of disaster, the army in the West was totally defeated by the Parliamentary commander Fairfax and the New Model Army at Langport, not far from Bridgwater.

The Prince by this time had moved back from Bridgwater to Bristol, and then after an outbreak of plague out to 'fine sweet' Barnstaple. But he was clearly no longer safe anywhere in the West. Once Prince Rupert had surrendered Bristol after a fierce siege, the question was not so much whether the Prince of Wales should be evacuated, but when he should go. Above all, it had to be resolved in which country he should take refuge.

14 June 1645. A detailed picture of the battle lines, with their commanders, drawn up before the decisive Battle of Naseby. It proved a triumph for Cromwell's New Model Army recently created on principles of military and religious discipline.

More was at stake than Charles' own safety. France, roughly speaking, represented the foreign Catholic interest, and the influence of Queen Henrietta Maria. Scotland stood for Presbyterianism (and therefore some kind of compromise on behalf of the Anglican King), but also for the British interest, since there it could legitimately be argued that the Prince of Wales was still on British soil. The problem of Ireland was that it was beset by so many different factions at this date that it was difficult to know whose interests would be served by the arrival there of the Prince of Wales. Perhaps distant and Protestant Denmark was the best solution.

At first the King himself took the line that 'France must be the place, not Scotland nor Denmark'. By December he had changed his mind: Denmark was now his first choice. Hyde remained strongly of the opinion that Scotland or Ireland (both British soil) were the obvious sites. The King began to bombard his son with letters to the contrary. The situation was further complicated by the fact that Queen Henrietta Maria herself had entered the fray. She was urgently demanding that her son should join her in France, in order to stir Cardinal Mazarin, the effective ruler of the country, to action on the King's behalf.

But throughout the autumn the Prince's entourage had been pushed further west into Cornwall itself. And as the campaign in the West reached its last stages the feared General Cromwell, the victor of Naseby, plunged into it.

On 15 February 1646 the final action of the campaign was fought at Torrington; two days later Charles with his Council took refuge at Pendennis Castle on the Falmouth peninsula. The Council hastily decided to favour a retreat to the Scilly Isles, off the Cornish coast. At ten o'clock at night on Monday, 2 March Charles went aboard the frigate *Phoenix* from Land's End, accompanied by Sir Edward Hyde and John Colepepper. He landed at St Mary's in the Scilly Isles on the afternoon of 4 March. It was exactly a year since he had left Oxford.

In one sense the journey itself was delightful and the consequences for Charles' future character radical. For it was during this brief halcyon trip aboard the *Phoenix*, in the course of which the Prince insisted on taking the helm himself, that Charles discovered that joyous taste for the sea which never deserted him, and was to unite him emotionally to so many of his subjects. But that was the pleasant side of the picture. Conditions on the island were rough, food inadequate, and since no one had been expecting the little court to arrive, accommodation lamentable. It was not long before the argument about where the Prince should now seek refuge began to rage again with renewed vigour. Hyde and Colepepper both voted for

Jersey, still British soil. The Queen continued to advocate France. The King, in beleaguered Oxford, was out of contact. At the end of April he fled from Oxford to what he mistakenly believed would be the protection of the Scottish army. As a result he was still further embroiled in political intrigue, still further distanced from his son.

It was not until 16 April that Charles set sail again, and then the destination was Jersey, not France. There was not much the Queen could do about the decision except bewail it, and the loyal islanders were granted the sight of Prince Charles dining in state. With great elegance, Charles accepted a gift of 1,500 pistoles (that is, money) from them – 'having not 20 in the world'. Soon Charles was able to set up a miniature court, according to the gracious tradition in which he had been raised.

Another pleasant aspect of that summer interlude was the relationship Charles formed with Marguerite, daughter of Sir George Carteret, governor of Jersey. This is Charles' first recorded love affair (as opposed to sexual experience) and his inamorata was about twenty, four years older than himself. The setting also seems appropriate. Love and the sea were two splendid new discoveries.

But they did not preserve Charles' summer from continued storms over his residency. Queen Henrietta Maria had succeeded in suborning Charles' attendant John Colepepper when he visited her for money and supplies. Hyde continued to maintain stoutly that it would be the greatest possible mistake for the Prince of Wales to desert British soil, but in the course of the summer the Prince of Wales was won round to his mother's point of view. This was not solely due to the vehemence with which Colepepper argued the case.

The King had become convinced that Charles should join the Queen in France, particularly since he had heard rumours of schemes afoot to make the young James Duke of York – a Parliamentary captive since the fall of Oxford – a puppet monarch. By 17 June the King was longing to hear that Charles was safe with his mother. Of course he was adamant that Charles must continue to protect the Church of England, stoutly and for ever. It was a strong directive, which lingered in Charles' mind throughout the years of exile. But that summer neither King nor Prince saw the maintenance of episcopacy as incompatible with Scottish and French aid. So the fateful decision was taken to embark at last for France.

Hyde had put every argument and failed. He had also correctly foreseen the suicidal divisions which the departure to France would spread within the Royalist ranks. Armed with melancholy thoughts, Hyde continued to lurk in Jersey, a prophet without honour, as the Prince of Wales, more cheerfully, sailed off on his French adventure.

Children: The Future of the Family

Nothing shows the development of the solid class of gentry better than the growing volume of family portraits commissioned increasingly in the sixteenth, seventeenth and eighteenth centuries from a country and urban, but by no means aristocratic, elite. At one level we can see their presence in the House of Commons and politics generally. At another in the complex web of property deals, marriage portions, and so on which placed their children at the centre of their families' future prospects and ambitions.

A highly decorative portrait of the mid-seventeenth century; the boy is shown in full-length embroidered coat, with a dalmatian on a Turkish carpet.

Sir Robert Vyner and his family, painted by John Michael Wright in 1673. The sheer number of such family paintings, increasing throughout and beyond Charles II's reign, cannot help indicating the confidence felt by many in the stability of future generations.

A delicate drawing of a young
girl by Peter Lely, foremost
painter of the reign of
Charles II.

James, the young fourth Earl of
Salisbury with his sister Lady
Catharine Cecil painted by
J. M. Wright c. 1669. The
inheritance of title, as with
that of an estate, was of course
a preoccupation of this age and
made the 'son and heir' so
prized.

In an age of high infant

mortality, familes were

always vulnerable.

Lely's graceful painting of a
girl with a parrot, 1670.
A century or so earlier parrots
were sometimes called the
'Devil's Bird,' objects of terror
to some, because of their
startling ability to talk.

CHAPTER TWO
INHERITANCE

The French Court had expressed in advance a flattering desire for the company of the Prince of Wales. Yet far from being greeted with open arms, Charles was not even officially received by the young King Louis XIV, his first cousin on his mother's side, for several weeks after his arrival. So Charles kicked his heels and resumed his long-interrupted relationship with his mother.

Henrietta Maria, living in the old palace of Saint-Germain, was in no fit state to handle a relationship with an adolescent son. Distraught, impecunious and possessive, her problems ranged from the financial to the emotional. She was paid a small pension of twelve hundred francs a day by the French government, but sent most of it abroad; in the meantime her love and concern for her afflicted husband racked her daily.

Officially, Charles himself received no money at all. This was a matter of policy. It was thought to be injurious for the Prince of Wales to appear as a pensioner of a foreign government. Therefore 'a mean addition' was made to the sum paid to Henrietta Maria. For funds Charles was expected to apply to her. It was of course a

Oliver Cromwell, painted by Robert Walker possibly in 1649.

Louis XIV, eight years younger than Charles, was to prove an important and sometimes dominating influence during Charles' reign.

George Villiers, Duke of Buckingham, Charles' playmate in the nursery and later mercurial companion in exile and at Court after the Restoration. Painting by J. M. Wright, 1660.

situation which was equally injurious in another way – to the relationship between mother and son.

Perhaps this relationship was doomed even if Henrietta Maria's agitated hands had not been left clutching the purse-strings. For one thing, the Prince of Wales could hardly be expected to regress into youth without demur. At sixteen he was of an age when many kings took over the reins of power. And yet the pattern of life which was now imposed upon him was at best adolescent. His childhood friend Buckingham was once more at his side. The two boys were allotted tutors but it was hardly surprising under the circumstances if they got a reputation for idleness. It is also worth recording that somehow or other Charles acquired 'a great compass of knowledge': we know this not only from the diarist John Evelyn but from the normally critical Bishop Burnet, the Scottish historian and author of the invaluable *History of His Own Time*. Like most young people, Charles did not want to be driven to study: but he was obviously capable of great application when his interest was aroused.

This was also the period blamed by the sober – and the priggish – in later years for inculcating Charles' taste for 'gallantry', though all the stories of Charles' 'debauchery' in exile must be treated with extreme caution. At the time it suited the Parliamentary book to spread such propaganda. Later the truth was embroidered, in the light of his subsequent career as a gallant monarch. The facts show him to have been really quite moderate in his tastes for a bachelor prince, by the standards of the time.

Certainly, as a boy of sixteen, the frolics which he enjoyed with Buckingham were comparatively mild. The one person who genuinely charmed him at this point, the delightful, tender Isabelle-Angélique, Duchesse de Châtillon, widow of the Admiral Coligny, was exactly the kind of woman to appeal to an inexperienced young man. Everyone adored Bablon, as she was nicknamed; her wit and softness captivated the entire French court. Alas for the youthful Prince, the affair was all the more romantic for being platonic. Henrietta Maria suggested that one solution to the royal finances would be to court the famous heiress, Anne-Marie Louise de Montpensier, known as the Grande Mademoiselle. Charles applied himself to the

La Grande Mademoiselle, the high-born heiress to whom Charles paid court in deference to his mother's wishes. A lack of enthusiasm was reciprocal. By P. Bourguignon.

task without enthusiasm. For one thing, he declared hopelessly that he really could not speak French. So the sweet nothings which might have made Anne-Marie overlook her cavalier's lack of fortune remained firmly stuck behind the language barrier.

The mixture of enforced idleness and poverty, stirred from time to time by a dash of bad news from England, made the court of Queen Henrietta Maria a fertile breeding-ground for quarrels and intrigues. The personalities of those involved did not help. There was Henry Lord Jermyn, Henrietta Maria's closest adviser, who was a man equipped neither with political experience nor, what was worse, with natural political understanding. The calibre of another adviser, George Lord Digby (later Earl of Bristol) was not of the finest either. Hyde accused him 'of perplexing and obstructing every thing in which he had no hand'. In August Prince Rupert appeared

Above: 'gley-eyed' Argyll, the implacable Covenanter whose dour disapproval did so much to alienate Charles from the Scots. Right: the Duke of Hamilton, leader of the 'Engagers', who sought a compromise between the Presbyterian Scots and the traditional Royalists. Below: James Graham, Marquis of Montrose, whose heroic efforts to raise the Highlands for the Stuarts led to his execution at the hands of the Covenanters.

at the Queen's court. Charles welcomed his cousin warmly. Nevertheless, the arrival of this experienced man of war only served to augment the disputes which had already arisen there because of clashes of personality. With the waiting and quarrelling, Charles' spirits sank. Except that he had youth and health, there was not much to be said for his two desultory years at the Court of France.

Meanwhile, at home, events were moving dangerously. Throughout the summer and autumn of 1646 the King was still under so-called Scottish protection. In January the following year he was handed over to Parliament, and the Scots, regarded by many as traitors as a result, retreated back across their borders. In June 1647 the King was abducted once more, albeit peacefully, at the hands of the Army; but in the autumn the Army leaders, headed by Cromwell, allowed the King to slip through their fingers. This was very likely deliberate. They were beginning to need support against their own extremists, the agitators in the Army ranks, and toyed with the possibility of working out some agreement with him. The King got as far as the Isle of Wight, in effect a prisoner, but from there began to negotiate once more with the Scots – and incidentally the Irish as well, although that was kept a secret.

The Scots were by now unhelpfully divided amongst themselves. There were those who adhered most strictly to the precepts set out in the National Covenant and wished to impose its oath upon everybody else. These Covenanters were headed by Argyll, dour, canny and a man of immense political perception. Then there was the group, also Presbyterian, which was more in sympathy with the King. Headed by the Duke of Hamilton and his brother, these men would come to be known as the Engagers after they had gone towards a private agreement, or Engagement, with Charles I. Hamilton was less tricky, but also less able, than Argyll. Thirdly, there were the followers of the great Royalist general Montrose: of all the Scots Montrose was a straightforward King's man.

Yet, for all their divisions, the Scots as a nation had enormous advantages as possible crusaders to rescue the King. They had an army, and they were the King's subjects. By December the King's secret negotiations with Hamilton's party were moving towards agreement on a possible Scottish army of rescue. The King promised to condemn all those Independent non-conformist sects detested equally by the 'Engagers' and their Covenanter comrades. Presbyterianism was to be established for three years.

Abroad however the line was still taken that the Scots were but one possible arrow in the royal quiver. France was unforthcoming, but there was also Holland. Here the eldest sister of Charles, Mary, and her youthful husband, the Prince of Orange, were loyally anxious to help her distressed father. Yet the Prince of Orange was much restricted. His position as Stadtholder of Holland was ambivalent: he was not, for example, an independent monarch and Holland was only one of those provinces which together constituted the United Provinces, each of which had its own Stadtholder. Nevertheless, William, together with the Duke of Lorraine, raised troops on his father-in-law's behalf – between five hundred and a thousand men – and encamped them at Borkum; he also chartered and equipped some ships at Amsterdam, and spent money buying munitions for the Scottish army.

It was natural under the circumstances that, like the other young and spirited Royalists, Charles Prince of Wales should prefer the prospect of action based on Holland to inaction based on France. By the beginning of 1648 Henrietta Maria herself had come round to that point of view and, still treating her son as one who could be despatched hither and thither without too much consultation, sent him off to Calais on the French border, to await developments. But here Mazarin stepped in and obstinately blocked the young Prince's progress, forbidding him to leave France. It was a time of exceptional frustration for Charles.

Meanwhile in England some at least of the Army and Parliamentary leaders were becoming ruefully aware of the underhand nature of their King. When rumours of the King's secret agreement with the Scots leaked out, the Army and the Independents in Parliament were together confirmed in their disgust. Negotiations with the King were formally broken off at the beginning of the year.

In fact the King's intrigues appeared to have had a successful outcome: they had combined Royalists and Engagers, which culminated in a Scottish invasion of England. This, the Second Civil War, was blamed by the Army leaders on the King's double-dealing: he earned from them the unpleasant sobriquet of 'the man of blood'.

By now the Engagers in Scotland were longing for the éclat of the Prince's presence. Charles, the boy who, at the age of twelve, had drawn his pistol at Edgehill and shouted, 'I fear them not!', was still kept prudently in reserve. Yet the moment of decision could not be much longer delayed. On 9 March a heated debate took place in the Prince's Council. The Queen had given way and agreed to his departure if, of course, this was permitted by Mazarin. Hyde's known views were overruled. At the end of the meeting 'the Prince's resolution was taken without more ceremony to come into Scotland'. By 23 March his offer was known in Edinburgh and on 1 May the Duke of Hamilton, the Earl of Lauderdale and three other Engagers formally requested the arrival of the Prince of Wales. On 30 May Charles himself wrote back in the most flattering terms that he was 'inexpressibly desirous of himself and impatient to be amongst them'.

Nevertheless, the Prince of Wales did not arrive in Scotland. By August, when the Scottish army passed lumberingly into England, he had still not arrived. His part in the Second Civil War was totally, not to say fatally, mismanaged by his elders and advisers. For what now transpired, put briefly, was the re-emergence of all the old worries in Royalist circles about the Scots. Instead of permitting the Prince to depart, his advisers sent off renewed enquiries concerning the use of an English prayer book in his private devotions, and similar questions which were surely of little import compared to the vast issue at stake – the defeat of the Parliamentary Army. On 25 June Cardinal Mazarin did indeed release Charles. Now, if ever, was the moment at which Charles should have joined the Scottish Engagers under their leader the Duke of Hamilton. The Scots were about to invade England. The presence of the Prince of Wales at its head, as the Scots themselves fully realized, would have enabled this force to present itself as a monarchical army of liberation – rather than an invading body of England's unpopular neighbours, the Scots.

But Charles, on leaving France, had been re-routed to Holland by the news that part of the English fleet had revolted against Parliament. At first this seemed

wonderful news. At Helvoetsluys Charles found the rebellious sailors, and also his younger brother James, whom he had not encountered for over three years, since he left Oxford. But alas, the revolt of these ships not only provided an additional and fatal motive for delay in joining the Scottish army, it also provoked a coolness between the royal brothers. For James, with joy, had placed himself at their head. He was after all titular High Admiral, and enjoying his first measure of liberty since his dramatic escape, dressed in women's clothes, in April: he naturally wished to spread his wings. But these wings his elder brother now proceeded smartly to clip. James was ejected from his self-appointed post of admiral 'much to his mortification'.

Charles I and James Duke of York, painted by Peter Lely. After Charles left his father at Oxford, he would not see his brother James until, three years later, they were reunited in dramatic circumstances in exile.

A portrait of Charles from the studio of Adriaen Hanneman, belonging to the period of his early command.

Despite the temporary rift between the brothers, the fleet, which had arrived 'full of anger, hatred and disdain', was restored to discipline and on 17 July Charles set sail. By 24 July the fleet was off Yarmouth.

Meanwhile, matters had already progressed in the North. Hamilton had actually crossed the border on 8 July. The Covenanters however did not join him and remained in Scotland, like so many Achilles sulking in their tents. The Royalists in northern England also failed to join in with the so-called Scottish army of liberation. The Scottish army's reputation for plunder, as it zig-zagged uneasily south, completed the sorry picture.

In the South, Charles, at the head of his newly acquired fleet, showed resolution and courage. It was born of a surge of new Royalist optimism, since he was in no position to appreciate how disastrously the northern situation was deteriorating. It was certainly in Charles' mind that he might soon be in a position to rescue the King, still in his Isle of Wight fastness, if this naval superiority was maintained.

At this point the Scots reminded Charles strongly of their prior strategic claims. On 10 August an emissary from the Committee of the Estates, in the shape of the Earl of Lauderdale, arrived in order to persuade Charles to fulfil his promise and join them. Yet, even at this stage, both sides continued to argue out the points of dispute – mainly religious – between them. Neither the Prince nor Lauderdale were aware that as these discussions on the finer points of Presbyterianism raged, General Cromwell was sweeping down on the hapless Scots.

They had reached Lancashire; he approached them across the Pennines. It was a dramatic tactical manoeuvre, the finest of Cromwell's career. It met its reward at the Battle of Preston on 17 August, at which Cromwell defeated the numerically far superior Royalists by pouncing on them from the rear.

The Second Civil War was in effect at an end, and with it had perished the Engagers' authority in Scotland. Ironically, Charles had in fact finally accepted Lauderdale's terms only the day before Preston. But it was now Lauderdale who was unable to return to a Scotland newly dominated by the Kirk, the Covenanters, and 'gley-eyed' (squinting) Argyll. Charles himself had little alternative but to head back to Holland. There, for the next six months he was, with his brother James, more or less dependent on the personal charity of the Prince of Orange.

It was a curious time in Charles' life, during which cares were not unalleviated by pleasures. The Hague itself was not a bad place in which to take up residence. Its cultural life flourished. While Amsterdam remained the commercial capital, bolstered by the prosperity brought by commerce and industry, Holland's painters, philosophers and theologians enjoyed the free and argumentative atmosphere of The Hague.

This was a time of development for Charles personally. At last he was free of his mother's apron strings. With James to care for, he moved to a position as head of the family – or those members of it who were at liberty, including his sister Mary. It had to be faced that Mary had not grown up into a particularly agreeable young woman, showing no tact whatsoever to the Dutch or her Dutch husband. Yet in the autumn of 1648 her devotion helped to support Charles' growing feeling of authority over his relations. And this family was in the process of being extended, on one side of the blanket at least, by the pregnancy of Charles' mistress Lucy Walter. The character of this straightforward young lady later became surrounded by myths. The truth about Lucy, 'brown, beautiful and bold', as John Evelyn called her, was that she was not a whore, as one legend suggests. She was not even of low birth, as the enemies of her son Monmouth would declare in later years. Lucy Walter's own mother was a niece of the Earl of Carbery; she herself came of a perfectly respectable Welsh family, hence her appealing, dark-eyed Celtic looks. On the other hand, she was certainly not sufficiently grand to be the chosen bride of the Prince of Wales.

Lucy Walter, the mistress who gave birth to the future Duke of Monmouth and whose degenerate ways led Charles to concur in the kidnapping of his son to protect him from her influence.

Englands Miraculous Preservation Emblematically Described, Erected for a perpetuall MONVMENT to Posterity.

One of the innumerable political sketches of the Civil War period shows the English Ship of State, guarded by the righteous figures of the Parliamentary commanders, resisting the assaults of assorted cavaliers, clerics and characters of easy virtue.

The child afterwards known as James Duke of Monmouth but first called James Crofts, after his guardian Lord Crofts, was born on 9 April 1649.

Hyde was now back at Charles' side. He had arrived at The Hague, exhausted from sea-sickness, continuing to preach against the Scottish involvement. On hearing of the previous Lauderdale agreement, disrupted by circumstances, he wrote to Henrietta Maria that, if another such concordat was proposed, he would have to move to another part of her service. He was thus hardly a figure of reconciliation. This meant that there were vital months of delay and indecision. And time and tide round the Isle of Wight had not waited. In England, divisions between Parliament and Army grew daily more pronounced. On 18 September a Parliamentary delegation arrived at Newport on the Isle of Wight in a final effort to negotiate with the King, animated not least by a wish to fend off the encroachments of the Army on their own authority. The King professed himself in principle prepared to make concessions, but although these abortive negotiations were known as the Treaty of Newport in the language of the time, no such treaty in our sense ever existed. And the King made it clear in a private letter that he had no intention of honouring it even if it had been concluded.

There was often a gap of some weeks between events in England and the Prince of Wales hearing what had taken place. One striking example of this was Colonel Pride's forcible purge of Parliament on 6 December. All those members who did not bow to the Army's increasingly radical demands – including the trial of the King – were ejected: a 'rump' of under sixty members was left. This meant that the Army leaders, including Oliver Cromwell, the victor of the Second Civil War newly returned from Scotland, and his son-in-law Henry Ireton, were in virtual control, with the aid of this Rump Parliament to carry out their behests. On the day of Pride's Purge the King was taking freezing walks along the shore of the Solent, Henrietta Maria crouched in poverty and misery at the equally cold palace of Saint-Germain, and Charles himself was by now at Breda, an ancient stronghold at the confluence of the Mark and the Pra, just north of today's Belgian border. He had decided to make the move, as the situation in Holland grew increasingly difficult. For all the amity of the Prince of Orange, an individual, even a royal one, could do little. The Dutch were embarrassed and slightly hostile.

Of Charles' counsellors at Breda not only Hyde, but the Marquess of Ormonde, still concentrated on the prospect of an Irish venture. The presence of Ormonde at the Prince's side at Breda was in itself reassuring. This splendid man of enormous vitality was head of the Anglo-Norman family of Butler. For the time being, therefore, with the experienced Hyde and the stable Ormonde to head them, the pro-Irish party of Charles' advisers was in the ascendant. As for Charles at Breda, much was traditionally expected of a royal prince in the way of benevolence and charity – whatever his fortunes. Desperately, his suffering followers (who had of course suffered in the royal cause) assumed that their prince or monarch could still exercise his ancient role as a fatherly protector, though in reality he was a provider who could not provide.

At Breda in December there was stringency, a certain amount of hope, a great deal of waiting. Elsewhere the pace was moving ever faster, but there was not much that Charles could have done at this point. He could not reach his father. He did not even know where his father was now held. In fact on 1 December the King was removed by the Army from his retreat at Carisbrooke on the Isle of Wight. He was confined first of all at Hurst Castle, a grim and isolated fortress on the Hampshire bank of the Solent, near Lymington – he observed later that he was leaving the best castle in England for the worst. A few days later, following Pride's Purge of the House of Commons, the Army officially seized power. On 17 December the King was taken at their orders to Windsor Castle.

About this time Charles at Breda was receiving his father's letters written from Carisbrooke at the end of the previous month. One particular letter was long and full of sage advice, couched in beautifully rounded phrases. Its final words were prophetic. 'We know not but this may be the last time we may speak to you or the world publicly ... To conclude, if God give you success, use it humbly and far from revenge. If He restore you upon hard conditions, whatever you promise, keep.'

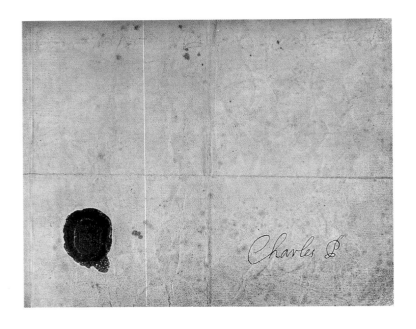

The famous blank sheet of paper, signed by Charles and once thought to be an invitation to Parliament to insert any conditions they liked if they would spare his father's life.

Charles returned to the Court at The Hague for Christmas, and it was a paradox that life there during that brief but festive season was cheerful while in England Christmas had been banished from the calendar, as being Popish and undesirable. It was not until 13 January that Charles was informed that the trial of his father was going ahead. The news was horrific enough – the trial of a reigning monarch by his subjects administered a shock wave throughout Europe. But at this point Charles did not seriously envisage his father's life being in danger. Deposition, a lifetime's incarceration: these were the possibilities, frightful enough in themselves. Charles wrote immediately to General Sir Thomas Fairfax. The letter was useless in an England now totally dominated by the revolutionary junta. Indeed a letter written by Henrietta Maria asking to be allowed to be near her husband, 'in the uttermost extremity', was not even read – it lay sealed for thirty-three years.

On 20 January 1649 the trial of King Charles I opened in Westminster Hall – the sombre scene of Strafford's ordeal eight years earlier. Two days later the Prince of Wales seemed to have realized for the first time that his father's life was actually in

Charles I, painted by Edward Bower supposedly during his trial.

danger. On 23 January one of the Prince's attendants, Boswell, pleaded in French on the King's behalf in front of the States-General. He was horrified to have to tell them, began Boswell, that an English prince came before them, seeking intercession for the life of the King his father. As a result of this personal appeal, two Dutch envoys set off for England, led by an emissary from the Prince in the shape of Sir Henry Seymour.

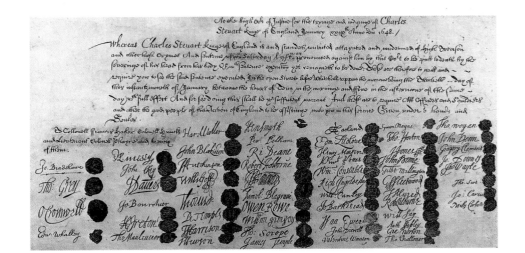

Right: The death warrant of
Charles I. Those who signed it
were condemned as regicides
at the Restoration, and those
still alive made the only
exceptions to a general pardon
issued by King Charles II.
Below: The execution of
Charles I.

The mission was irrelevant. By the time the Dutch reached England the King had already been condemned to death. Some of the most determined judges had already signed the death warrant by the Friday, 26 January. On Saturday the King was brought back into the court to hear the sentence of death read out. On Sunday, at St James's Palace, to which he had been brought from Windsor, the King was allowed to receive Seymour, who was thus able to receive the last messages for Charles, and the King's final letter to his wife.

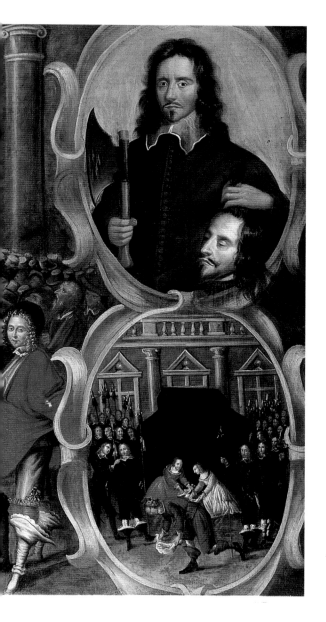

On the next day, the last day of his life, the King was permitted to see those two touching little figures, Princess Elizabeth and Henry Duke of Gloucester, who had remained as captives in London since the collapse of their father's regime. It was fifteen months since they had set eyes on the King. Princess Elizabeth had grown into a delicate but intelligent girl of thirteen: the tears rained down her face as she clasped her father. That set her brother off crying too. It was a scene which wrung all who witnessed it, including the King's custodians.

Later that night the Princess wrote down the contents of the interview in full, the first and most affecting of all the many documents which form the martyrology of King Charles I. The King spoke to the girl of her mother: she should tell Queen Henrietta Maria 'that his thoughts had never strayed from her, and that his love should be the same to the last'. To the eight-year-old Harry the King said 'that he doubted not but that the Lord would settle his throne upon his son …

An embroidery, based on the design of the frontispiece to the *Eikon Basilike*, a compilation commemorating Charles I as a martyr. Here we see the devout King casting off his corruptible crown which descends rightfully to his son.

and that we should all be happier than we could have been if he had lived'.

That son was in the meantime in a state of turmoil and despair. He thrashed about him, looking for foreign aid. Letters were sent on behalf of Louis XIV to the English Army commanders. They had no effect.

Tuesday, 30 January was the appointed day. Then, at the very last minute, there was a hitch. It was suddenly realized that the execution of King Charles I was not enough. That would simply leave the junta and England itself with the spectre (or vision) of King Charles II. It would be a powerful case of 'The King is dead, long live the King'.

In the course of that freezing January morning an urgent measure was passed 'that no person whatsoever should presume to declare Charles Stuart (son of the late Charles) commonly called the Prince of Wales, or any other person, to be King, or chief magistrate, of England and Ireland … ' Only then was it time for the King, wearing two shirts against the cold so that he should not shiver and be mistaken for a coward, to step out of a window in the Palace of Whitehall towards the ready scaffold.

'I go from a corruptible crown to an incorruptible crown,' the King told his chaplain, Bishop Juxon. To the Bishop also he entrusted his last letter to his son, a long message of advice and blessing. It was a sad and sapient document, in which Charles was pressingly advised to take his stand on goodness and piety: how much better to be 'Charles le Bon' than 'Charles le Grand', how much better to be 'good than great'.

Just after two o'clock in the afternoon that day the King went finally to his incorruptible crown.

Not until 5 February did Charles, in Holland, learn that the corruptible crown was now his. It was his chaplain, Stephen Goffe, who entered the room and, after a slight hesitation, began: 'Your Majesty –'

To the agonized son, he needed to say no more. After the weeks of uncertainty, Charles burst into bitter weeping. To Goffe he could not speak. Eventually he made a sign for him to leave. For several hours, Charles II, King of England, Scotland and Ireland, otherwise Charles Stuart, son of that man of blood Charles Stuart the elder, remained quite alone.

This frontispiece from a history of the period dates from 1682, showing that by then the idea of Charles the Martyr and the ruin of the kingdom by Satanic forces had taken strong hold in its portrayal of Britannia's sorrows.

An engraving by Hollar for the title page of one of the increasingly popular travel books of the time. The bustle, activity and sense of diversity comes across quite clearly in Hollar's detail.

Plymouth, 1673 by Hendrik Danckerts. The predominance of the citadel reminds us that these busy seaports were expected to undertake sterner duties if needed.

England: Length and Breadth

Focusing on the life of Charles II it is sometimes easy to overlook the developments in town and country way beyond the confines of London. The ports, merchant towns, villages, farms and parish churches were just as much the pulse of the nation as the Court. Charles' reign produced travellers eager to visit all parts of the country and proudly note improvements in the houses, roads, commerce and manufacture.

Charles's kingdom was diverse and active.

Henley-on-Thames by Jan Siberechts. Waterways were crucial arteries before the age of canals, surfaced roads and of course rail. English rivers, most obviously the Thames, virtually dictated the site of settlements for centuries.

Nottingham, 1683 by Nicholas Hawksmoor – the site of the raising of the royal standard at the outset of civil war. This important city, located on the Trent, which was navigable to the sea, commanded access to much of the Midland areas around it.

Beeley, near Chatsworth, Derbyshire, by Jan Siberechts, 1694.

THE KING'S CAUSE

The shock of the King's execution failed to bring action from the other crowned heads. France was between periods of civil war known as the Frondes, and her protracted war with Spain would drag on until 1659. Europe as a whole, and German lands in particular, were suffering in the aftermath of the Thirty Years' War whose ravages had closed with the Peace of Westphalia in 1648. If Charles was to succeed his father in more than name it was clear that he would need military support from within the domains he now claimed to rule. But where could he look? Jersey was loyal, proclaiming the new King Charles II on 17 February. But Jersey, in such a context, was insignificant. The Scots were not disposed to having their monarchy abolished for them by the English, but any terms they might agree for an actual royal restoration would be religiously abhorrent to Charles.

In fact, with England now secured under her kingless, godly Commonwealth, to look for salvation within the United Kingdom was bound at once to raise up those twin religious spectres: the employment of Ireland brought with it a whiff of Popery; that of Scotland involved taking the Oath of the Covenant. The original Oath of the Covenant of 1638 had been reinforced by the Solemn League and Covenant in 1643. It is probable that a message was sent by Charles to Argyll, suggesting that he would join with the

Opposite: the title page of *The Leviathan*, 1651, by Thomas Hobbes, and his portrait (below) by J. M. Wright. Hobbes, the greatest English thinker of his age tutored Charles in exile but is better known for his analysis of the legitimacy of governments.

The Royal Oak of Britain, carrying its fruits of liberty and its institutions, under assault from the devil's agents in the wake of Charles I's execution. Engraved 1649.

Scots – if the Solemn League and Covenant was not pressed upon him. But the Covenanting Scots were still cock-a-hoop at the fall of the Engagers, and as a result more insistent than ever on the Oath as a price of their assistance.

Under the circumstances Ireland was once more considered to be the more alluring prospect. In preparation it was decided to take Charles and his Court back to Jersey. He landed at St Helier on 17 September 1649, accompanied by James Duke of York.

This new sojourn in the island – which was to last for five months – was of a very different nature from Charles' jaunt three-and-a-half years earlier. Quite apart from the desperate cause of a King without a kingdom, money was, and continued to be, an obsessional concern. And of course the personalities surrounding the King continued to clash. Throughout the autumn, as preparations for the Irish venture, supported by Hyde and Ormonde, were made, disputes among other advisers smouldered on, with the occasional spark flying. The King himself came in for criticism: he was not attending to his business sufficiently. During this troubled period Charles had a habit of meeting a situation in which nothing could be done with an assumption of indifference, even indolence, and for that he should not necessarily have been blamed. But the active members of his entourage fretted at the delays, and looked round for a scapegoat: the King's reputation for laziness was always conveniently to hand.

For better or for worse, the Irish plans were destined to come to nothing. The earnest little court at Jersey plotted

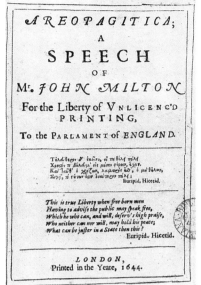

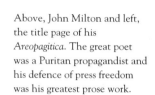

Above, John Milton and left, the title page of his *Areopagitica*. The great poet was a Puritan propagandist and his defence of press freedom was his greatest prose work.

and prepared and nagged throughout the autumn; all the while the victorious campaign of Oliver Cromwell had quite put an end to any possibility of the King landing there. It was in September at Drogheda, north of Dublin, and in October at Wexford, on the south-east tip of Ireland, that Cromwell instigated those fabled blood-baths which conquered Ireland and, incidentally, blackened his reputation for ever. And, with hopes of Ireland gone, the situation in England was hardly more encouraging than it had been immediately after the execution. As one correspondent wrote in the spring of 1650, the King's party there was 'so poor, so disjointed, so severely watched' that they could do nothing on their own. The same source suggested that 'a good understanding' between the King's party and the Presbyterians might at least enable the English Royalists to rise again. It was a conclusion which could no longer be avoided.

Given that King Charles II had a moral duty to try to recover his throne as soon as possible, he had absolutely no alternative at the beginning of 1650 but to try Scotland once more. He was a monarch. He had inherited a kingdom. He must seek to wrest that kingdom from its unlawful possessors. It was up to him to establish who, if anyone, could help him in the task. This explains, among other things, how Charles, having decided to try the Covenanters once more, also gave a commission to their sworn enemy, the Marquess of Montrose. As a result, Montrose landed at Kirkwall in the Orkney islands in January 1650. But it was

M. MONTROSE.

This Original at the Duke of Montrose.

Montrose, who 'went to his death like a bridegroom to a bride' and whose apparent desertion by Charles left an indelible stain on the King's reputation.

most unfortunate that Montrose landed there before he received a crucial letter from the King, written from Jersey and dated 12 January. In this letter Charles broke the news that he was once more contemplating the terms of the Scots. Montrose, in his ignorance and innocence, campaigned in Scotland quite unaware of what was taking place elsewhere in Europe.

Charles finally left Jersey on 13 February 1650 and went first to meet his mother. How much – all tragic – had happened in the two years since their last encounter! Now the Queen's own poverty was fearful: she relied on scarcely concealed acts of charity among the kinder of the French nobility. Even so, the main burden of Henrietta Maria's conversation was to beg her son never to sign the Covenant.

The new battle joined between the King and the Covenanters – a battle of words, and certainly of wits, from which in the end neither emerged triumphant, was joined at Breda on 26 March. Both parties arrived there on that date within a few hours of each other. The King's deliberate and delightful courtesy was from the first very much to the fore, but regrettably the three chief commissioners chosen, Alexander Brodie, Alexander Jaffray and the Earl of Cassilis, belonged to the sternest faction of the Covenanters. On 4 April the most domineering terms were laid before the young King at Breda. Not only was he himself to take the Oath, but he was also to swear to establish the Presbyterian form of worship in England and Ireland, as well as Scotland. Furthermore, he was to permit no other form of worship within his own household.

Despite the loftiness of these claims, Charles was still prepared to accept them, so far as Scotland itself was concerned. What he could not do was impose them on 'his other kingdoms'.

So the battle at Breda raged. But there were two new weights on the side of the Covenant which were to be of considerable significance in the final decision. First, the Engagers, or at least some of them, had returned to the fold of the Scottish counsels, and as a result Lauderdale, amongst others, was back at Breda. The fact that this Scot, whom Charles both liked and trusted, advocated agreement, was important.

Even more influential was the advice of the Prince of Orange. William's reflection on hearing the news of the Irish defeat must stand for a whole body of judicious monarchical opinion: 'It is obvious that God wishes him [Charles] to understand that Scotland is the only way to his restoration.' Under the circumstances, William urged Charles to go the whole hog – to follow Presbyterian worship himself while in Scotland.

At last, on 27 April, Charles returned a formal and favourable answer to the commissioners' proposals. He would swear the Oath of the Covenant. He would grant everything demanded as regards Scotland herself, including the establishment of the Presbyterian Kirk and the ratification of the Scottish Parliament and its Acts.

He still would not accept Presbyterianism for England, the abandonment of the Catholic Irish treaty – in short, all those demands which were not strictly speaking

John Speed's 'Kingdom of Scotland'. Of the many possible places planned as a springboard from which to reclaim his kingdom, Scotland alone proved practical for Charles. The results, though, were disastrous.

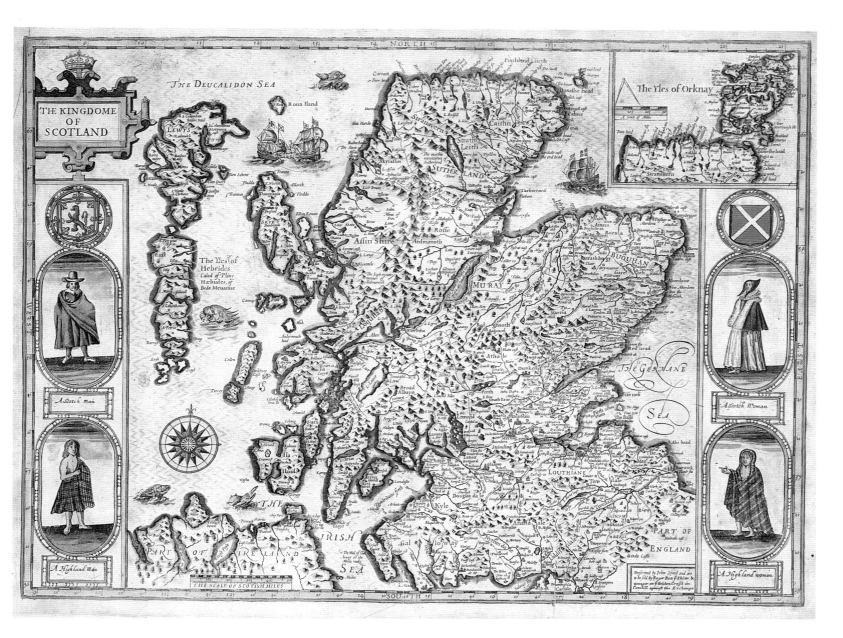

pertinent to Scotland. But it was implicit in the agreement as it stood that Montrose no longer held the King's commission.

In Scotland Montrose heard the glad news that the King had bestowed upon him the Garter and the bad news of the talks at Breda in one and the same letter. By the time the King wrote a rueful letter telling Montrose that he now had to look after himself, the Marquess had already been captured by the gleeful Covenanters. On 18 May he was led through the streets of Edinburgh like a captive in a Roman triumph. On 21 May he was executed.

He went to his death, they said, like a bridegroom. As the ghost of Strafford haunts Charles I, so Montrose's ghost continues to haunt the reputation of Charles II. But it was in the gloomier shades of desperation that the younger Charles' treatment of Montrose took place: in this light it should be judged.

On 24 May Charles set sail for Scotland. In general, if he went with the natural dismay of the English Anglicans, he went with the approval of Europe.

Charles' journey, and indeed his arrival in Scotland, was not auspicious. His voyage was tormented by contrary winds, and, even before he sailed, the Scottish Parliament had made some stringent new demands, believing that the King was now 'safely caught in the springe [trap] of the Kirk'. Charles himself was unaware of this, but the unpleasant news caught up with him when a storm obliged his vessel to anchor just off Heligoland at the mouth of the Elbe. There were new arguments and disputes.

It was on 3 July, still on board ship, but by now at anchor in the mouth of the River Spey, on the north-east coast of Scotland, that Charles capitulated for the third and last time. For him personally it had been a painful progress, from the first agreement to negotiate, via the terms proposed in April, to the final humiliation of accepting these new and pungent conditions.

So it was that Charles II came at last to swear that great oath, so solemn to so many, so odious to so many more, so invidious to a Stuart king. It began: 'I Charles King of Great Britain, France and Ireland, do assure and declare by my solemn oath, in the presence of Almighty God, the searcher of all hearts, my allowance and approbation of the National Covenant and Solemn League and Covenant above written …' It ended menacingly on the subject of Presbyterian government and worship, as approved by the General Assembly of the Kirk and the Scottish Parliament: 'And I shall observe these in my own practice and family, and shall never make opposition to any of these, nor endeavour any alteration therein.'

There can be no question that Charles swore the Oath in the cause of expediency and nothing else. This point was appreciated by the Covenanters themselves in their hearts. Alexander Jaffray, one of the commissioners, wrote in his Diary, 'We did both sinfully entangle and engage the nation ourselves and that poor, young Prince to whom we were sent, making him sign and swear a Covenant which we knew from clear and demonstrable reasons that he hated in his heart.'

But that was after the event. At the time Kirk and politicians were triumphant, combining to keep a strict watch over their King and making his first few weeks in Scotland ones of unimaginable gloom and depression. There was an actual day appointed to bewail the sins of the late King and the royal family. The King yawned his way through the sermons, which were both infinitely long and very frequent. And the Scots' social life was as bleak as their church-going. Grace before a meal could stretch interminably: 'At dinners, they lay as fiercely about 'em as in the Pulpit.' The mixture of religious fanaticism and low living did not endear itself to the newly acclaimed King of Scotland. He kept a perfect composure in public. But inside himself he brooded and observed in conversation, 'The Scots have dealt very ill with me – very ill.' It was an ominous remark.

The final irony of all came when, exactly two months after he swore the Oath of the Covenant at Speyside, the entire justification for his climb-down, the Scottish army, was vanquished beneath the hoofs of Cromwell's victorious cavalry at Dunbar. The Covenanter Scots, far from constituting that mighty host which would place the King on his English throne, became a spent and impotent force, as once the Engagers had been. For on 3 September Cromwell won one of his greatest victories against vastly superior forces. There is one story that Charles actually fell on his knees in thanksgiving when he received the news, and another that he threw his cap in the air for joy. Both are probably apocryphal, but they symbolize the resentment the King now felt against the Scots.

In personal terms, Charles was far more devastated by the news of the death of his sister Elizabeth, shortly after the defeat at Dunbar. The poor young Princess died in captivity at Carisbrooke Castle, only two days after permission arrived from Parliament for herself and her brother Henry to leave at last for the Continent. As a final horror little Henry was informed that his sister had died of grief because Charles had taken the Oath of the Covenant, though in fact she died of consumption.

In Scotland Charles was young and human enough to rejoice in his heart at the humiliation of his own persecutors. As for their reaction to the defeat inflicted on them, its flavour may be judged by a letter shortly afterwards to Charles from Robert Douglas, one of the moderators of the General Assembly. Douglas implied that the defeat had in fact been due to the 'Guiltiness' of the royal family: perhaps a new day of 'Humiliation' should be kept? It was no wonder that when he was adjured to repent yet again, Charles observed wearily: 'I think I must repent me ever being born.'

On 4 October 1650 King Charles rode carelessly out of Perth, 'as if going on hawking' – and only came to rest forty-two miles later. This attempt to escape his Covenanter captors, as they had virtually become, was known as the Start. It finished almost as soon as it began. Two officers from Perth soon caught up with him. By 6 October he was back there, listening to yet another sermon.

But the Start, significantly, demonstrated in terms which the Kirk could not miss that Charles had reached the limits of his endurance. Charles' disgust with the Covenanters had been growing apace since Dunbar. Politically and strategically, it was madness on the part of the Covenanters to suppose they could defeat Cromwell without the help of all the pro-monarchical forces in Scotland: these obviously included the northern Royalists, whom they had so unhelpfully termed the Malignants, while putting their celebrated champion Montrose to death.

Charles II crowned King in Scone, Scotland, New Year's Day 1651. During his unhappy stay in Scotland Charles found himself subject to many indignities at the hands of the Covenanters.

It was with a view to creating some kind of national unity, even at this late hour, that the project of the King's coronation was expedited. Enormous trouble was taken over the details of the coronation, which was appointed to take place on 1 January 1651 at the Cathedral of Scone. Still, the restraining hand of Presbyterianism was not lacking from the order of the day. It was noticeable that Charles received the crown from Argyll and the sceptre from the Earl of Crawford, both Covenanters. Shortly afterwards John Middleton, a leading 'Malignant' soldier who wished to return to the Covenanting fold, did penance in sack-cloth – a strange epilogue to a coronation.

But to a certain extent the gambit worked. King Charles made a series of progresses in that part of eastern and northern Scotland not controlled by the Commonwealth troops. In general, Charles bent every effort to make this new deal towards national unity work. At Aberdeen in February he persuaded the ministers to assist General Middleton in recruitment. That was one coup. Another took place in March, when he persuaded the Scottish Parliament to approve the raising of troops generally in the Highlands. The Engagers were in principle allowed back.

In the early summer of 1651 King Charles rode high. Argyll's influence diminished as his own authority increased. Charles' twenty-first

A caricature of the treatment meted out to Charles by the Scots Covenanters – possibly not too far from the reality.

birthday, 29 May 1651, was declared in the Scottish Parliament the day of 'the King's Majestic Majority'. And Charles' enormous physical energy was coming into its own. He thought nothing of riding, two or three times a week, between Stirling and Perth in order to display himself alternately at the head of his forces and in Parliament. As to his own commitment, he told them genially that he had only one life to lose.

The question was rapidly arising: where and in what direction was this life, and indeed this army, to be deployed? The obvious decision was to march on England. But the Scots still wavered. Their army lurked uncertainly west of Fife, near Stirling, leaving the initiative to Cromwell. The actual march began as late as 31 July. The Duke of Hamilton agreed that marching on England was probably the

best course. Or at any rate he called it 'the least ill'. Yet he added, 'It appears very desperate to me.' Now the fatal divisions, the doom of Scottish society for so many years, began to appear in their ranks once again. Argyll, for example, retreated morosely from the scene and refused to join the army. At this the Engager Hamilton was full of glee: 'All the rogues have left us.' But by the time Charles reached England he would need all the rogues he could get.

It was thus a listless and troubled force which crossed the border into England on 5 August. Charles was in fact proclaimed King of England at Penrith, a northern

Stirling and its castle, painted by Johannes Vorsterman. Stirling was among the places visited by Charles in his efforts to arouse enthusiasm and gather recruits for his march into England.

market town, and later at Rokeby, where a flourish of trumpets attended the ceremony. But it was significant that the important border town of Carlisle had refused to surrender to his call. And as their native country receded, all too many of the Scots decided to recede from the army back to it. Practically no one in England joined the royal standard to replace them. The optimistically held notion of English Royalist help was an illusion for the grim reason that the English Royalist movement was itself a myth. Of this the King's intelligence, such as it was, had been quite unaware. And the King was after all at the head of a band of Scots Presbyterians.

Nothing seemed to go right. When the Earl of Derby, the great magnate of Lancashire, landed from the Isle of Man to bring his followers to the King's aid, he was instantly defeated at Wigan. Only the Earl himself, and a handful of his men, escaped to join the King further south. And the King's fortunes got no better as he moved south. If anything, the patriotic revulsion of the English against the Scots increased.

The Duke of Hamilton had written, 'I confess I cannot tell you whether our hopes or fears are greatest, but we have one stout argument – despair; for we must either stoutly fight or die.' It was in this mood that King Charles, at the head of no more than sixteen thousand men, most of whom were by now utterly exhausted, arrived on 22 August at the city of Worcester.

By now Cromwell, supported by his experienced commanders Lambert, Harrison and Fleetwood, had arrived from the north. With his usual strategic flair, he decided to cut off Worcester from the south and south-east in order to obviate the risk of the King reaching London. The royal party inside Worcester were like settlers within a defensive circle of their upturned wagons; they soon found themselves ringed by the Indians.

The final Indian charge could not be long in coming; indeed, there are grounds for believing that Cromwell actually delayed the assault to coincide with his 'most auspicious day' – 3 September, the first anniversary of his victory at Dunbar. When the first noise of firing was heard, the King climbed up the fine fourteenth-century square tower of Worcester Cathedral. This watchpost surveyed (and still surveys) an imposing panorama of water and wood, as the rivers Teme and Severn were spread out beneath his gaze.

The King was armed with a spy-glass and, from his lookout, could see the bridge of boats being towed by Fleetwood up the Severn, which Cromwell with most of his cavalry had crossed in support. The King concluded that this must have considerably weakened the main Commonwealth force to the south-east and therefore ordered his own men to charge out of the Sidbury Gate and attack them. He himself promptly joined in the fray.

At first this brave essay was successful. The Royalists, covered by their own artillery, attacked up hill, and for three hours conducted themselves with an unparalleled energy and venom. Their King was there with them, on foot, fighting at their side, cheering them on. Once their meagre ammunition was exhausted, they still went on at push of pike, butting with their muskets where they were too closely engaged to use pikes. It was here that the gallant Duke of

Hamilton fell, mortally wounded. Some of the enemy's artillery was captured, and for a brief moment their troops fell back.

It has been proposed that, if the Scottish infantry under its commander David Leslie south-west of the city had been moved in support at this juncture, victory might have been grasped. Nevertheless, one cannot genuinely believe that the King had a chance, Leslie or no Leslie. The Parliamentary forces were superior in every respect – and numerically by this point nearly tripled those of the King.

As it was, Cromwell, when he took in what was happening outside the Sidbury Gate, immediately recrossed the Severn. The Commonwealth counter-attack was all too potent. It was with the greatest difficulty that the King, amongst others, got back to the Sidbury Gate at all. There was chaos outside and inside the city. The Scots, let it never be forgotten, were far from home. At some point Leslie's nerve certainly collapsed: he was glimpsed in the mêlée 'as one amazed or seeking to fly he knew not whither'.

One man however who kept his head and his courage to the last was the King. There were many tributes to Charles' valour on that dreadful 'black and white day', as a contemporary narrative called it, when the King's men were 'ravished at Worcester by numerous overpowering force'.

Once having beaten his way back into the city via the Sidbury Gate, the King stripped off his armour. Calling for a fresh horse, he rode amongst the soldiers, urging, pleading and commanding them to stand and fight.

'I had rather you would shoot me,' he cried, 'rather than let me live to see the consequences of this day!'

It was too late. The cavalry were finished. 'Neither threats nor entreaty' would persuade them to make a fresh charge. Charles could not even get them to shut the gates of the city.

Even so, it was towards dusk, when over two thousand of his own men – compared to two hundred odd of the enemy – had been killed, that Charles at last consented to withdraw. The exact details of his escape from the town are obscure, but we know that Charles left by St Martin's Gate, to the north of the city. And now Charles was quite clear where the duty of a sovereign lay. He must escape. A dead king might be a martyr, a captive king would be a pawn. Nine thousand of the Scots had already been taken. The rest of the roaming, hopeless men were easily harvested. The Royalist cause was in ruins.

It remained only to scoop up the person of the fugitive King.

Plays, Poems and the Literary Arts

The Restoration of the King saw an outpouring of literature, most notably for the theatre, as if the repressions of the Cromwellian period had suddenly given way to an outburst of energy. Certainly the London theatre flourished, and the 'wits' produced their plays and verses for the amusement of the court. Meanwhile figures like Milton and Bunyan survived into this new age.

Above, John Bunyan and, right, an illustration from his great work *The Pilgrim's Progess*. Bunyan was a Baptist who spent many years in jail under the Restoration acts against nonconformists. *The Pilgrim's Progress* was completed in 1678.

John Dryden, a central figure of the Restoration Theatre whose *All for Love* (1678), was a great success. He was also a poet and royalist propagandist, and his poem celebrating the year of the Great Fire and Dutch War popularized the phrase *annus mirabilis*. By Godfrey Kneller.

Andrew Marvell, poet, parliamentarian and friend of Milton. In his own time he was well known for his Puritan propaganda, but later generations have seen him as a significant poet.

The Restoration saw an outpouring of literature in all forms.

The first page of Milton's immortal *Paradise Lost*, finished and published some half a dozen years after he became blind in 1663. Although forced into hiding at the Restoration, Milton was included in Charles II's general amnesty.

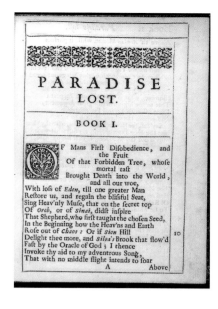

Thomas Killigrew by William Sheppard, 1650. One of the playwrights who gained favour at Charles II's court, he built the first Theatre Royal at Drury Lane.

CHAPTER FOUR
THE FUGITIVE

As the King vanished through the northern gate of Worcester, on that tragic night of 3 September, he was attended by only a few gentlemen. But they included some of the most notable figures in his entourage – the egregious Buckingham, the powerful Earl of Derby and the Scottish Lauderdale, less recognizable in England but an equally desirable prize for the Commonwealth to capture.

The royal party soon found themselves quite lost in the darkness. They knew that they were somehow north of Worcester – but that was about all, since the trooper who was supposed to know the district proved alarmingly ignorant. Lord Derby suggested that the King should continue to head north and try to hide out in the Brewood Forest. He also mentioned the name Boscobel, where he himself had hidden after the disastrous rout at Wigan: he knew the people living there, the Giffard family, to be kind, hospitable and, above all, loyal.

They were also Catholics. The position of Catholics in England at this date was both melancholy and irksome. Officially, their religion was forbidden: those who did not attend Church of England services were termed recusants and heavily fined. Their priests in particular were in danger of death if apprehended. During the Civil War the Catholics had suffered from the assumption that they must inevitably be supporters of the King, though in fact most Catholics were more concerned to preserve the practice of their precious religion in private.

Nevertheless, a sort of Catholic underground continued to exist, which handed the forbidden priests from hiding-place to hiding-place. It was an odd chance

Detail from a silk embroidery, dating from about 1665. It celebrates the restoration of the King. Charles and Major Carlos are hiding from Cromwell's troops up the by now immortalized oak tree.

which brought King Charles II in touch with this underground while on the run himself. This secret world was so very different from the kind of Catholicism which Charles had known before – the foreign confessors of his mother, the French, Spanish and even Irish Catholics of the Continent. He discovered for himself that the English Catholics were then (as now) a very special breed in whom national loyalty was far from being extinct. In time he would wish to act upon this knowledge.

For the present however it was more a case of what the Catholics could do for their King. It transpired that Charles Giffard, the owner of the Boscobel estate, was actually amongst the little body of gentlemen still with the King.

Giffard recommended not Boscobel itself (which was let to a Catholic family of yeoman farmers named Penderel) but another house close to it, Whiteladies, which the King reached at dawn. The plan now devised was for Charles to disguise himself in country clothes belonging to William Penderel, who was the tallest brother – a green jerkin, grey cloth breeches, leather doublet and greasy soft hat. It was of course essential to rid himself of his entourage. He must survive, and he would only survive alone. One of the King's attendants was Lord Wilmot, a man of considerable style – he refused to disguise himself during the escape, saying 'he should look frightfully in it'. The only concession he eventually made was to wear a hawk on his wrist, a gentlemanly form of disguise. Nevertheless, Wilmot, presumably because he was a much less conspicuous figure than the rest of the lords, was the only one entrusted with the King's secret decision. He would head for London, rather than the Welsh ports or Scotland; this would be all the safer for being unexpected.

The King agreed with Wilmot on an address where they might meet. The secrecy was made easier by the fact that the other lords, far from pressing for information, begged not to be told, 'because they knew not what they might be

Boscobel House, and nearby Whiteladies, where the King first sought refuge after his defeat at Worcester. Painted for Charles II c. 1670 by Robert Streeter.

forced to confess'. Indeed, very shortly afterwards nearly all the lords except Buckingham were captured. The Duke, born under a lucky star, made his way to France. But Derby was condemned to death, on the grounds that, being an Englishman, he had acted as a traitor by joining the Scots; Lauderdale, for being a foreigner (a Scot) and knowing no better, was let off with imprisonment.

Meanwhile the sun was up. The house was no longer safe from search. The King stole out of Whiteladies by the back door and took refuge in a nearby wood, the Spring Coppice. John Penderel went off to find a more secure hiding-place, depositing Lord Wilmot at Brinsford. Penderel's search was fruitless, but it was on the way back, by an extremely lucky chance, that he met someone whom he recognized as the chaplain in secret attendance on another local Catholic gentleman, Thomas Whitgreave of Moseley Old Hall. This was Father John Huddleston. Penderel tested the temperature of the water. Would Whitgreave be prepared to harbour the fugitive King? The answer was encouraging, although it is an indication of the isolation of this particular piece of country that Huddleston actually thought the King had gained the day at Worcester until Penderel disillusioned him.

An oak chest carved with a scene showing Charles' escape at Boscobel in 1651. The chest is on display at Boscobel House.

The King's day in the Spring Coppice was far from tranquil. Accompanied only by Richard Penderel, he suffered from both hunger and thirst, and he also had the unpleasant experience of observing some troops on the road, evidently searching for fugitives. Only an unexpectedly heavy shower over the copse itself and nowhere else – which the King described as 'remarkable enough' – saved him from their attentions.

While in the wood however Charles changed his mind about heading for London. Penderel could think of no 'man of quality' to harbour him on the way there. Besides, Charles himself knew of several 'honest gentlemen' in Wales. So it would be the Welsh ports after all.

Under cover of darkness the King and Penderel left the wood, and, nourished only by some more bread and cheese taken at the door of another Penderel house, set off for the Severn. There were several more adventures, including an encounter with a miller who chased them off, shouting 'Rogues, rogues!' – for the ironical reason that he was harbouring a number of fugitive Royalist soldiers. Indeed, the Midlands were still in a state of chaos, which contributed materially to the King's preservation. It was not until 9 September, six days after the battle, that the first proclamation was put about seeking his capture. The day after that the reward was announced for laying hands on this 'malicious and dangerous traitor' – one thousand pounds, an absolutely vast sum at the time. Posters were put out by Parliament seeking 'a tall black man, over two yards high'. It was lucky that so many of the English had not seen him in the flesh since boyhood, if at all.

The King spent the night of Friday, 5 September, in a barn about seven miles from Whiteladies. It was then discovered that the Severn was heavily guarded and impractical to cross. The only solution was to return to the Boscobel area. They had to ford a river on the way back: Charles was a strong swimmer – it was one of the many forms of physical exercise for which he had a passion – but Richard Penderel, who could not swim at all, pronounced it to be 'a scurvy river'. Charles remembered with pride that at least in this instance he was able to help Penderel by enabling him to cross the river safely.

They got to Boscobel at five o'clock in the morning, where the first news which greeted the King was about Wilmot: he was safely stowed at Moseley Old Hall. He also learnt that a particularly gallant Royalist soldier, Major Carlis, who had stayed till the end at Worcester, was at this very moment concealed in the thick Boscobel Wood. The Major knew that his own home nearby would undoubtedly be searched. It was thus that Carlis – or Carlos, as he has gone down to history, having changed his name later to mark his association with the sovereign – found himself in the legendary royal oak, sharing it with King Charles II.

In those days the tree was a large and particularly bushy pollard oak. It still had some space around it, however, which the King decided would give them a good view. Here the pair remained all day, the King sleeping from time to time, with his head in Carlos' lap, on a cushion provided by the Penderels. As Charles told Pepys, 'We see the soldiers going up and down, in the thicket of the wood, searching for persons escaped, we seeing them now and then peeping out of the wood.'

It was not until the evening of what must have been another very long day that the King and Carlos dared to venture back into the house. It was at supper that night that the King first heard from Humphrey Penderel of the price on his head – 'If it were one hundred thousand pounds, it were to no more purpose,' exclaimed the gallant Carlos. The night at Boscobel was spent in a priest's hiding-place at the top of the house, but soon Charles was passed on to Moseley Old Hall, about five miles away, where he was reunited with the flamboyant Wilmot.

The upstairs bedroom, where the King was installed at Moseley, had its own convenient hiding-place nearby. The usual incumbent of this nook, Father John Huddleston, now enters King Charles'

The King's hiding place at Moseley Old Hall; the existence of such priest holes in the homes of loyal Catholic subjects was to prove a significant influence on his attitude to religious toleration.

story properly for the first time. Coming from a Lancashire family, and having served in the Royalist Army during the Civil War, Huddleston represented in his own person all that was best about that kind of patriotic English Catholicism which Charles was just discovering for himself.

Huddleston was outspoken, saying that the King now resembled him, being 'liable to dangers and perils'. He had already shown Charles the secret chapel, 'little but neat and decent'. Charles looked on it, crucifix, candlesticks and all, respectfully. He then observed, according to Huddleston, 'If it please God I come to my crown, both you and all of your persuasion shall have as much liberty as any of my subjects.' There is no reason to doubt Huddleston's story: Charles' generous intention to right a wrong was certainly always there once he had encountered the sufferings – and the loyalty – of the English Catholics.

Significant also was Charles' conversation with Huddleston on the subject of the Catholic faith. Charles was encouraged to look at a Catholic catechism. Of the tract, according to Huddleston, Charles spoke the memorable words: 'I have not seen anything more plain and clear upon this subject. The arguments here drawn from succession are so conclusive, I do not see how they can be denied.' This exchange has sometimes been cited as evidence of Charles' early conversion to Catholicism. In the context, it is more plausibly regarded as evidence of Charles' natural curiosity, coupled with politeness.

No refuge, it was understood, would remain a safe house for very long. Besides, the net was closing in. On the Monday Boscobel was searched. The Penderels had their remaining provisions confiscated by the troops. The next day, 9 September, the date of the first government proclamation, Whiteladies was also searched. Giffard was badly man-handled, but kept his head admirably; he did not attempt to deny the visit of 'some unknown Cavaliers', but said that he had absolutely no idea whether the King had been amongst them.

That evening the danger was even more acute when a party of soldiers actually came to Moseley itself. The King was bundled into the nook, remaining undetected. The next day the King and Wilmot departed for Bentley Hall, the home of a Colonel Lane. The fugitives' desperate need was for some convincing cover story. It was discovered that Colonel Lane's daughter, Jane, was due to visit her sister, Mrs Norton, at Abbot's Leigh, for the impending birth of the latter's child. If Charles went in Jane Lane's company as a servant, he might conceivably get clean away.

Bentley lay three miles outside Walsall. Here Charles was transformed, from his disguise as a woodman, up the social scale to being a servant. He was to be William Jackson, son of a neighbouring tenant, which was slightly more plausible than his previous manifestation – though only just. The little train duly clattered off on Wednesday morning. Jane Lane's horse lost a shoe and it was Charles' duty to oversee

A painting by Isaac Fuller, c. 1660-70, glamorizes the King's flight in disguise to Bristol accompanied by Jane Lane.

Mrs Iane Lane and King:

the Kings escape in the sea Adventure

A sequence showing the most dramatic moments of the flight – defeat at Worcester; the oak tree; the journey with Jane Lane; the final escape.

its replacement. With characteristic bravado, Charles chatted freely to the smith as he worked, asking him, 'What news?' 'There is no news, except the good news of beating those rogues the Scots,' replied the smith. This gave Charles the irresistible opportunity of asking if 'that rogue Charles Stuart' had been captured, 'who deserved to be hanged more than all the Scots for bringing them in'. 'Spoken like an honest man,' said the smith.

At Long Marston, further on the road to Abbot's Leigh, Charles was set by the cook to wind up the jack for roasting the meat in the fireplace. He did it clumsily, but at least he demonstrated what he had learnt at the Penderels: he explained that, being a poor tenant's son, he seldom ate meat or used a jack.

Abbot's Leigh, which was reached on Friday, 12 September, lay three miles beyond Bristol, and there the mixture of farce and danger which characterized the King's escape continued. In the buttery Charles heard himself minutely described

– except that the missing King was authoritatively pronounced to be 'three fingers' taller than the present Will Jackson. But when Charles discovered that one of the talkers had been in his regiment of guards, he beat a hasty retreat upstairs. He was infinitely more afraid of the fellow, now he knew him to be one of his own men, than when he had believed him to be an enemy.

The royal party tried in vain to find a ship at Bristol and so decided to strike southwards, where one of the sleepy south Dorset ports would provide the kind of inconspicuous transport to the Continent they needed. As their base, they would use Trent Manor in Somerset, home of Colonel Francis Wyndham, a member of a family with long Royalist connections.

Of course, Jane Lane was still needed to cover the journey, and there was a distressing last-minute hitch when her sister gave birth to a still-born child; it seemed a heartless moment to be leaving her. In the end it was the King who devised an excuse: a fictitious letter from Colonel Lane, pleading illness and summoning his daughter back to his side. Wilmot wrote ahead to warn Wyndham: they all realized that he would know nothing of what had been going on ever since Worcester. It was now Tuesday, 16 September, the day on which the Council of State issued new instructions 'to use the best means they can for the discovery of Charles Stuart'.

It was pure bad luck that, in the event, the King could not make his escape from the Dorset coast. The reason for the eventual failure was the coincidental Commonwealth campaign against Charles' old refuge, Jersey. As a result, the so-called sleepy ports of Dorset and Devon had been transformed, and there were a quite unaccustomed number of Commonwealth troops in the area.

At Trent Manor, however, lying in a lost village between high banks and steep lanes, they were not to know of this development. The manor was next to the village church: not a very fortunate locale. For when the bells began to peal unexpectedly, and Charles was sent to know the reason, he was told it was for the 'joyful news' of his own death!

Lyme – the Regis came later, as a reward for its loyalty – was the obvious port for the getaway. Peters, the Colonel's valet, was entrusted with the commission, and since there was a fair at Lyme, Charmouth, a nearby fishing village set in the wide bay which ends at Bridport, was selected. There, on Monday, 22 September, it was finally arranged that one Limbry, the master of a coasting vessel, would convey them to France for £60, although the tide would not let him sail until eleven o'clock that night. Peters, a practical man, immediately engaged a room in a Charmouth inn where the King and Wilmot could lurk; as a romantic, or at least a person of imagination, he explained the need for this limited late-night rendezvous by saying that he was assisting a runaway bridal couple from Devonshire.

Charles had said goodbye to Jane Lane. He arrived at Charmouth that night, riding double with another young lady, Juliana Coningsby, a Wyndham cousin. Her existence gave plausibility to the wedding story at the inn.

With the King and Miss Coningsby at the inn at Charmouth, Wyndham, Peters and Wilmot went down to the shore and awaited the ship. Nothing happened. The tide came in, went out, and there was not a trace of Limbry. Cold, disconsolate and perplexed, they were forced in the end to return to the inn and confess failure. The reason for Limbry's non-appearance was in fact a quite ridiculous marital escapade:

his wife, aware of the government's proclamation about Royalists, suspected Limbry of being up to no good with his nocturnal project (although she did not conceive it was the King he was helping). She followed him, and ended by locking him in his bedroom. In vain the captain raged. She would not budge.

In the absence of any explanation, however, the royal party were left with the problem of the next move. It was Charles, characteristically, who thought it the best course to head for Bridport, a much larger town, and stuffed with troops on their way to Jersey and Guernsey. There he could go 'blundering' among the soldiers and keep his rendezvous with Wilmot. Suiting the action to the word, he pushed his way through the concourse to the largest inn, with his horse, annoying the troops in the process. One ostler did remark that his face was strangely familiar. Charles kept cool, even when he discovered that the ostler had worked close to the house of a Mr Potter who had entertained the Royalists at Exeter during the Civil War.

'Friend,' he replied easily, 'you must certainly have seen me then at Mr Potter's for I served him above a year.' The two 'servants' parted with jolly vows to drink a pot of beer together at their next meeting. In spite of all this bravado, when Wilmot, based at another inn, joined Charles, they decided that the best course was to get back to Trent Manor. There in effect they would start all over again.

In the meantime the danger of discovery had not diminished. Another ostler, that of the Charmouth inn, had become very suspicious as he pondered on the horseshoes of the royal party, those luggage labels of the past. He recognized one as having been cast in Worcestershire. But by the time the hue and cry was raised, and the local magistrate had alerted the troops, the scent had gone cold. The soldiery set off in the direction of Dorchester – that is, to the east of Bridport. But the King, Wyndham and Wilmot were by now about five miles north.

As a matter of fact they were lost; Wyndham had to ask the name of the village where they decided to spend the night (it was Broadwindsor). Here, occupying upper rooms under false names, the King and his party got involved in a hilarious caper, since by complete coincidence a party of about forty soldiers on their way to Jersey also decided to put up in and around the same inn. One of their female followers gave birth to a baby during the night: the village was selfishly concerned that the baby should not be abandoned there, as a charge on the parish. In the hullabaloo which followed the presence of the King remained undetected.

By the next night, 24 September, the King was back at Trent Manor; here he was to remain for the next two weeks while deliberations were made for the next throw. On Monday, 6 October, considerably rested, the King set out yet again with Juliana Coningsby. He was heading for Heale House, near Amesbury, and was there five days, using yet another hidey-hole: it was no wonder that the King, once restored, would be a prey to claustrophobia, and that sauntering in parks at his ease would be his idea of daily recreation.

It was not until 13 October that Charles was able to set out on his adventures once again with the hope of a Sussex boat. Wilmot had contacted a useful ally, Colonel Gunter of Racton, near Chichester, one who exclaimed, 'God be blessed!' when told that the King was well and safe. On the next day Charles finally reached Brighthelmstone (as Brighton was then known) and was installed at the George Inn, on the site of the present King's Head in West Street.

Now everything seemed to be going smoothly. Gunter had fixed up a boat with a merchant named Francis Mansell, by the simple expedient of getting him drunk: the payment was to be sixty pieces of silver. Officially, his cargo was billed as a party of illegal duellists. The master of the promised brig, Captain Tattershall, also met the King. He recognized him immediately, but held his peace until they were alone. He then fell to his knees and kissed the King's hand, declaring that he hoped to be a lord and his wife a lady when the great day came.

The rendezvous was for nearby Shoreham: Charles spent his last night in England at Bramber, a little village just to the north. Even at this stage there was danger: Charles narrowly escaped running into some Commonwealth soldiers in the area. But he did finally make the appointed hour at Shoreham harbour.

And so at last it came about. On Wednesday, 15 October, at four o'clock in the morning, King Charles II finally departed England's shores. He had been on the run for six weeks; he had slept on pallet beds, hidden in trees, crouched in innumerable hiding-places, his lanky frame doubled up in holes for recusant priests, his large body fed by the food of the poor. In all this time, his spirit never failed.

The journey was a straightforward one. The wind blew from the north all night long, so that the brig merely had to run before it. Just before dawn the French coast came into sight. There was one more alarm as a ship which might have been a privateer hove into view. The King and Wilmot were put into a cock-boat, manned by a Quaker named Carver, who was the brig's mate.

On the very day of his embarkation, the Earl of Derby, last seen before dawn at Whiteladies, was executed. Had he been captured, Charles Stuart the younger, a tall black man over two yards high, would likely have met the same fate.

Furniture and Clocks

A Charles II beechwood sofa illustrates superbly the overall simplicity of design married to the intricately woven turkeywork on the back, seat and armrests.

Marquetry was among the developing crafts of the age. This elaborate lid of a box dates from 1670.

Restoration furniture combined solid and functional aspects with the extravagent and spectacular. It was distinguished by elaborate work on panels and embroidery. The great clockmaker Thomas Tompion was an appropriate figure to emerge in an age obsessed with instruments.

The Groombridge Cabinet,
c. 1670. Needlework reached a
high point of precision as can
been seen here on the panels.

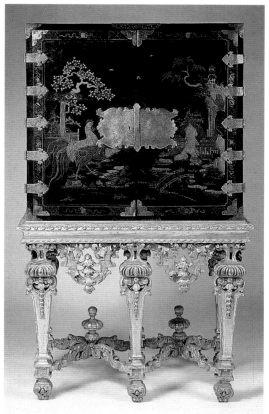

A black and gilt lacquer
cabinet on a silvered stand.
The decorative motifs –
Chinese pavilions, water
gardens, cockerels, foliage –
are reflective of growing trade
with the East, from where
sheets of such lacquer were
imported.

A sleeping chair in the
Queen's closet at Ham House,
it remains covered in its
original silk.

It was a decorative

and mechanical age.

The Lonsdale Tompion –
a small (8 inches high)
travelling alarm clock and an
example of the work of one of
the master-craftsmen of his
age. The clock was made
about 1680.

A gilt brass lantern, about
12¹/₂ inches high, by Thomas
Ford of Buckinghamshire.
Charles II's obsession with
clocks is famous.

A Charles II ormolu mounted
architectural longcase clock.
Attributed to the Fromanteel
workshop, it stands 6¹/₂ feet
high.

Opposite: Silver furniture in
the King's Room at Knole,
1676-81. This is the most
famous set of silver furnishing
in Great Britain. Such
furniture was confined to the
period from 1660 to about 1710.

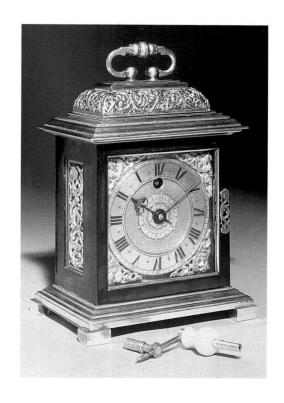

CHAPTER FIVE

THE KING ACROSS THE WATER

The King who arrived back at the Court of France at the end of October 1651 was so emaciated, even dirty, that many failed to recognize him. After the first rapturous welcome, Charles was described as both 'sad and sombre'. Writing gloomily to Jane Lane a year later (she had escaped to become lady-in-waiting to Charles' sister, the Princess of Orange), he deplored his inability to express his gratitude in some practical form, despite her need: 'I believe it troubles me more that I cannot do it yet, than it does you.'

France herself was in the midst of the second Fronde, which had broken out in September. Basically, it was a struggle for power between Cardinal Mazarin and the Prince de Condé. As a result, the French royal family was in a state of alarm and tension, which spread to all its dependants, including Queen Henrietta Maria. That in turn affected Charles. His mother's mood was grim. And unlike his younger brother, the Duke of York, there could be no question of the English King joining the army of the great Marshal Turenne and going into the field against Condé. Handsome, energetic James, tired of kicking his heels near his mother, applied for some active post and was granted permission, on condition that it was a purely personal gesture.

He was a natural soldier, easy, practical and talented. One can understand how at this point Hyde regarded James as a more hopeful character than his elder brother, condemned to stay behind in Paris for an infinitely less agreeable life of poverty and negotiation. Charles' situation in the spring of 1652 was 'the most painful that can be imagined' – at least, that was how it would be described in

Henriette-Anne Duchess of Orléans dressed for a masque, by Pierre Mignard. Also known as Minette, she was Charles' favourite and their mutual affection was endearingly evident.

One of Van Dyck's portrait of Henrietta Maria, Charles' mother, whose attempts to dominate him in exile in France proved so deleterious to their relationship.

James' memoirs. The sufferings of mother and son, now ensonced at the Louvre, were acute. They were not even receiving the French money on which they so depended, and they had no one else to approach.

It was a sad truth that the status of Charles II amidst the crowned heads of Europe was declining all the time. The summer of 1652 had seen the outbreak of a war between the England of the Commonwealth and the Dutch. Naturally Charles tried to prise some advantage out of this, beginning with the suggestion that he might come on a personal mission to the United Provinces. But the Dutch, for all their problems with the Common-wealth, had reason to regard the Stuart connection warily.

One of the cruel blows of fate which had befallen the Stuart family shortly after the Scottish catastrophe of Dunbar was the death of Mary's husband William II. He died in November 1650, at the age of twenty-four. Six days later Mary gave birth to a son, another William, the heir to the house of Orange (and also of course within the Stuart succession). The guardianship of this baby produced an instant quarrel between the various interested parties in the United Provinces. In the end Mary, the Dowager Princess Amalia and the Elector of Brandenburg (husband of Princess Louise Henrietta of Orange) were appointed co-guardians; but not before the Dowager Princess had carefully denigrated Mary by suggesting that she herself, not Mary, stood for the nationalist aspirations of the Dutch. It was a damaging charge to make at this juncture against a member of the vulnerable Stuart family.

In the summer of 1652, therefore, it is understandable that the Dutch were in no hurry to accept Charles' offer of assistance against the Commonwealth. What assistance, after all, could he provide?

Of course there remained Scotland. The price of Worcester – total defeat at the hands of the English – had been immediate occupation of the country. Legalization of this occupation followed, then union of the two countries, imposed from England. The situation was naturally inimical to many of the Scots, foremost amongst them the Highlanders, whose geographical situation enabled them to breathe defiance with virtual impunity if they so wished. But the King was by now profoundly sceptical about the Scots and events soon proved him right. A rising in the Highlands in the summer of 1652 proved abortive and all hopes from that quarter were dashed following the collapse of another rising and the defeat of the Highland commander John Middleton at Dalnaspidal in July 1654.

The King's options were running out. Meanwhile in England the elevation of Oliver Cromwell to the quasi-royal rank of Lord Protector was another blow. It was a far more conventional concept than that of a 'headless' republic and negotiations between England and the various European powers were eased as a result. The melancholy observers of the exiled Royalist set began to suspect that yet another blow might be in store for them: the alliance of France and Commonwealth England, which would be the death-knell to Royalist hopes in France. Yet there was really nothing that King Charles, penniless, depressed and helpless, could do to avert it. He was thrust back on a series of diplomatic missions and enquiries – to the Danes, to Hamburg, Danzig, Poland, Queen Christina of Sweden, the German Diet and so forth – which, totted up, might win a prize for optimism and perseverance, but achieved little positive result.

Relief when it came, came in the form of change, rather than any true lightening

A portrait of Charles in exile by an unknown artist. The traumas of his youth and the grief he suffered are all too apparent in his countenance.

A hostile Dutch lampoon of 1649 shows the coronation of King Cromwell. To the Royalist exiles such an event seemed disconcertingly likely.

of the situation. Nevertheless, to the King a change – any change – was welcome. As the steps of the diplomatic dance in which Protector and Cardinal were involved quickened, it suddenly suited the French to be rid of their dependant. Having been at times cozened by Mazarin, at times virtually imprisoned by him, Charles now found himself offered the full payment of his French pension – on condition that he left the country within ten days.

The gesture had very little grace about it: the French made it clear the step was a necessary preparation for an English alliance. Yet at least Charles was once more on his own, without his mother. As the years drew on and their differences increased, her presence aroused in him a combination of profound irritation and melancholy affection, which he was glad to avoid.

Indeed, first at Spa and then at Aachen Charles, for a month or two, actually found life rather fun. The decision to go to Spa was not of course taken from a very wide choice: Holland, no longer at war with the Commonwealth, would not have him, and the various territories within and around the Holy Roman Empire, on the borders of the Spanish Netherlands, offered the best alternative.

At Spa, the impoverished little band whistled to keep up their spirits, and, as descriptions of their life show, to a certain extent succeeded. It was high summer. All the afternoon the courtiers would dance, then take supper, then dance again in the evening light in the meadows: 'I think the air makes them indefatigable' was one comment. A more stable side of Charles' entourage was represented by the Marquess of Ormonde. And the mimic court was further gilded by the arrival of Mary Princess of Orange. The mutual devotion of brother and sister was the subject of sentimental and approving comment. They went together to Aachen where there was plenty of mirth and dancing and drinking. It was all very jolly and apparently carefree and gracious at the same time. Charles was described as winning universal regard by his 'affable and free carriage'. It was left to an English spy to write a secret report to John Thurloe, Cromwell's Secretary of State and master of the Protectoral intelligence network: 'For all his dancing, I believe he [the King] has a heavy heart.'

By the beginning of autumn that was undoubtedly true. The upsurge of optimism consequent on departure from France had waned. The courtiers' obsessional interest in their own poverty had taken over from their gaiety: Aachen was described as 'a most expenseful place', at five pence a night for a bed.

When the King and his sister decided to pass on to Cologne in early October it was in part because of its convenience as a collecting station for the money granted to him by the Imperial Diet. And that money proved as difficult to elicit as the French pension … The Elector of Cologne only paid up 'his small quota', as Hyde described it, after an importunity 'unfit to have been

James Butler, Duke of Ormonde, studio of Peter Lely. Ormonde was one of the truly great figures of the age and a strong influence among the exiles.

pressed upon any other prince or gentleman'. So when the Count of Neuburg invited King Charles and Princess Mary to Düsseldorf, they accepted with alacrity. On 29 October they repaired there by water, floating down the Rhine in a kind of Siegfried idyll. Then, from Düsseldorf, King Charles and Princess Mary ventured daringly a little way into the Spanish Netherlands, although Charles had no permission to do so. Then it was back to Cologne, where, after the Düsseldorf jaunt, the rest of the winter passed somewhat sadly and even sourly.

Under the circumstances, it was natural for all concerned with the royal fortunes to cast their eyes anew at England where after 1653 some kind of revival of Royalist spirit had at last taken place. In November 1653 King Charles gave the first written credentials to an organization terming itself the Sealed Knot, as the official organ of Royalist conspiracy in England. It was Hyde's view now that the King was most likely to be restored from within England. But it was also part of his policy, with which the King heartily agreed, that the English rising, when it came, should be a co-ordinated once-and-for-all affair. The Sealed Knot was given its commission as much to hold in check other unplanned and thus doomed risings, as to set in motion its own.

The trouble was that the English conspirators were as disunited at home as the English Court abroad. The Sealed Knot could not prevent the eruption of two irresponsible plots in the summer of 1654, or the activities of a splinter group, calling themselves the Action Party, which decided to plan a major coup for the spring of 1655. The King found himself in a highly awkward situation as regards the Sealed Knot. First, he was well aware that without the active participation of the Knot the rising was hardly likely to succeed. Secondly, the leading members of the Knot declined to take part, unless actually ordered to do so by the King. Thirdly, the Action Party made it clear that they intended to go ahead in any case, with or without the Knot. The King vacillated, and took no clear decision.

It is difficult to criticize him too harshly but the result, when the rising came, was disastrous. Nothing happened at all in Leicestershire or Staffordshire (where plans collapsed). These conspirators were the lucky ones. In the North too nothing of any great consequence happened. In fact the rising itself was officially postponed – except that the news did not reach the West.

There Colonel John Penruddock, a member of the Action Party, did enter Salisbury and seized the town on 12 March. This merely gave the Protectoral government an excellent excuse for repression via a much-increased militia, once ·they had put the rising down with comparative lack of effort. Indeed, the regime of

Princess Mary whose marriage into the House of Orange was to result in the accession of a Dutchman to the English throne. By Adriaen Hanneman, 1659.

the Major-Generals, a military rule by districts instituted in England shortly afterwards, was happily attributed by the government to the necessities imposed by the Penruddock Rising. Yet the Rising never posed the faintest danger to the established regime: what with the infiltration of the Sealed Knot organization by government spies and the uncertainties of the English Court abroad, there was little to fear.

Naturally the King in Cologne knew nothing of this. He went as far as to move secretly to Middelburg in Zeeland, hoping from this convenient spot to be summoned to England. The whole episode was abortive and slightly ludicrous. On 9 April the King, disillusioned and despairing, went quietly back to Cologne. He maintained his spirit in his public verdict on the Penruddock Rising when he criticized his critics: 'Those people, who take upon them to censure whatsoever I do … They who will not believe anything to be reasonably designed, except it be successfully executed, had need of a less difficult game to play than mine is.' And he ended with a jocular boast: 'I shall live to bid you welcome to Whitehall.'

But of that coming to pass, in the summer of 1655, there seemed but a slender chance. Hope, indeed, was the necessary diet of all the exiled Royalists. Above all, it was the food on which their King had to live. It was more through hope than conviction that King Charles now concentrated his ambitions on a Spanish treaty.

The failure of the Penruddock Rising made it abundantly clear that the English Royalists were good for nothing of consequence at the present time. To balance the decline of Hyde's pro-English policy came the rise of Protectoral aggression towards Spain. The summer of 1655 saw an expedition on behalf of Cromwell to the West Indies, whose most significant achievement was the capture of Spanish-held Jamaica. Optimists in Royalist circles thought that hostilities between Spain and England must soon follow – in fact, it was not until the spring of 1656 that war was actually declared. Pessimists paid more attention to the development of the alliance between Cardinal Mazarin and Oliver Cromwell, two men who had in common strength and initiative, the qualities of the self-made.

John Penruddock, whose ill-fated rebellion against Cromwell's republic gave the English government an easy excuse for tightening its grip. By John Hayls.

At the same time, there were startling whispers that Cromwell himself might take the crown. These insinuations had their own impact on the Royalist frame of mind. There was a divinity which hedged a king, a divinity which had so far hedged King Charles II in so far as it hedged anyone at all. The Protector did not finally reject the notion of a royal crown until April 1657, and then only at the end of a period of agonized indecision. Meanwhile the 'dead calm' in England from the summer of 1655, and the renewed talk of 'making a king' (namely Cromwell), combined to render the state of the exiled Royalists particularly harsh.

It was in this context that the prospects of Spanish assistance were assessed with mixed hopes in the autumn of 1655. One step which the English King now felt it essential to take, if he was to make any progress at all with the Spanish, was to move nearer the centre of things. His aim was to reach the Low Countries, preferably the Spanish Netherlands, where the presence of the influential governor, Don Juan (an illegitimate son of the Spanish King), would surely expedite a Spanish alliance. Finally, Charles secured permission to come to Brussels, the capital of the Spanish Netherlands, arriving there in March 1656. The crucial negotiations – from the English point of view – began.

Projected clauses of the Spanish Treaty (which was not actually signed until 2 April 1658) included a monthly allowance of three thousands crowns for Charles himself and half that amount for James. The Spanish ports would in future welcome the English Royalist privateers, while, most important of all, Spanish armed help was promised to place the King of England on his throne. In return, Charles promised the suspension, and if possible the Parliamentary revocation, of the penal laws against English Catholics once he had been restored; he also swore to maintain an alliance with the Irish Catholics. Lastly, the existing Royalist soldiers abroad, notably the fair number of Irish soldiers currently serving with France, were to be pressed into service with Spain – against France.

One may believe that Charles gave the promises concerning English Catholicism with a light heart, since he was evidently a very long way off being able to implement them. But the clause concerning the Royalist soldiers had the immediate effect of angering his brother James. The Duke of York had enjoyed service in the French Army; prospering, he had been offered a French command in Italy by Mazarin. Now he was expected to transfer his allegiance and also his fighting command to Spain. In an understandable huff, James declined to come to his brother's side but went instead to the United Provinces. It was left to Ormonde to act as peacemaker and conciliate James; in the meantime, Henry Duke of Gloucester served as a volunteer with the Spanish.

In Holland, too, Mary Princess of Orange was not best pleased by the Spanish alliance. Her beloved brother had joined with the hereditary enemy of the United Provinces. For once Mary had something in common with her mother, since Henrietta Maria naturally abhorred the Spanish trend, which made her own position in France similarly awkward.

Henry Duke of Gloucester, who shared his brother's exile and successfully resisted the vigorous attempts of their mother, Henrietta Maria, to convert him to Catholicism. His death at the age of twenty-one is widely regarded as a tragedy for the Stuart dynasty.

Of course, the bickering of brother and sister, brother and brother, was as nothing beside the fundamental division which existed within the structure of the family, between Queen Henrietta Maria on the one side and King Charles on the other, concerning the vital and now highly political topic of religion. It sprang both from Henrietta Maria's missionary Catholicism, and from her son's rejection of it.

Much has been written on the subject of the religion of Charles II, about which only two things can be stated with absolute certainty: that he was born a member of the Church of England (like his father), and that he died fifty-five years later a member of the Roman Catholic Church (like his mother). The exact moment at which the change was made, first in his own heart, secondly in the form of an official conversion divulged to a Catholic priest, can only be suggested, not known. It is nevertheless important to point out the savagery with which Charles II denounced his mother's Catholic fervour in the 1650s, in order to refute firmly the proposition that this conversion took place in exile.

On the evidence, nothing was further from King Charles' mind. He was horribly aware that even a rumour of his conversion might fatally damage the prospects of his restoration to the English throne. The crucial incident in all this is the attempt of Queen Henrietta Maria to convert Henry Duke of Gloucester to Catholicism in the autumn of 1654, when he was fifteen. First the King wrote 'Harry' a very strong letter on the subject, sufficiently vehement to dispose of any idea that he himself was contemplating such a step. Then he wrote to his mother in even plainer terms: 'And remember the last words of my dead father (whose memory I doubt not will work upon you) which were to charge him – Harry – never to change his religion, whatsoever mischief shall fall either upon me or my affairs, hereafter.' Harry duly remained a Protestant and in September 1655 joined Mary at The Hague. The ghost of King Charles I, like Hamlet's murdered father, was quite enough to prevent his son from forgetting the Anglican cause for which he had died.

Hyde's attitude was slightly different. His eyes ever turned towards the English phoenix from whose ashes he expected restoration, Hyde was concerned that the King should preserve the allegiance of the English Catholics. King Charles, he wrote, was the sole ruler from whom they could hope for 'repeal or modification of the penal laws'. But by the time Oliver Cromwell was well settled in his Protectoral role, that was no longer true. Cromwell, and the Protectoral government generally, showed considerable brilliance in the way they dangled before both Pope and Cardinal Mazarin the prospect of toleration for Catholics, without ever quite granting it officially. As a result, the condition of English Catholics did generally improve in the mid 1650s, before the demands of Cromwell's anti-Catholic Parliament of 1657 reversed the trend.

King Charles enjoyed Brussels after Cologne. But he was not allowed to remain there long by his new allies, the Spaniards, and soon took up his residence in the beautiful town of Bruges, a watery paradise of light and ancient buildings about nine miles from the North Sea. Here rows of gabled houses were mirrored in the calm surface of the canals. It was a city redolent of the great days of Flanders and the Burgundian Dukes. Now however it was a backwater. Especially did it appear as such to Charles, anxious to prosecute his affairs at the centre.

Nevertheless, it was here that the King was destined to spend a large part of the remainder of his exile. And gradually he established himself. The burghers treated him with great courtesy. The King was made patron of the Guilds of St George and St Sebastian – for crossbowmen and archers respectively. The Flemings, said Charles, were 'the most honest and true-hearted race of people he had met with'.

How debauched was this court at Bruges? It is necessary to ask this question, since rumours concerning the dissipation of the King's entourage, spread by English government propagandists, were on a level with the stories of his extravagance – and of course his Catholicism. In December 1656, for instance, one of Thurloe's spies wrote with contempt of 'Charles Stuart's court' and how 'fornication, drunkenness and adultery' were esteemed 'no sin amongst them'. The spy went on to comfort himself with the reflection that God would certainly never 'prosper any of the attempts' of such people.

As for the King himself, the same zealous vigilantes were anxious to discover fresh mistresses for him by every post. Indeed, by the Restoration, Charles had been endowed with three more illegitimate children to follow James Crofts. Charlotte Jemima Henrietta Maria Fitzroy, born in 1651, was the daughter of Elizabeth Killigrew, a Royalist lady some eight years older than Charles. Charles' principal mistress at Bruges, Catharine Pegge, the beautiful daughter of a Derbyshire squire, presented him with a son in 1657 and a daughter in 1658. The girl died, but the son, Charles Fitzcharles, survived to enjoy the patronage of his restored father: he was nicknamed Don Carlo, commemorating his 'Spanish' origins. In the nine years between Worcester and the Restoration there were also encounters with pretty women who, like Charles himself, saw nothing wrong in such dalliance between consenting adults.

By the standards of the time none of this amounted to profligacy in a young unmarried monarch. The truth is that King Charles II was at this time the reverse of high-spirited, and he did not try to cure his melancholia by debauchery.

Lucy Walter, mother of James Crofts, was the one who had gone from the King's embraces to lead a life of genuinely tragic dissipation. Her alleged misdeeds included procuring the abortion of two further illegitimate children; she was also accused of murdering her maid – the charge was later dropped. It became essential to remove Lucy's son from her care. Repeated efforts were made – abduction, if not outright kidnapping, was planned in what the King called 'the matter of the child'. By 1658 James had been successfully transferred to his grandmother, Henrietta Maria, in Paris. In view of the fact that Lucy died shortly afterwards of venereal disease, the removal, however callously performed, was clearly in the child's best interests.

Any emotion that the young Charles might have felt for the young Lucy back in those halcyon days before his father's death had certainly been exhausted many years back. But to the years of his exile belongs the story of one romance which clearly did mean something more to him than mere dalliance and desire. The extent of King Charles' feeling for the Princess Henrietta-Catharine of Orange, daughter of the Dowager Princess and sister-in-law to Mary, has recently come to light, revealed in a series of letters written in Charles' own hand to his friend Lord Taaffe, a bosom companion of his court in exile.

Princess Henrietta-Catharine, a Dutch Protestant, was a perfectly reputable match for Charles. Nevertheless, it was as much her character as her eligibility which attracted Charles. She matched Charles' loving protestations with her own, and there was enough passion in Charles' own utterances to suggest that he was only too pleased to give himself up on this occasion to a courtship which was both materially suitable and romantically inspiring.

If love burgeoned in the King's heart at Bruges, to that town also fell a more surprising honour: it could claim to be the founding place of a famous regiment, for it was here in 1656 that Charles formed his own King's Regiment of Guards, much later – after Waterloo – officially known as the Grenadiers. The reason for the formation was rooted in that clause of the Spanish treaty concerning Royalist troops. It was not only a question of transferring Irish soldiers from the French Army: King Charles also undertook to raise some troops of his own. As a result, one regiment of English guards was formed under Rochester, a Scottish unit under Middleton and an Irish one under Ormonde. Several further regiments were added and later the Duke of York was put in overall command. This international brigade went into service under the Spanish flag in June 1657. One day it would form the nucleus of the post-Restoration Army.

However formidable it may sound on paper, this army was a motley and disreputable collection. The men, underpaid if paid at all, were ill-equipped and thus ill-disciplined. Hyde referred to these new regiments as 'naked soldiers' – a sad spectacle. For the lamentable truth was that the fabulous Spanish gold had failed to materialize. In some ways, King Charles was even worse off than he had been before the move to the Low Countries: in Cologne he had lived off hope and the French pension. Now the latter source had, naturally, dried up. For all the bright horizons extended by the Spanish treaty, 1657 proved to be a year in which the English King touched the depths of depression. The King's melancholia was once again the subject of comment. The fate of his younger brothers James and Harry, permitted to shine at the front, was enviable.

Refuge was taken in absurd schemes, and still more absurd rumours.

A glimpse of things as they really were was provided when Buckingham decided to desert; returning to England, he married the heiress daughter of Sir Thomas

Mary Duchess of Buckingham, painted by J. M. Wright. Mary Fairfax was the daughter of the Parliamentary general Sir Thomas Fairfax, the marriage typifying Buckingham's unstable character, as it was performed when he deserted the exiles for England towards the end of the Protectorate.

Fairfax. In the autumn of 1657 Hyde summed up the mood of the Royalists at home as 'heartbroken': as a result, they looked for redress from 'some extraordinary act of providence' rather than from any endeavours of their own.

Nor, by the autumn, had the Spaniards shown any sign of mounting that extraordinary force against England, based on Flanders, the promise of which had been the mainspring of the projected treaty. In December it was the bright suggestion of Don Juan that some further light might be cast on the English situation if Ormonde reconnoitred it. Ormonde, with great personal bravery, did so, and suggested that the King could land near Yarmouth with safety – a view for which there was no real justification. But Ormonde found himself coping with the renewed demands of the Action Party in England for the presence of their sovereign, to which once again they attributed miraculous powers of rallying otherwise reluctant insurgents. In the event, the petty risings of 1658 were easily, almost effortlessly, put down by the Protectoral government.

King Charles now moved to Antwerp, a more convenient jumping-off ground for a projected invasion than Bruges. Not that an invasion was in prospect. The summer saw the climax of the seemingly endless war between Spain and France. The Spaniards were defeated, by the French and the English combined, at the mighty Battle of the Dunes; as a result, Dunkirk was given over to the England of the Protectorate. If anything, the course of the war had assisted revolutionary England rather than the exiled Royalists. It ended altogether the following year.

Disconsolately, Charles set off on a hunting and hawking expedition from Antwerp. Even that seemed to suffer from a kind of doom. He found too few partridges and too much standing corn. He was actually at Hoogstraeten, on the borders of the Netherlands, and playing tennis – rapidly becoming his favourite game – when, on 10 September 1658, he was told a remarkable piece of news. A week earlier, in the words of one of Hyde's correspondents, 'it had pleased God out of His infinite goodness to do that which He would not allow any man the honour of doing'.

Oliver Cromwell had died of natural causes.

There was a short burst of wild but foolish rejoicing when the news of Cromwell's death on 3 September 1658 reached the Netherlands. Some people who should have known better danced in the streets. But about the most significant immediate effect of the Protector's sudden death – he died after a short period of illness, and the Royalists in Europe were taken unawares – was to forward

Dunkirk, the Spanish possession seized for the Protectorate following the Battle of the Dunes. Every success of Cromwell's was of course a body blow for the exiles.

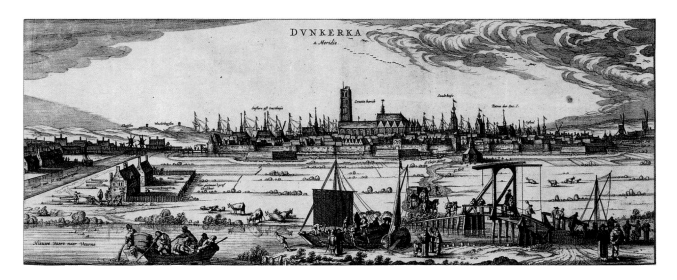

the suit of King Charles to his 'best friend' Princess Henrietta-Catharine. King Charles himself did not let the opportunity slip and proposed immediately. Henrietta-Catharine became ill with emotion. Yet by November the Dowager Princess, in common with the rest of Europe, had realized her mistake; King Charles found coolness where once there had been ardour. Early next year, a 'new gallant' for Henrietta-Catharine made his appearance, John George of Anhalt-Dessau whom she subsequently married. The King was philosophical as well as generous. He told Taaffe that his fondness for her inspired in him a real wish for her true happiness. Towards her mother he showed less tolerance, referring to her privately as 'an old strumpet' and suggesting in even cruder terms that the Dowager Princess had resented his lack of attentions to herself.

The news of the Protector's death did not merely fail to crown Charles' efforts as a romantic lover, it also ushered in an even more extraordinary phase in a life already full of paradox. Nineteen months were to pass between the death of Oliver and the restoration of Charles. To those interested parties abroad, including the King, the last act seemed interminable.

The first figure to occupy the stage vacated by Oliver was his son Richard Cromwell. Theoretically chosen by his father's dying voice, Richard was immediately confirmed in his new position by the Council of State; Protector Richard was thus easily and uncontroversially substituted for Protector Oliver. Like the sons of Charlemagne, Richard Cromwell was a fainéant, a weak plant who had grown up thinly in the shadow of the strong stem of his father. But he was not a bad man, and therefore not a bad figurehead for the English state as it now stood.

At the time a pervasive hopelessness spread like a wide, calm surface of water over the shifting sands of the King's affairs. The death of Cromwell had broken this surface with a sudden sharp splash. Now even the ripples caused by it appeared to have died away. The real trouble was the strange tranquillity which settled over England, as Hyde put it: 'the same or a greater calm in the kingdom than had been before'. This serenity was attested on all sides, both Royalist and Cromwellian.

Nevertheless, the next stirring came from within England herself. But it was not an 'extraordinary act of providence', as the death of Cromwell had been – merely an inevitable development of the feeble new Protectorate. By January 1659 a body of Army officers, including Lambert and Oliver Cromwell's son-in-law, Fleetwood, and his brother-in-law, Desborough, had come to feel in themselves rather than in Richard the source of the true power in England. They caused a Parliament to be summoned, sometimes known as Richard's Parliament. In this assembly, republicans, Presbyterians, and secret Royalists jostled with each other: from the other side of the water the King had at least managed to encourage some secret Royalists to put themselves up for election.

The Protectoral Parliament was dissolved on April 22. Protector Richard was transformed into Tumbledown Dick and slipped away to silence and exile in his turn. A Council of State became the new titular head of government. A slightly desperate expedient, the return of the Rump Parliament – elected, in its original form, an unbelievable nineteen years previously – was employed. But desperation did not imply in any sense a return to monarchy. It is notable that at this critical juncture nobody suggested for a moment recourse to Charles Stuart.

The vital element in this summer's royal plans was deemed to be the army of King Charles, not the reappearance of the Rump. He now had as many as 2,500 men with him in the Low Countries, the effect of the new military organization following the Spanish treaty. Perhaps it might find a use in support of a Royalist rising in England? Plans were indeed made, and Charles had even sanctioned a new action group to the annoyance of the Sealed Knot. But the eventual course of the rising showed that, like the Bourbons after the French Revolution, the Royalists in England had learnt nothing and forgotten nothing since their last disastrous concerted effort. Once again the affair went off at half-cock. It became popularly known by the name of Sir George Booth, because his force, easily put down by Lambert at Chester, was all that properly featured of the various para-military bodies promised. Shades of 1655!

The Rump and dreggs of the house of Com remaining after the good members were purged out.

A playing card makes fun of the Rump Parliament, the residue of some sixty 'hard-core' Puritans left after Pride's Purge in December 1648. Its recall after the collapse of the Protectorate was an act of desperation.

King Charles, disillusioned yet again, resolved to seek his fortune in Spain herself. Perhaps he could galvanize that long-promised assistance by his presence. He was unaware that the single man who would play the most crucial part in his restoration had already come to a private conclusion which favoured the return of the monarchy.

George Monck was a professional soldier, who, being born in 1608, belonged more properly to the generation of King Charles I than to that of his son. Not only had the army been in a large measure his career, but he also took his high standards of order and efficiency from the conventional military ideals. In Scotland, where he not only held down but positively governed the Scots with his Cromwellian army, his rule was both wise and firm. He had been loyal to Oliver Cromwell. He would have been loyal to Richard too, had he considered that the younger Protector had any capacity for maintaining within England that law and order which he found so precious. As Monck expressed it, 'Richard forsook himself, else I had never failed my promise to his father or regard to his memory.' It is the contention of a recent biographer that Monck had already reached a decision in August 1659. Indeed in order to explain the suddenness of the events of 1660 one is forced to the conclusion that by the autumn of 1659 not only Monck but also some of the other leaders, and even more of the ordinary people, were in their heart of hearts beginning to explore this possibility.

George Monck, by Peter Lely. Monck was the kingmaker whose decision in favour of the monarchy made possible the peaceful Restoration.

Under the circumstances, King Charles' foray to the Spanish borders at Fuenterrabia in the winter of 1659 proved unnecessary. Moreover, by this time the news had spread that the English ice was thawing. This put the King's advisers in a panic. It was suddenly dangerous for the King to seem too dependent upon Spain.

But the expedition did have one consequence of great importance in the King's personal life. In December he rediscovered his youngest sister, Henriette-Anne. They had not met for over five years, since the involuntary retreat from France. Charles remembered Henriette-Anne (or Minette, as she was occasionally known) as a thin little girl living in straitened circumstances with her mother. Henriette-

Anne was still physically delicate yet in other ways she had changed and blossomed so much that the court women tricked the King agreeably by introducing the wrong young lady as his sister. It was her brilliant colouring, combined with her doll-like figure, which made Henriette-Anne so captivating. She had bright chestnut hair and eyes of a startling blue (the traditional colouring of the later Stuarts, Charles being the exception). Her teeth, unlike those of so many beauties of the time, were white and regular, and she had a smile of exceptional sweetness.

But the real secret of the enchantment which Henriette-Anne undoubtedly exercised over her contemporaries was her ability both to give and receive love. A childhood deprived of physical necessities had left her rich in love, at least, from her widowed mother. Naturally King Charles fell under her spell. They got on immediately, in spite of the long absence and enormous age gap. Early on, Charles asked Henriette-Anne not to put so many 'majesties' in her letters: 'for I do not wish that there should be anything between us but friendship'.

By now the King's relationship with his mother was thoroughly soured. Mary in Holland had her own drawbacks of temperament. James had an awkward sense of his position as his brother's heir: besides, he tended to side with his mother. But with Charles' 'dear dear sister' all was pleasure and lightheartedness, the thrill of discovery and rediscovery. 'I am yours entirely,' he ended a letter dated 26 May 1660, written on board the boat which was taking him towards England. Charles did not fail to think of Henriette-Anne even in the hour of his glory. It was a portent of the important role she would play as his ambassadress.

In the memoirs of James II (dealing with his campaigns as Duke of York) the beginning of 1660 was described as the 'lowest ebb' of Charles II's hopes, a time when all his optimism had left him. Yet, when only a few short months had passed, King Charles was to be restored 'without one drop of bloodshed, to the astonishment of all the Christian world'. How did this seemingly amazing reversal come about? As Samuel Pepys, an up-and-coming young civil servant, noted in the diary which he had only just begun to keep, 'Indeed it was past imagination both the greatness and the suddenness of it.'

The first thing to be noted is that the Restoration of King Charles II was a strictly internal process. The final irony of the years of exile lay in the fact that King Charles was in the end restored not by any efforts of his own, but because the mighty tide of revolution had somehow exhausted itself quite early in the Protectorate. Stability and order had become the concern of almost everyone in

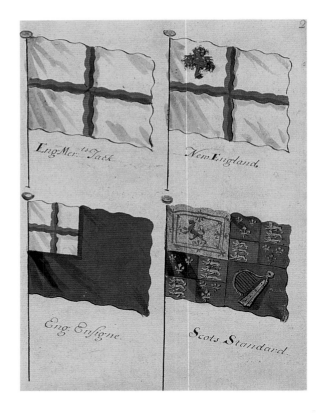

Top and above: Pepys' naval flags and a motif carrying his credentials as Secretary of the Admiralty.
Right: Hayls' portrait of the outstanding civil servant, amateur musician and most celebrated diarist in history.

the state. That had been satisfied by the old Protector, but ever since, a series of political experiments had gradually led men of good sense (such as Monck) to think longingly of the old monarchy. In these, the King was not contaminated. That was his strong – unconscious – appeal. Moreover, in exile, he had won high opinion for resilience in adversity; he had maintained his Protestantism against the wildest rumours of a Catholic conversion; he had not allowed his personal reputation to become tarnished by inevitable slanders; and even his many foreign intrigues had left him unscathed in the minds of most of his subjects. In short he did not scupper his own cause.

Early in 1660 there were visible fissures in the surface of England. On 1 January Monck marched from Scotland, not only in search of pay for his woefully deprived men, but also with the avowed intention of restoring the sovereignty of Parliament. When he reached London, he forced the Rump Parliament to admit to its ranks a number of members hitherto excluded for political reasons.

Pepys' reportage of the situation in February 1660 is as vivid as any: 'Boys do now cry "Kiss my Parliament" instead of "Kiss my arse" so great and general contempt is the Rump come to among all men, good and bad,' he wrote. A few days later there were thirty-one bonfires to be seen at one glance at the Strand bridge: and everywhere 'rumps' (of beef) were being roasted. One notes the progress in Pepys' Diary, from the man who showed him a clandestine Lion and Unicorn at the back of his chimney on 5 March, to the prevalent clamour on 16 March when people were beginning to 'talk loud of the King'. It was on that date that the Rump finally dissolved itself, and a free election was announced – although a last-ditch attempt was unsuccessfully made to block the sons of former Royalists from standing. By the end of March, effigies of King Charles were being made.

At Brussels the King, now being acclaimed, played the hand superbly – that is to say, with an air of universal friendliness. On 27 March he sent Monck a letter which was in itself a masterpiece of tact: it was certainly the kind of missive which his father had never learnt to write. First he paid diplomatic tribute to Monck's demonstrably strong position in England: 'I know too well the power you have to do me good or harm, not to desire you should be my friend.' Then King Charles protested his own desire for peace and happiness – in words which do have a gleam of his characteristic humour: 'And whatever you have heard to the contrary, you will find to be as false as if you had been told that I have white hair and am crooked.' There is a blandness too about the King's phrase of desiring to secure 'all good men' in the possession of 'what belongs to them'. Who these good men might be, and in what those belongings might consist, was left charmingly vague: yet these would of course be two of the most vexed points concerning the Restoration settlement, as in the aftermath of any civil war.

King Charles ended on a note of enormous warmth: 'However I cannot but say, that I will take all the ways I can, to let the world see, and you and yours find, that I have an entire trust in you, and as much kindness for you, as can be expressed by Your affectionate friend. Charles R.' As a result Charles received from Monck at the end of March a piece of kindly advice in the form of a secret message: to remain at Brussels, under Spanish sovereignty, when Spain and England were officially at war, would be imprudent. As once before, the King retreated to the useful quasi-neutral town of Breda. He had absolutely no wish to show himself imprudent – now.

It was thus from Breda that on 4 April King Charles wrote formally to the Speaker of the House of Commons. On the same day he gave out the Declaration of Breda. The letter to the Speaker was a triumph of double-think, far in advance of his communication to Monck. It referred constantly to the need for Parliaments, and how the presence of a monarch was justified by his role in preserving them. 'We look on you,' wrote the King, 'as wise and dispassionate men and good patriots, who will raise up those banks and fences which have been cast down.' And he boasted of the Protestantism from which he had not swerved. There was only one drum-beat of revenge – his pointed allusion to his father's death. That 'crying sin' he believed that they would be quite as anxious to avenge as he was himself, being equally 'solicitous' to redeem the nation from 'that guilt and infamy'. Yet he ended on a touching note: 'And we hope that we have made that right Christian use of our affliction, and that the observations and experience we have had in other countries hath been such as that we, and we hope all our subjects, shall be the better for what we have seen and suffered.'

The Declaration of Breda was largely the work of Hyde. Unlike the King's letter to Parliament, it was a deliberately bold document. First it granted a free and full pardon to anyone appealing to the King for his 'grace and favour' within forty days, with only a few exceptions to be decided by Parliament. The thought of the regicides continued to outrage the King. Otherwise no one would be punished for their behaviour to either Charles I or Charles II; nor would their properties be touched.

Even more strikingly, the Declaration of Breda referred to the 'passion and uncharitableness of the times' which had resulted in many differences in religion. The King promised, via an Act of Parliament, 'a liberty to tender consciences'. No man was to be in future 'disquieted or called in question' for differences in religion, so long as these differences did not threaten the peace of the kingdom. Alas, for the Act of Parliament: it was not to be. Nevertheless, the intention at least in that brave, happy April was there. Furthermore, it was for Parliament to deal with all the various transactions concerning property, inevitable after 'so many years, and so many and so great revolutions'. Last of all, the arrears of pay of the Army and its officers, under Monck, should be paid.

The Declaration of Breda was a remarkable piece of clemency combined with statecraft. But these were remarkable times: King Charles II at Breda was living through a situation which even in his wildest fantasies of exile he cannot have envisaged. By mid-April in England it was reported by one of Hyde's young relations, an apprentice in the City, that 'those formerly called Cavaliers begin to appear in garbe fit for gentlemen, and their masters "turn tide"'. About the end of April there was actually a muster in Hyde Park, with trumpets sounding through the streets: the cry was heard loud and without fear that 'the King shall enjoy his

own again'. By the end of April too, Buckingham, a most reliable guide to the way the wind was blowing, was wearing his Garter in public.

It was on 1 May that Charles' letter and the Declaration of Breda were officially read out in the House of Commons. And on the same auspicious day – a day of national mirth and rejoicing which the Puritans had tried hard to obliterate – the House of Commons passed an official resolution to desire Charles to take the government of the kingdom upon his shoulders.

Most remarkable of all these remarkable events was the fact that not one single condition was suggested, let alone imposed upon the King. The storm of revolution had blown itself out so thoroughly that those Presbyterians reported by Pepys as wanting to bring back Charles tied by such conditions 'as if he had been in chains' could find not the slightest support. Instead, the scenes on May Day itself were so ecstatic as to turn Pepys' stomach. He witnessed people actually drinking the King's health on their knees in the streets, which he described as 'a little too much'.

Charles decided to move on from Breda to The Hague in order the better to receive the delegation of Parliamentary Commissioners who were coming to offer him the government of his own kingdom. It was indeed a precious and solemn moment when Sir John Grenville arrived and asked to present the letters of the House of Commons, not least because he employed with veneration the sacred title of 'majesty', 'which not long since was the aversion of varlets and fanaticks'. The King, for his part, graciously did find his way to accepting the invitation to return.

The Declaration of Breda, a masterpiece of diplomacy paving the way for the Restoration. Illustration from Sir William Lower's *Voyage of Charles II*, 1660.

Charles dancing with his sister Mary at a ball given at The Hague just before the King's departure for England.

At The Hague these were never-to-be-forgotten days. The 'wonderful changes which were almost daily produced' in England had taken Europe by surprise. Now there were rival French and Spanish dinner-parties to toast the future ruler. The Catholic–Irish clique joined with the Spanish–French clique in seeking promises of Catholic toleration for the future.

As for the petitions, the letters, the reminders of favours and loyalties past, the pleas for forgiveness of (regrettable but surely explicable) disloyalties – these all flowed in a happy, bubbling current towards the person of the twenty-nine-year-old King. Again, it was hardly surprising that amidst such amiable sycophancy Charles was in the 'best of humour that ever he was seen to be'. Nor was his enjoyment lessened by the presence of a laughing young woman called Barbara. She had been born Barbara Villiers, a cousin of the Duke of Buckingham, and was married to a Catholic Royalist named Roger Palmer; but she was already in the months before the Restoration contributing in her way to the King's royal good humour. Of less cheerful links with the past, poor Lucy Walter had died in Paris a year back. The King's son, James Crofts, now renamed Fitzroy, remained in the care of Queen Henrietta Maria. There, with his grandmother, the handsome, engaging young man had his head thoroughly turned. That too was an omen for the future.

Now the good ship *Royal Charles* was riding at anchor and waiting to convey him towards England herself. (It had, as a matter of fact, only just stopped being the good ship *Naseby*.) A hundred pounds of roast beef had been put aboard, and silver plate on which to serve it. On the night of 23 May more than fifty thousand people went to watch the departure of the English King. But in fact there was no night: the torches and flares of the royal equipage illuminated the darkness. The drums beat a heavy and continuous assembly. Mary Princess of Orange broke down in tears and the tender-hearted Charles wept in sympathy.

The sea was calm, the heavens clear. Charles Stuart, the second, went up onto the poop of the ship to take a last look at Holland. It was also to be his last true sight of foreign parts. For the rest of his life he would not set foot outside England again. The King was coming into his own.

Charles at his last celebratory banquet at The Hague.

Charles' flotilla prepares to leave Holland, by Lieve Verschuier. After the Restoration he never set foot on foreign soil again.

A 'vanitas' still life by Evert Collier. By the age of Charles II stringed instruments like the violin, with their scope for decoration, had become highly prized as items for collection.

Virginal by Adam Liversidge. The seventeenth century saw great developments in most keyboard instruments, this one being in the Ashmolean Museum, Oxford founded by Sir Elias Ashmole, himself a collector of instruments.

Dr John Blow, 1649-1708, the celebrated composer and teacher who was organist of Westminster Abbey in the Restoration period.

Musicians and Musical Life

The Restoration age was a crucial one in the development of music in England, culminating at the end of the seventeenth century in the compositions of Purcell and, at another level, in the superb organs of Smith and Harris commissioned for Whitehall and great cathedrals. Yet these achievements are not specifically English, and the influence of France and Italy in particular, looked forward to a period of decline in the English tradition. Beyond this, however, was a widening of musical interest, in collecting, in court performances and of course in the type of amateur pursuits recorded so regularly by Pepys.

A painting, c. 1665, of the Yarmouth Collection in the Castle Museum, Norwich. It records just a fraction of the magnificent collection assembled by the Paston family in the seventeenth century.

Foreign influence guided musical development.

The frontispiece of Henry Purcell's *Ode to St Cecilia*.

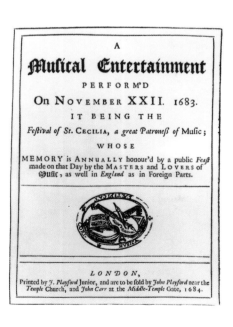

A

Musical Entertainment

PERFORM'D

On NOVEMBER XXII. 1683.

IT BEING THE

Festival of St. Cecilia, a great Patroneß of Music;

WHOSE

MEMORY is ANNUALLY honour'd by a public *Feast* made on that Day by the MASTERS and LOVERS of Music; as well in *England* as in Foreign Parts.

LONDON,

Printed by *J. Playford* Junior, and are to be sold by *John Playford* near the *Temple* Church, and *John Carr* at the *Middle-Temple* Gate, 1684.

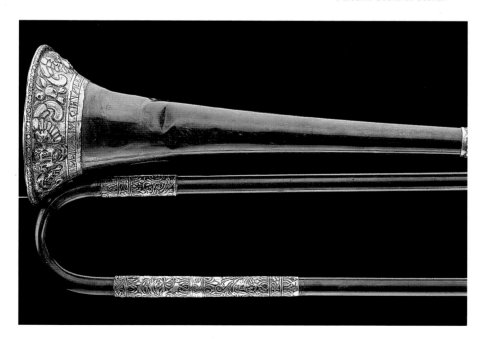

A silver-mounted trumpet by Bull and Dudley c. 1680. Metallic instruments were more durable and offered greater scope for decoration than traditional woodwind instruments, and partly for this reason became more popular.

CHAPTER SIX

INTO HIS OWN

A t Dover on 25 May 1660 the flags waved, the trumpets blew, and high above the heads of the crowd could be seen the royal arms, publicly flaunted in joy.

The King was rowed ashore about three o'clock in the afternoon. Monck was the first to receive him, with all obeisance and honour. And now it was time for the ordnance to speak. The thunder started with guns and cannons there in Dover, and spread all the way to Tower Hill in London, just as the bonfires sprang from hill to hill, as from Dover Charles went on to Canterbury, and thence to Rochester. He took his time in treading the triumphal route, now lined by the local militia of Kent, as well as more gracefully strewn with herbs by Kentish maidens. It was part of the perfect timing of things, the way everything now fell into place with such marvellous felicity, that the King would be able to take possession of his capital on an auspicious day.

It was on horseback and bareheaded, riding between his two brothers, all three in silver doublets, that on Tuesday, 29 May, the King finally entered the capital. Met by the Lord Mayor at Deptford, he first rode through the borough of Southwark and then, preceded by the Mayor, crossed London Bridge. So clogged was the structure with wooden houses on both sides, that the royal party had to be content with a twelve-foot passage, while heralds and maids and other attendants milled about them.

The pomp of this first royal procession indicated that King Charles II did not intend to return as a supplicant exile. Not only a monarchy but a whole way of life was being restored. The noise remained fulminating, above all the noise of the

Charles II in his Coronation robes by J.M. Wright, 1661. Twelve years after the death of his father, England was again ruled by a crowned, anointed sovereign.

To His Moſt
Excellent Maieſtie
KING
CHARLES
The Second, our Moſt Gracious
SOVERAIGN.
The humble Addreſs of the Officers of the ſeverall Regiments of Horſe
under the Command of his Excellency the
Lord General *MONCK*, as it was pre-
ſented by them to His Majeſtie at *Dartford*
Heath in *Kent* this preſent Tueſday , *May*
29. 1660.

LONDON:
Printed by *S. Griffin*, for *John* P*layford* at his
Shop in the Temple, 1660.

The loyalty of the Army.
An address presented to the
King on his thirtieth birthday,
on his triumphant progress to
the capital.

people – over twenty thousand of them, laughing, shouting and crying and jostling to see the King. That day and night they were all Royalists. The streets literally flowed with wine: the Venetian Ambassador kept a perpetual supply on tap outside his house. It was seven o'clock in the evening before the King, surrounded by this happy tumult, reached Whitehall.

Here he was addressed by the Speakers of both Houses of Parliament. The Earl of Manchester, for the peers, began his address in a style which was almost ludicrously obsequious: 'Dread Sovereign!' he cried, 'I offer no flattering titles, but speak the words of Truth: you are the desire of three Kingdoms, the strength and stay of the Tribes of the People, for the moderating of Extremities, the reconciling of Differences, the satisfying of all Interests', and so on. The King's 'Gracious answer', as it was afterwards described, was very short. To excuse its brevity, he said that he was disorientated by his journey and above all by the noise; but 'I confess [it] was pleasing to me, because it expressed the affections of my people'. He was too tired to attend a Thanksgiving service at Westminster Abbey, but at the end of it all he still had to dine ceremoniously in public, showing himself to his people at his food, as his ancestors had always done.

Was the weary King solaced that night by his mistress Barbara Palmer? Legend has it so. And in view of the birth of Barbara's daughter Anne, almost exactly nine months later, on 25 February 1661, the legend seems plausible. It is true that Barbara's husband, Roger Palmer, did acknowledge Anne as his own at the time of her birth, but as Anne grew up her royal paternity became quite obvious. She was officially designated the King's daughter at the time of her marriage, created Countess of Sussex in her own right, and, with Charlotte Countess of Lichfield, Barbara's second daughter by the King, came to form an important part of his inner family circle.

The man the crowds cheered through London on his thirtieth birthday was an engaging but not a merry monarch. This is confirmed by all contemporary accounts. For one thing, Charles II was no longer young by the standards of the time. His appearance had much changed from those far-off days when Cromwell was wont to refer to him jocularly as 'the young man' and 'the young gentleman'. Undoubtedly his face was much leaner. The nose too had markedly lengthened.

Already the characteristic deep lines which are seen in all the later portraits had formed from nostril to chin, curving round the wide mouth.

In general, it was majesty, not youth, which supplied the charm of his appearance. 'You may read the King in every lineament' was the general verdict on his face. His tall figure, 'so exactly formed that the most curious eye cannot find any error in his shape', was as appropriate in a monarch as it had been inappropriate in a fugitive. Once again, there was favourable comment on his

Barbara Palmer, later Lady Castlemaine and Duchess of Cleveland, by J.M. Wright, 1670. The mistress in whose arms the King allegedly spent the night following his return to London.

shining black hair, which had not yet started to go grey. However, even Charles was not to enjoy his thick black locks for long: three years later he went in his turn 'mighty grey' and adopted a periwig in consequence like everyone else.

It was hardly surprising if the new King was at heart sober, serious, even melancholy, rather than merry. Here was a man who had been undergoing harrowing experiences since boyhood: including his father's death, his family's poverty and his own humiliation. It is useless to pretend that this 'black grim man', as he was described by a witness of the procession, was the same brave boy of Edgehill, or even the spirited general on the eve of the Worcester fight. He was determined never to be subjected again to the experience of humiliation, accompanied by helplessness. With this resolution went the presentation of a public mask of cynicism, gaiety, indifference — it could take many forms, according to the interpretation of the beholders. Behind the mask lay a melancholy which nothing, not all the fabled delights of the Restoration Court, quite dislodged.

As the bells rang out and finally died away, and the myriad bonfires were reduced to ashes, the King remained wary. Outwardly, he could and would forgive the past — except for those directly involved in his father's murder. Even then he showed himself more merciful than those around him. The corpses of Cromwell, Ireton and Bradshaw (President of the court which tried Charles I) were exhumed and publicly hung at Tyburn, a gesture which did little harm to the deceased. Of the forty-one surviving regicides, those who had signed the warrant and a few others closely associated with the King's death as well as the two (unidentified) executioners, twelve died altogether. It was the King who prevented a further nineteen of their number, those who had given themselves up, from being pursued by the law; he told Hyde that while he could not pardon them, he was 'weary of hanging'. He did not save Argyll in Scotland, but then Argyll was responsible for the death of Montrose.

Nevertheless, in Charles II a temperamental disinclination to vengeance was not at all the same thing as an inclination to forget the past. Revolution, and its possible consequences, was one spectre which stalked the corridors of the King's palace from the inception of his reign to its end. To understand this, one has to be wary of hindsight. Unlike us, the monarch riding down towards Whitehall on 29 May had no knowledge that he would die in his bed twenty-five years later.

Thus one finds the implicit fear of another revolution expressed continuously and in all sorts of different ways in the early years of the reign. There were significant details such as the preference for Windsor Castle as a royal fortress, not simply because it was 'the most romantique castle that is in the world', but because it could be properly garrisoned. There were broader policies, such as the concentration on forming a proper body of guards to surround the monarch. Still more important is it to realize that in the early years plots were not only feared, but existed. In January 1661, for instance, the Fifth Monarchy men, members of a millenarian sect, ran amok. The year 1663 produced quite a serious republican plot in Ireland.

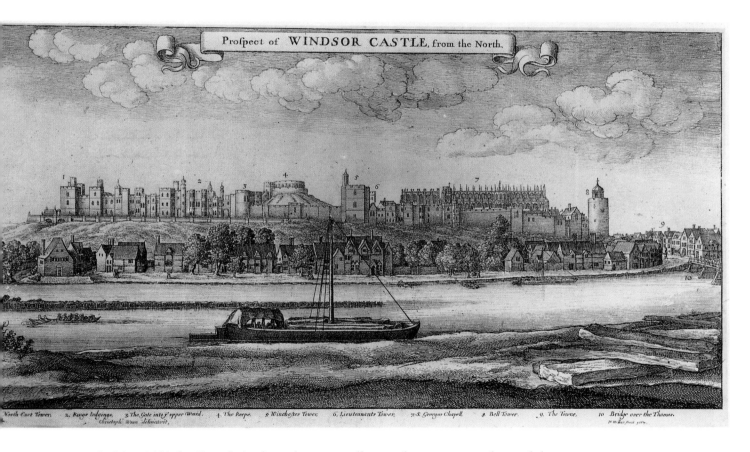

Prospect of **WINDSOR CASTLE**, from the North.

North East Tower, 2. Kings Lodgings, 3. The Gate into y' upper Ward. 4. The Keepe, 5. Winchester Tower, 6. Lieutennants Tower, 7. S. Georges Chapell, 8. Bell Tower, 9. The Towne, 10. Bridge over the Thames. Christoph: Wren delineavit,

In May 1664 the French Ambassador, an intelligent observer, wrote that it did not seem impossible that the English would 'be tempted again to try and taste a Commonwealth', remembering their greatness under Cromwell. The glorious 29 of May, then, ushered in an age of anxiety as well as an age of rejoicing.

Yet King Charles II arrived in a healing mood. The only trouble was that healing involved another twin pair of considerations: conciliation and reward. One or the other he might have achieved: the conciliation of the Cromwellians, the reward of

An etching of Windsor Castle by Hollar; this was 'the most romantique castle that ever there was in the world', and also stoutly defended.

the exiled and wounded Royalists. To do both was likely to prove difficult, if not impossible. Nevertheless, the King set out with the highest intentions.

The loyal petitions began to flood in at once: in fact, many of them had already been received before the King's arrival, and throughout May Hyde had been deluged with petitions for peerages, ecclesiastical preferments and the like. How many of these petitions related to Worcester! It was not only the King who looked back to that fearful time. One Mary Graves petitioned for having provided twelve steeds: one of these, she was reliably informed, had been shot down from beneath the King during the battle and 'the other I heard was that happy horse His Majesty got from Worcester upon ...' Less romantic were the drapers of Worcester who had been commanded to clothe the life guard in red cloth and had never been paid; they wanted £450.

Through the petitions and the Restoration settlement itself, we can discern the obsession of the loyal not only that they should, understandably, be rewarded, but less attractively, that the disloyal should not. Yet the King had to go forward and reconstruct the government of the country, and former foes were vitally important for the kind of healing settlement he had in mind.

The first body of men who surrounded the King was of necessity a combination of the old and the new. It was of course dominated by the trusted counsellor Hyde, and the veteran Sir Edward Nicholas was given the other secretaryship of State. The Marquess of Ormonde was made Lord Steward of the Household to compensate for the fact that Parliament had appointed Monck Lord Lieutenant of Ireland – although the following year Ormonde was restored to the post for which, as a man who loved and cared for the country, he was so well equipped; he was also given a dukedom. But the Lord Treasurer was to be the Earl of Southampton, a magnate who, if he had had no truck with the Protectoral government, had not shared the exile either; and, even more significantly, his nephew, Anthony Ashley Cooper, who had been a member of the republican Council of State, was made Chancellor of the Exchequer. This group formed, in Hyde's words, 'a secret committee'.

Beyond them lay the Privy Council, numbering between forty and fifty. Beyond that lay Parliament, once again two-housed. What were its powers? For that matter, what was its relation to the monarchy? What indeed were the powers of the monarchy? It was one of the remarkable consequences of the King's unconditional Restoration that in spite of years of argument, civil war, discussion and experiment, no one in 1660 yet had a clear idea as to what the proper answers to these questions were.

In so far as an accepted theory existed, it gave the King wide powers. Although the whole Restoration was based on an optimistic feeling that the King and Parliament would in future amicably share power, there was absolutely no indication as to how this was to be worked out in practice. In the meantime, the King retained his prerogative untouched, and with it the right to prorogue or dissolve Parliaments at will, to control foreign policy and, when necessary, to wage war. As against this, Parliament, it was understood, would vote him the extra monies he might need for such matters.

It was a measure of the uncertainty of the times that the moment was not felt appropriate for a general election. Although the sitting House of Commons had not been elected legally (they lacked the King's writ), they were confirmed in their existence, and kept there till December to carry out all the vital post-Restoration legislation. This Convention Parliament thus passed a general Act of Indemnity and Oblivion, from which only fifty named individuals were excepted.

Equally important was the settlement of the Army. A measure was passed to the effect that Commonwealth salaries need not be repaid – this reassured General Monck, amongst others – while of course the Act of Indemnity affected the soldiers as much as any section of the community. At the same time, King Charles took a prudent decision to alter the entire composition of the future Army.

Disbanding the old Cromwellian soldiers at considerable financial cost, he welded together by degrees a totally new kind of force out of his former Royalist regiments and whatever military elements in England were indubitably loyal. He retained, for example, the Coldstream Guards, who were a Cromwellian creation. It was, to be frank, the first English standing army – in the sense of a non-political military body in support of the civil power. But considerable effort was made to camouflage the fact: references were made to 'guards' and 'garrisons' rather than to the dreaded word 'army'. And the King's army was incidentally a convenient source of reward for that other army – of needy place-seekers.

Where the law was concerned, conciliation was more obvious, innovation less apparent. The vital principle was established that service during the Interregnum should be no disqualification: thus both Sir Matthew Hale and Edward Atkins, who had been esteemed judges under Cromwell, were reappointed.

There was one area where public innovation simply could not be avoided, and yet conciliation of all parties was absolutely vital, and that was the vexed area of religion. The question of what sort of State church should exist in England after the

Restoration was, like the constitution itself, left wide open at Charles' return. The promises given at Breda had been generous in scope. The King was personally inclined to toleration and on 25 October 1660 issued a declaration in favour of a modified episcopacy, which it was understood that the Presbyterians would also accept. But this solution, most unfortunately, even tragically, was rejected by the Commons in November. It was a defeat, not only for moderation and toleration (leading the way to the much harsher Clarendon Code), but also for the King's own plan for the English Church. It arose through the failure of the English Parliament in 1660 to follow their King's admirable lead in promoting an established Anglican Church, with the ability to tolerate other law-abiding sects in the wings of its many mansions.

The land settlement was in general more successful than the religious settlement, because here the status quo could be, and was, respected – except in the case of Crown and Church lands – even at the cost of the Royalists: it has been established that surprisingly little land actually changed hands at the Restoration. The Crown and Church lands were, however, successfully restored, despite the conflict of interest with those who had acquired them, as a result of the successful manoeuvres of Hyde and the King.

Where pomp was concerned, Charles II knew that he had, after all, been brought back to incarnate not a republican head of state, but the beloved old monarchy for which the people yearned. Thus the immediate needs of a restored sovereign were felt to include tradespeople of all sorts: an arras worker, a bookbinder, a brewer, a coffee-maker, a fishmonger, mat-layer, milliner, fruiterer, saddler, milkman, woollen draper, clock-maker, comb-maker, corn cutter (awarded a special scarlet livery, as was the royal rat-killer). On a grander level, the King needed, naturally, a Master of Tents, a Surveyor of Stables, Falconers, Cormorant Keepers. On the most important level of all, he needed to reorganize the entire paraphernalia of the royal existence. Here the King's return was to take a palpable form, in terms of building and artistic commissions.

The tastes of the new age dictated many of the earliest pieces of renovation: within the Whitehall complex the Cockpit Theatre was soon made ready. By June, over £1,200 had already been spent in furnishing the royal apartments. A sun-dial in the Privy Garden was given priority, as was the 'King's Tube', or astronomical telescope. That was another indication of the way the new reign would go. The King's own natural bent for scientific discussion and discovery could now be given a free rein. Like the jackdaws who were his favourite birds, he was not only a great collector of curiosities, but inquisitive to boot. It was the kind of mind peculiarly suited to a monarch, who could engage his subjects in conversation as and when he pleased, on what topics had currently seized his fancy, without fear of seeming to bore them.

He adored all clocks and watches. In the end there were no fewer than seven clocks in his bedroom (their ill-synchronized chiming drove his attendants mad), while another clock in the antechamber told not only the hour but also the direction of the wind. Hooke's balance-spring action was demonstrated in front of the King, while the royal accounts contain many items for the purchase of further clocks.

When the Royal Society came to be formed in November 1660 it was not mere flattery which caused the King to become its Fundator (or founder): he granted the Royal Charter on 15 July 1662. The man who was obsessed by the need to possess a lunar globe, with the hills and cavities of the moon's surface as well as the degree of whiteness solidly moulded, was well fitted to occupy the position.

At first the King was so zealous that he wanted the Society to examine every philosophical or mechanical invention before the patent was passed. In later years his acute interest in it faded, but his interest in mathematics, navigation and laboratory experiments – his own and others' – did not. He was responsible for the founding of the Mathematical School at Christ's Hospital in 1673 to instruct boys in navigation as well as mathematics. He was also responsible for the foundation of the Royal Observatory at Greenwich two years later. This was designed by Wren, as he himself confessed, 'for the Observator's habitation and a little for Pompe'. Where science was concerned, Charles II made an excellent natural leader of post-Restoration society.

Only the chronic want of money hung over the new reign. In August 1660, just a few months after his return, the King observed ruefully: 'I must tell you, I am not richer, that is, I have not so much money in my purse as when I came [back] to you.' A year later Pepys was describing how 'the want of money puts all things … out of order'. As a result the search for a bride for the King was much influenced by the question of her dowry. The lot would fall upon the well-endowed Portuguese Infanta; it was a further sign of the King's financial straits that the dowry would already be pledged as a security for loans eight months before the bride herself actually landed in England.

How much was the situation of the King's own making? Critics at the time, and ever since, have accused him of extravagance and mismanagement. Yet Charles II had been brought back to personify royalty, that in itself necessitated all the traditional trappings of a king. Again, the sums of money Charles II was originally voted by Parliament, although seemingly adequate, proved difficult to collect and in any case the yield had been over-estimated. In this way, from the very beginning, the Crown was immersed in a mire of debt from which it had little hope of escaping – by natural means. As we shall see, the King eventually resorted to unnatural means. But it was hardly his own fault that he found himself floundering in the first place.

The King's annual peacetime expenses were estimated by Parliament at £1,200,000: war was to be considered an extra, as had been customary in previous reigns. The sum itself was comparatively generous by the standards of the time – if not lavish – but the income which the King actually received was appreciably smaller. It has been estimated however that, on average over the course of his reign, the King received of those monies about £945,000 a year, increased to something under £980,000 by his private income. Assuming he kept within his theoretical income, that in itself already produced a gap between this annual income and his annual expenditure which Mr Micawber would have aptly summed up as 'result misery'. In fact, a paper on the state of the revenue shows that between Michaelmas 1661 and Michaelmas 1662 the King's expenditure was roughly £1,500,000.

Yet Charles II had little room for manoeuvre. Not only was austerity in a sovereign impossible to conceive in a body politic where rank was very much demonstrated by outward display, but the very prestige of the nation seemed bound up with the appearance of the monarchy.

It was in keeping with his subjects' aspirations, therefore, as well as his own, that the King now embarked on preparations for two ceremonies with their origins rooted deep in English history. He would hold a ceremony for the installation of the new Knights of the Garter – the first for twenty years. And after that, with even more magnificence, would follow the coronation, the joyous celebration of all that had happened over the last glorious twelve months. Both events took place in April 1661, the coronation following the Garter ceremony on the 23rd.

The coronation procession demanded an early start; everyone had to be mustered on Tower Hill by eight o'clock in the morning. Once again the conduits in the streets ran with wine, as on Restoration Day. But this time the streets were railed, and gravelled. As the foot guards of the King passed, their plumes of red and white feathers contrasting with the black and white of the Duke of York's guard, they represented the established order – and monarchical strength. The coronation medal bore the royal oak bursting into leaf and the appropriate motto Iam Florescit – now it flourishes. This was the Crown triumphant, come out of its hiding-place.

The total cost was over £30,000. The figure however was not really surprising, considering the determination to crown the King in style, and the elaborate paraphernalia needed, including two crowns (one of which was known as St Edward's crown, as before) and a quantity of ceremonial apparel for the King himself. The coronation ceremonial demanded, it seemed, an unceasing change of clothing for the monarch, most of it made of cloth of gold or some equally costly substance.

The culmination of the ancient and solemn service in Westminster Abbey was the moment the King's crown was finally placed on his head by the Archbishop of Canterbury. 'A great shout' began. Immediately afterwards the whole nobility swore fealty. Thus they 'firmly ascended the throne, and touched the King's Crown, promising by that Ceremony to be ever ready to support it, with all their Power'. The ceremonies were rounded off by an ostentatious post-coronation feast held in Westminster Hall. The King's official champion, Sir Edward Dymoke, was there on his white charger, and made a grand entry preceded by trumpeters. Throwing down his gauntlet, he made the traditional challenge: 'If any person of what degree soever, high or low, shall deny, or gainsay our Sovereign Lord King Charles the Second ... here is his champion, who saith that he lieth, and is a False Traitor.'

This was the very Hall in which twelve years earlier the King's father had been tried for his life. But the ghost of Cromwell did not answer.

Henry Fagel, a 'Foreigner at the Court of Charles II', had described the English ladies at the coronation with enthusiasm as 'everyone dressed as a Queen'. But the position was in fact vacant: and Court and King alike stood in need of an incumbent

Design, attributed to Balthazar Gerbier, for a triumphal arch in Fleet Street, one of several erected along the route of the coronation procession.

Dirck Stoop's painting of the King's coronation procession, 1661, as it leaves the Tower of London for Westminster.

Right: A painting of Charles II's coronation regalia, recently bequeathed to the Museum of London.
Far right: the King's enthronement in Westminster Abbey, engraved by Hollar.

and an heir. The royal family had recently been depleted by two deaths, both by smallpox: Mary Princess of Orange at the age of twenty-nine, and Harry Duke of Gloucester at the age of twenty-one. The demise of this promising young man, described by Hyde as being 'in truth the finest youth and of the most manly understanding that I have ever known', was far more than a family tragedy. As it was, the Duke of York remained in effect the only heir to King Charles II throughout his reign who was both male and legitimate – and wholly English. But he was first a suspected, then an acknowledged Catholic. If the 'sweet Duke of Gloucester' had lived as an alternative Protestant heir, matters might have gone very differently.

The Duke of York's prestige and importance were inevitably increased by his brother's death. At the same time he had recently forfeited much of his previous popularity in Court circles, as well as his suitability to follow Charles II on the throne, if necessary, by what was generally regarded as a most unfortunate marriage. It was ironic that the lady in question was actually the daughter of Charles' faithful servant Sir Edward Hyde (he had been raised to the rank of Earl of Clarendon at the coronation, by which name he will in future be known). James had seduced Anne Hyde while she was acting as a Maid of Honour to his sister Mary; as a result she became pregnant. James then made a secret contract with Anne and was married to her privately by his chaplain on 3 September 1660.

Once the marriage had taken place, James had second thoughts. Now he behaved in the most ungentlemanly fashion; he ignored the contract and tried to wriggle out by suggesting that others than himself could have been the father of the child. But he was unable to make the mud stick. On 22 October the child was born; it was a boy, who died. The marriage itself was generally known by the end of the year.

The irony lay in the fact that Clarendon himself was furious at the match. Marriage to his own daughter was no part of his elaborate web of marital plans, redolent of diplomatic alliances and wealthy dowries, for the two bachelor princes under his sway. At the same time, he incurred a great deal of odium for having apparently aimed to make his daughter Queen of England. It was unfair, but, given the relationship, natural. Really the only person who came out of the rather squalid incident of the York marriage at all well was King Charles. He refused to have the match declared invalid and ostentatiously visited Anne during her confinement, showing a lead which the Court reluctantly followed. As for the idea of having Parliament annul the marriage, he refused to allow Parliament to interfere with the succession – a reason for which James would one day be grateful.

DVKE AND DVTCHES OF
YORK WITH PRINCES
MAREY AND ANN

The untimely death of the Duke of Gloucester, the unsuitable marriage of the Duke of York: both of these increased the urgency to marry off the King. The eventual choice, the Infanta Catharine of Portugal, was no new candidate. Her father, King John IV, under whom Portugal had become liberated from Spain in 1640, had suggested it long ago when the bride and groom were respectively seven and fourteen. For sentimental reasons, it was pleasant to know that King Charles I had at the time favoured the match. But of course the point of the union to Portugal was very far from nostalgic. Put at its simplest, marriage into the Portuguese royal family brought England down firmly on the Portuguese side against Spain, and again, any support of Portugal was welcome to Spain's other neighbour, aggressive France.

This painting of James, Anne and their daughters was begun by Lely and completed by Benedetto Gennari. The comfortable scene contrasts with the discreditable behaviour of the Duke at the time of his marriage and his wife's first pregnancy.

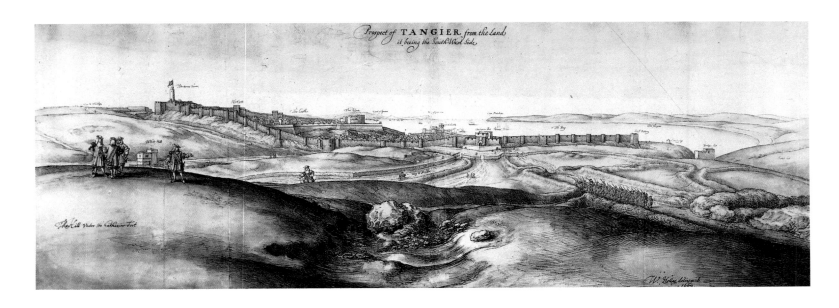

Prospect of TANGIER from the Land it being the South West Side

Tangier by Hollar – part of the dowry brought by Catharine to the King, though few Englishmen knew where it was.

The Book of Common Prayer with the royal seal, 1661. To establish a form of worship, neither 'Popish' or Puritan, was one of the most urgent tasks of the Restoration government.

Republican England had of course been the official ally of France; in consequence, King Charles had been forced to throw himself on the mercies of Spain. Despite this disagreeable memory and the perfidy of his French relations, the King was by temperament far more in sympathy with the French than with the Spaniards. After his Restoration, he was prepared to let bygones be bygones. Forgiveness was made easier by the fact that the young King Louis XIV, now grasping the reins of power for the first time at roughly the same moment as Charles II was restored, had not been responsible for the French betrayal. The moment the Restoration was effected, the English royal family tilted back contentedly to their French-oriented sympathies. It was a fact underlined by the betrothal of Charles' surviving sister, the beguiling Henriette-Anne, to Louis XIV's brother, Philippe Duc d'Orléans (generally known as Monsieur, as she will now be known as Madame). The marriage took place shortly before the coronation.

French influence doubtless played its part, but above all the English showed themselves mesmerized by the enormous fortune offered with the hand of the Infanta. Her dowry, dangled before English eyes, was to be two million crowns, or about £360,000 (then), the possession of Tangier on the Mediterranean coast, Bombay on that of India. Clarendon swore to the Portuguese Ambassador that the principal inducement to the marriage was the 'piety, virtue and comeliness' of the Infanta: but then gave the game away by asking for Tangier to be handed over 'quickly' to reassure the English ...

A proxy courtship was carried out on the King's behalf in Portugal by the English Ambassador, Sir Richard Fanshawe. Charles himself was soon writing as flowery letters as could be managed, not only to the young lady herself but also to

The Comming of ye King's Ma.ties and ye Queenes from Portsmouth to Hampton court.

Passage del Rey de gran Bretanha Carolo II.e o Rainha Dona Catarina de Portsmuit ver a Hampton-court

her powerful mother. To Catharine he referred to his sanguine feelings for the future; she responded in kind. By May 1661 the King and Clarendon were able to inform the English Parliament that negotiations were complete.

Nearly a year elapsed before Catharine made the journey to her new home. She arrived at Portsmouth on 13 May 1662. One of her first actions was to ask for a cup of tea. It was in its own way a milestone in our social history. It is true that tea-drinking had been known in England before this date but it was extremely rare. Subsequently Queen Catharine did a great deal to popularize the general drinking of tea.

Meanwhile, still for the time being tealess, the English worried over the delivery of the dowry, the garrisoning of Tangier and other practical considerations. Once the Queen's arrival was imminent, another practical arrangement occupied Clarendon and his master. Some sort of wedding had, finally, to take place. The Queen could not simply assume the married state. The question was, what sort of wedding?

Queen Catharine was of course a Catholic. In the Privy Council Clarendon had already written some of his masterful notes to King Charles on the subject of the wedding: he must have a Bishop with him when he arrived in Portsmouth, and he must have a Protestant ceremony for the sake of the legitimacy of the children. Queen Catharine, Clarendon had been assured, was prepared to submit to this. The King scribbled back, 'I hope she has consulted the Jesuits.' 'She will do that [which] is necessary for herself and her children,' wrote Clarendon firmly.

And that proved to be the case. A brief and secret Catholic ceremony was held first in Catharine's own room, as a concession to her piety. The legal marriage took place on 21 May in Portsmouth. The King and Queen sat on two specially made thrones, behind a rail to keep off the press of spectators. Catharine wore rose colour, covered in lovers' knots of blue ribbons. Afterwards they were cut off, according to Portuguese tradition, at her request; everyone was given a piece. The lace of her veil was however covered with patriotic emblems of her new country, including Tudor roses.

After that, things did not go quite so swimmingly. The Queen's state of health did not permit the marriage to be consummated that night. The King jokingly

The King and his bride approach Hampton Court after their journey from Portsmouth.

A medallion of 1662 commemorating the marriage of Charles and Catharine.

Catharine of Braganza, by or after Dirck Stoop c. 1661. She is shown wearing a farthingale which, like those worn by her Portuguese ladies, caused contemptuous comment among Englishmen.

reported to his sister Madame that he thought it was just as well that the long sea journey had upset her cycle, for he himself had had such a terrible journey down to Portsmouth that he was afraid that 'matters would have gone stupidly'.

The one thing which had troubled no one throughout all these prolonged negotiations towards matrimony – least of all the King – was the character of the bride herself. Convent-bred – and certainly reared in a most secluded fashion, having made very few appearances in the outside world – Catharine of Braganza was already twenty-three years old, which one sour commentator said was like a woman of forty in English terms. The suite of over a hundred people that she brought to England sounded more like the cast of a grandiose opera than something suitable to the informal English way of life. Her ladies-in-waiting in particular – 'six frights', wrote the wicked Comte de Grammont – aroused English national prejudice, in their vast skirts, known as farthingales, or *gardas Infantas*, because no man could get near them.

It was unkindly rumoured that the Queen herself clung obstinately to these Portuguese fashions, so unalluring to English eyes. In fact, she was on arrival pathetically anxious in all ways to do whatever might please the King, and first set foot on English soil wearing English clothes; it was the Duke of York, out of curiosity or a desire to put her at her ease, who desired her to change back into her own national dress.

Warrant for the Great Seal, October 1662. Within a short period following the Restoration the full panoply of royal rule, ritual and administration was back in place.

Catharine of Braganza also came to enjoy such typically English preoccupations as fishing and picnics. For all her slight frame, she was not unathletic, particularly for one who had been nurtured in such a claustrophobic fashion. Catharine's skill at archery was noted; she was sufficiently interested in the whole sport to become patroness of the Honourable Fraternity of Bowmen.

But that of course was once the Queen had learned to relax. The first impression given to the English was of a hieratic, almost doll-like figure. Her tiny stature also militated against her at first sight. It is unlikely that King Charles exclaimed that they had brought him a bat, not a woman, when he first saw her: such an unchivalrous remark would have been quite out of character. But the malicious tale does reveal how Catharine must have appeared to the English: small and dark and very, very foreign.

As against this, the King himself, the person most intimately concerned, was charitable; 'her face is not so exact as to be called a beauty,' he told Clarendon, 'though her eyes are excellent good, and not anything in her face that in the least degree can shock one. On the contrary she has as much agreeableness in her looks altogether, as ever I saw.' Moreover, he went on, 'And if I have any skill in physiognomy, which I think I have, she must be as good a woman as ever was born.'

Yet the first crisis of Queen Catharine's married life nearly undid her. At the court of King Charles II there was already an uncrowned queen in the shape of Barbara Palmer. Barbara, later Countess of Castlemaine and later still Duchess of Cleveland, has had a bad press from historians who have been only too well aware of her greed, extravagance and tempers and have been therefore inclined to agree with John Evelyn's verdict – 'the curse of the Nation'. They have not had the opportunity to admire at first hand her sheer physical appeal, like that of a magnificent animal. Grammont described her as having 'the greatest reputation of the court beauties'. Pepys made her out of all the royal mistresses his firm favourite: she was his 'lovely Lady Castlemaine'.

But she had a famous temper and the King, like many another man, quailed before her furies and gave in to them. Nevertheless, Barbara when young was clearly great fun, unlike her husband. Roger Palmer appears as a somewhat gloomy figure, his depression hardly surprising in view of the outrageous cuckolding by his young wife. In the autumn of 1661 he accepted the title of Earl of Castlemaine, with the further humiliation that its inheritance was limited to 'heirs of his body gotten on Barbara Palmer his now wife' – making the source of the honour quite clear. Now, in a series of hideous scenes, Barbara demanded, besought, and implored Charles to make her Lady of the Bedchamber to the new Queen. Eventually, he agreed, but in doing so risked an extraordinary insult to his wife. Catharine was not a fool. She certainly recognized Barbara's name, having been doubtless warned of her existence in advance, and, on seeing it in the list of Ladies of the Bedchamber presented for her agreement, angrily crossed it out. However, when she was first presented with Barbara in person, she received her rival cordially, her poor understanding of English preventing her from realizing who Barbara was. The moment she discovered, Catharine's eyes filled with tears of rage; her nose began to bleed and she collapsed to the floor in hysterics.

It took Queen Catharine a little time to discover that hysteria and threats were no way to play her cards where Charles was concerned – those were best left to Barbara, the mistress. In repose, Catharine discovered the strength of her own hand: not only was her sheer goodness of character her strongest suit, but it was also as effective in its own way, where Charles was concerned, as sensuality and tantrums.

A year after the marriage, relations between the royal couple had settled down most amicably, thanks to Catharine's tact and restraint. Once she had actually supped in Barbara's apartments. The crisis was over. In time, Catharine was notably more spontaneous with Charles in public – grown quite 'debonair', as it was described; she even hugged him in public, something unthinkable to that grave Portuguese Infanta who had arrived at Portsmouth.

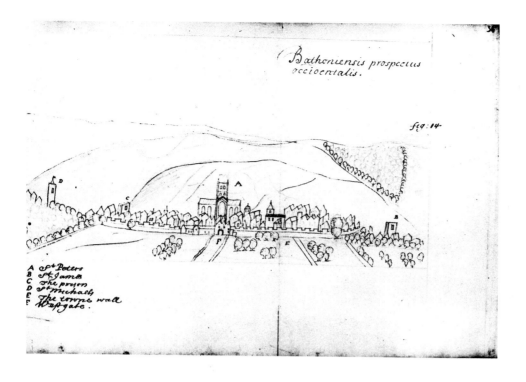

Bathoniensis prospectus occioentalis.

fig: 14

A St Peters
B St James
C The proson
D St Michaels
E The towne wall
F Wapgate.

Nicholas Hawksmoor's sketch of Bath, a town renowned since Roman times for its natural spring waters and visited unsuccessfully by Catharine in her quest for fertility.

Only one thing was lacking: an heir. It was not for lack of effort on the King's part. It was reported that he slept regularly with the Queen. But royal brides were watched for signs of pregnancy virtually from their wedding night. Any failure to conceive immediately was converted into total barrenness by the unkind rumour-mongers within and without the Court. Catharine had only been married a year when she was to be found taking the waters at Tunbridge Wells, as her mother-in-law had done a generation earlier. Catharine took the waters repeatedly that summer without success. Later she turned to the spa at Bath.

It was hardly surprising that, during her severe illness in the autumn of 1663, the delirious Queen raved of pregnancy and childbirth. To the King at her bedside, Catharine confided that she had been delivered of a 'very ugly' boy.

'No, it's a pretty boy,' Charles answered gently.

'If it be like you, it is a fine boy indeed,' whispered the Queen. There followed further rambling remarks on the same subject: at one time the Queen thought she had three children, including a girl who did look like the King.

'How do the children?' she enquired anxiously.

The King might equip her chapel, redecorate her apartments, employing Catharine's favourite greens and yellows, start to build her a new palace at Greenwich – none of this could bring the Queen true security or happiness without the longed-for heir. Yet the day would come when Catharine's unarguable goodness would stand her in good stead. As we shall see, by the time of the Popish Plot, even the prickly, suspicious English had been won to the side of their little foreign Catholic Queen. No–one could seriously believe ill of her. This was a major achievement in such an age.

Gardens and Agriculture

John Tradescant, son of the more celebrated plant hunter and gardener to Charles I. John the Younger introduced to England the Virginia creeper, phlox and the michealmas daisy from America.

One of the characteristics of the growth of a 'landed gentry' class was the increasing attention paid to improvements in property. Thus building, landscape, gardening and methods of husbandry became a concern of the prosperous middle classes as well as of the nobility.

Much planting was done for future generations.

The Restoration was an age of curiosity. This famous painting shows Charles II being presented with a pineapple by the royal gardener John Rose, supposedly the first grown in England. Painting attributed to Hendrik Danckerts, *c.* 1675.

The Duke and Duchess of Lauderdale in their splendid garden at Ham House, Surrey. The prevailing classical approach to garden design is evident.

Robert Robinson's painting of an idealized garden dates from the 1670s. Everything about its style, formalism and classicism is characteristic of the age.

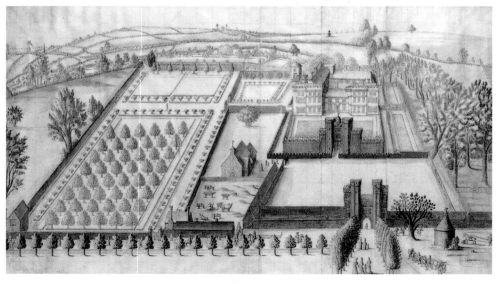

Gardens at Llanerch, Denbighshire. The garden was begun by the Royalist Mutton Davies in about 1660. It is a magnificent example of how a privileged lifestyle could be envisaged far from the hot-house of Whitehall and Westminster.

The garden layout at Lullingstone Castle, Kent, shows, almost to a caricature extent, the period's preoccupation with symmetry.

The frontispiece of John Worlidge's *Systema Agriculturae*, 1668. Many farming methods can be seen in the illustration; the book ran to five editions during the author's lifetime.

Jan Siberecht's painting, 1681, of Cheveley Park near Newmarket, an area which of course benefited greatly from the King's patronage.

Sir Henry Capel whose collection of plants was the starting point for the botanical gardens at Kew.

VII

O n 8 May 1661 King Charles II opened the newly elected Parliament: it was twenty years since a reigning English monarch had given the traditional speech from the throne. It was more than twenty years since there had been a legally elected Parliament. A comment was made on the youth of the members. 'I will keep them till their beards grow,' replied King Charles ominously. And he was as good as his word. This body, known as the Cavalier Parliament, would yield little to its predecessor in longevity, for it was not to be dissolved until 1679.

Yet its first tasks were still redolent of the past. One outstanding question was of course religion. That wonderfully open, peaceful desire of Breda, that no one should be 'disquieted or called in question' for their religious opinions, still remained to be implemented after the fiasco of the previous autumn. What finally emerged as a religious settlement – the so-called Clarendon Code enacted between 1662 and 1665 – was however as far from the heady spirit of Breda as could be imagined.

The Clarendon Code consisted of various Acts – the Corporation Act, the Act of Uniformity, the Conventicle Act, the Five Mile Act – which amounted, in effect, to the Anglican revenge. Harsh restrictions were placed on dissenters who refused to acknowledge a standard liturgy or the episcopal government of the Church. For example, all those who would not take the sacrament according to the rites of the Church of England were debarred from holding municipal office. Nonconformist ministers were compelled to vacate their livings as the Victorian division between 'church' and 'chapel' was for the first time introduced into the fabric of English society.

1-4 June 1666. The Four Days Battle, in which the English lost 6,000 men and were routed by the Dutch Admiral de Ruyter. Detail from a painting by Abraham Storck.

These Acts went further than Clarendon himself would have wished, and were certainly abhorrent to the King's instincts for toleration. Yet when Charles proposed a Declaration of Indulgence – an attempt to exempt certain individuals from the consequences of these measures – it was rejected by the House of Lords. It was a clear indication of how ineffective the King was in controlling the Parliamentary will when it went contrary to his own.

The picture was little better in Ireland and Scotland. In Ireland the Duke of Ormonde sought valiantly to produce a land settlement fair to Catholics. He failed, and the Catholic Irish found themselves subjected to an unequal settlement under the control of a Protestant ascendancy. In Scotland Lauderdale – though he happily concurred in the execution of Argyll – was only too aware of the strength of the Covenant. He suggested to the King that while he should denounce it in public, in private he should leave matters as they were. But there was no effective reconciliation. The Presbyterian Scots would remain obdurate, refusing to accept the episcopal church rule of the bishops they so detested.

The King, in fact, was far from the free agent his theoretical prerogative rights seemed to imply. The mood of the Restoration Parliament, elected on a heady tide of Royalist sentiment, underwent subtle but swift changes, not least because as members of the Commons were elevated to the Lords by appointment or inheritance new members, differing in character from the 'Cavaliers' of the Restoration election, took their places. As early as April 1663 Pepys described Parliament as being 'in a very angry pettish mood'.

There was then little appreciation of the importance of the composition of Parliament in the 1660s. This did not mean that no effort at all was made to carry through the royal policies. In Clarendon's attempts to form some kind of Court party in the Commons – rather than in later Whiggery – have been sought the origins of the English party system. Through these manoeuvres a new kind of man emerged to represent the King's interests in Parliament. Such a figure was Henry Bennet, created Baron Arlington in 1665.

Arlington, twelve years older than the King, ten years younger than Clarendon, was in essence a civil servant. Clarendon wrote of him crossly that he 'could dictate; he could not lead'. But Arlington could also serve, and that was the type of man the King was beginning to need in an age where the theoretical rights of King and Parliament were amorphous, yet their practical relationship had to be hammered out day by day.

For one thing, the King did not share Clarendon's great belief in the Privy Council as an instrument. In Clarendon's declared opinion, this body was 'the most sacred, and hath the greatest authority in the government next the person of the King'. He envisaged a constitution in which the legislature consisted of the King in Parliament and the executive of the King in Council – with the two completely separate. In Clarendon's view, Parliament was there to vote the money – but the Council, dominated of course by himself, was there to spend it.

But to King Charles II, aristocratic control via the Privy Council was scarcely more appealing than that by Parliament. When the King expatiated in 1664 on his affection for Parliaments, his honeyed words were not pure hypocrisy. 'I need not tell you how much I love Parliaments,' he declared. 'Never King was so much beholden to Parliaments as I have been …' There was much truth in the sentiment.

Whatever difficulties Charles was having, and would have, with his subjects at home, he was at least united to them by his love of the sea. King Charles' concern with the sea had international consequences as well. One incident gives a clue. In late 1661 King Charles waxed extremely indignant when the French King jibbed at the tradition by which 'ships belonging to the Crown of England' (that is, men-of-war on the high seas) were formally saluted. Charles instructed his ships not to tolerate any diminution in the reverence which was their due, adding that he would be quite unworthy if he quitted a right, and went lower 'than ever any of my predecessors did'. As he later wrote, 'It is the custom of the English to have command at sea …'

King Charles' conception of England's maritime role was also central to his relations with the Dutch. They had not treated him notably well during his exile, but though at first he had no inclination for the pursuit of vendettas abroad, it was the premature death of Mary Princess of Orange which, in December 1661, upset the equilibrium. Her brother and mother were left as joint-guardians of the eleven-year-old William, with no mention at all of the States of Holland. It was hardly surprising that the States refused to confirm the guardianship of a foreign monarch, whatever his blood relationship.

King Charles' annoyance over the whole affair was in direct proportion to his rising anger with the Dutch on more fundamental matters. In this, as in his love of the sea, he echoed the prevailing emotion of his people. For the Dutch cut across the English in certain vital areas: in Baltic trading, for example, and in distant lands, such as the West of Africa, and trade to India in the Far East. As the Dutch were clearly stronger than the English in distant waters, it was in the interests of English traders to have the Dutch defeated in a European war.

As King Charles came to share these feelings, he was further influenced by his own preference for the French. The use of Madame as a conduit for correspondence with Louis XIV – 'this private channel' – arose naturally enough in the first place out of her marriage to the French King's brother. It was fostered by the deep and growing love they felt for each other. It is Madame whom we find in the Dutch War burning with English patriotism. 'It is only with impatience that I can endure to see you defied by a small handful of wretches,' she wrote to her brother.

Such English sympathies of course only increased Madame's value as an intermediary with Louis XIV. Following the Restoration the King had already made his choice of France over Spain according to his personal inclination. This orientation became more obvious after the Cromwellian acquisition, Dunkirk, was sold to France. It was true that financial necessity played some part in Charles' decision: quite apart from the high price paid by France (some £400,000), Dunkirk cost a fortune to maintain. But the drift of the English King's diplomatic desires was clear. Thus the Franco–Dutch defensive treaty of 1662 came as an unpleasant reminder of the French King's priorities.

It was a question of the future ownership of the Spanish Netherlands, which in itself formed part of the general problem of the Spanish succession. In 1660 Louis XIV had married another farthingaled Infanta, Maria Teresa, daughter of Philip IV of Spain. As early as December 1661 letters from France were warning Clarendon, for example, that 'the King of France, when the King of Spain [Philip IV] dies, will send an army into Flanders to seize the country in the right of his wife'. Under the circumstances, Louis XIV looked on Holland less as England's commercial rival than as Flanders' potentially aggressive neighbour.

Sporadic fighting broke out during the winter of 1663–4, in Africa, where the English enjoyed success, and America, where the New Netherlands were seized. Nearer at hand in the Channel, the English fleet acquired a series of Dutch ships as prizes, victories which neatly combined prestige and profit. Already by November the sheer aggression of ordinary Englishmen, and of Members of Parliament in particular, towards the Dutch was making it difficult for the King to delay much longer. As he admitted to Madame in September, 'the truth is they [the Dutch] have not great need to provoke this nation, for except myself I believe there is scarce an Englishman that does not desire passionately a war with them.' On 24

November the King gave vent to a calculatedly patriotic speech to Parliament on the subject of his preparations for war: 'If I had proceeded more slowly, I should have exposed my own honour and the honour of the nation, and should have seemed not confident of your affections.'

It was significant that the King also had to dismiss as 'a vile jealousy' the rumour that he might graciously accept the war subsidy now voted by Parliament, and then, having made a sudden peace, turn it to his own use. War did pose an acute financial problem to a Crown already heavily embarrassed. It was true that the nationalistic optimism which pervaded the period, in the matter of this Dutch War, made light of such difficulties: Dutch prizes were expected to compensate for military costs. It was better to concentrate on the magnificent possibilities of war. In December 1664 Captain Thomas Allin was ordered to attack the Dutch merchant fleet, homeward bound from Smyrna: in the event, the attack did not produce much effect. In February of the following year King Charles, tired of waiting for King Louis, declared war.

The Dutch War brought in its train a series of humiliations. First, there were the Dutch victories, which, in view of English complacency beforehand, were as unexpected as they were unwelcome. Then there was the discrediting of those who could be held officially responsible for the war – principally Clarendon. Thirdly, for Charles II, there was the tarnishing of the King's own royal image.

To Charles the prosecution of the Dutch War seemed at first a not unenjoyable occupation. At the beginning of the war the English had about 160 ships, with 5,000 guns and something over 25,000 men; the Dutch had fewer and smaller ships – but these were of course easier to manage in shallow waters; they also had more guns and more men. The English Navy was put under the command of the Duke of York, who had been confirmed in his boyhood title of Lord High Admiral at the Restoration. The appointment was not purely nepotistic; James, like his brother, was fascinated by the sea and had already gained much popularity within the Admiralty Office.

At the first proper engagement of the war, the Battle of Lowestoft on 13 June 1665, the Dutch were resoundingly defeated by the English under James' command. But the position deteriorated rapidly. The daring Dutch Admiral de Ruyter – who had not been present at Lowestoft – captured a rich merchant fleet in northern waters. As England's fortunes declined at sea, she was also beset by an enemy within. It was during the summer of 1665 that the ominous and disgusting

signs of plague began to be found in London. The first Bill of Mortality, giving it as the cause of death, occurred in the parish of St Giles in the Fields in early May. The June heatwave which followed gave a fatal impetus to the spread of the disease. In one week alone at the end of June, one hundred plague deaths were registered. Soon the thin summer darkness was illuminated by the lights of innumerable night burials. By the end of the month, burial in consecrated ground had been abandoned in favour of communal plague pits.

The King and Court remained in the capital till July and then headed for Oxford. Parliament was prorogued, and the Exchequer transferred to Nonsuch, a palace near Ewell. This made it possible to criticize the Court for cowardice, though clearly to have had the monarch die of plague would have served no particular purpose. The same excuse cannot be made for the flight of the President of the Royal College of Physicians, which was indeed culpable. Yet it is true that the Court's departure did nothing to arrest a general breakdown of the central authority. The primitive Anti-Plague Laws of 1646, advocated by the College of Physicians, simply meant that the inhabitants of a plague-ridden building were immured behind a sealed door until they either died or recovered (generally the former). In the meantime, the restrictions were easily flouted by the upper classes, who either did not report the existence of the disease, or had themselves smuggled away from their sealed houses to the country.

Although the plague was found to have reached its peak during the week of 17 September, with a total of seven thousand deaths recorded, it was slow to die away. The official total of deaths exceeded sixty-eight thousand, but the true figure may have been something over one hundred thousand, all this occurring at a

Opposite: The Duke of York as head of the Admiralty by Henri Gascars. The Dutch War proved ignominious for the British fleet.

Admiral de Ruyter. The Dutch naval commander, one of the greatest seamen of his age, was a constant thorn in the side of his British enemies.

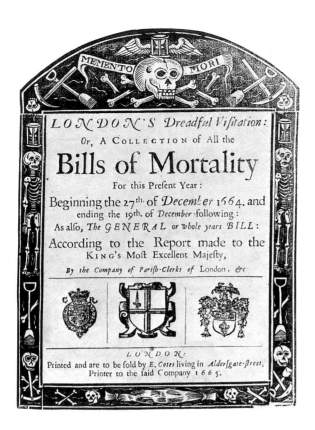

LONDON'S *Dreadful Visitation*:

Or, A COLLECTION of All the

Bills of Mortality

For this Present Year:

Beginning the 27th of *December* 1664. and ending the 19th. of *December* following:

As also, The *GENERAL* or *whole years BILL*:

According to the Report made to the KING'S Most Excellent Majesty,

By the Company of Parish-Clerks of London, *&c*

LONDON:

Printed and are to be sold by *E. Cotes* living in *Aldersgate-street*, Printer to the said Company 1665.

The Diseases and Casualties this Week.

	Imposthume	11
	Infants	16
	Killed by a fall from the Belfrey at Alhallows the Great	1
	Kingsevil	2
	Lethargy	1
	Palsie	1
Abortive	5	Plague — 7165
Aged	43	Rickets 17
Ague	2	Rising of the Lights 11
Apoplexie	1	Scowring 5
Bleeding	2	Scurvy 2
Burnt in his Bed by a Candle at St. Giles Cripplegate	1	Spleen 1
		Spotted Feaver 101
Canker	1	Stilborn 17
Childbed	42	Stone 2
Chrisomes	18	Stopping of the stomach 9
Consumption	134	Strangury 1
Convulsion	64	Suddenly 1
Cough	2	Surfeit 49
Dropsie	33	Teeth 121
Feaver	309	Thrush 5
Flox and Small-pox	5	Timpany 1
Frighted	3	Tissick 11
Gowt	1	Vomiting 3
Grief	3	Winde 3
Griping in the Guts	51	Wormes 15
Jaundies	5	

Christned { Males — 95 { Females — 81 { In all — 176

Buried { Males — 4095 { Females — 4202 { In all — 8297   Plague — 7165

Increased in the Burials this Week — 607

Parishes clear of the Plague — 4   Parishes Infected — 126

The Assize of Bread set forth by Order of the Lord Mayor and Court of Aldermen, A penny Wheaten Loaf to contain Nine Ounces and a half, and three half-penny White Loaves the like weight.

Above: one week's mortality list for the City of London shows the unimaginable ravages brought by the plague. Above right: the title page of the collected edition of the Bills of Mortality for 1665. Right: scenes from the capital during the year of the plague.

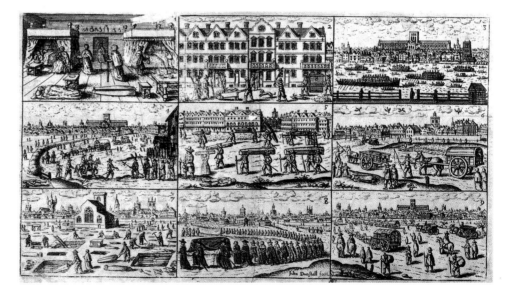

moment when the honeymoon of the King and his people was fast approaching its conclusion. A sick people, who are also at war, are hardly likely to love their monarch the more for such disasters. Nor had the events of the Great Plague increased the popularity of the Court, as may be imagined, particularly as news of their merry debaucheries was already beginning to spread downwards.

At Oxford on 28 December 'my lady Castlemaine', as Barbara was now generally called, had given the King a very public Christmas present in the shape of a son, born at Merton College, where she was lodged. She was not otherwise having a very fruitful time in the university city, since the ties of affection, if not sensuality, which bound her to Charles were being alarmingly stretched from a new quarter.

It was not the little Portuguese Queen who was the danger, but a girl called Frances Stewart. Here was a most disquieting kind of rival. It could not be denied that Frances had a sense of style which the French Ambassador complacently attributed to her education in his country – she had been at the court of Henrietta Maria and was now a maid of honour to Queen Catharine. Barbara, constantly pregnant, can hardly have shone, for all her voluptuousness. Frances, with a lovely figure and long legs, was also eight years younger than Barbara, never the happiest of situations for the older rival.

But Frances' youth was not the worst of it. Most dangerous of all, Frances Stewart was actually virtuous! There was indeed something child-like, even childish, about Frances which accorded with her virginity and her determination to preserve it. She loved, for example, to play Blind Man's Buff, to build card castles, amusements which were harmless, if slightly frivolous. At the same time, she tantalized: as when she had an exciting dream that she was in bed with three French Ambassadors (what could the explanation for that be?) and told it to the Court. The combination of provocation and virtue drove the King mad. He was discovering the fatal appeal of innocence.

And there was a further complication, still less pleasing to Barbara's jealous ears. Queen Catharine still had not succeeded in becoming pregnant. Were the Queen to die – and she had been extremely ill in 1663 – the King would be free to marry again. Frances came of a good Scottish family. Her very virtue, her youth, her good spirits, all made her a not implausible candidate. It was happily appropriate that King Charles had her image engraved with helmet and trident as Britannia, to preside over the British coinage for three centuries. She was a charming symbol of womanhood.

Then in April 1667 Frances suddenly eloped with the Duke of Richmond. She did so, exhausted by the pressures put upon her, and as if to prove once and for all that she valued a wedding-ring over the perquisites of a royal mistress. The King was appalled, writing to Madame: 'You may think me ill-natured, but if you consider how hard a thing 'tis to swallow a injury done by a person I had so much tenderness for, you will in some degree [understand] the resentment I use towards her.' The next year Frances caught smallpox and the King's better nature returned when he heard that she was untouched: he told Madame that her affliction had brought

him to overlook the past, and 'I cannot hinder myself from wishing her very well.'

In the spring of 1666 the King's campaign to gain allies against 'the Hollanders' was not much more successful than his pursuit of Frances Stewart. It was true that Louis XIV's support of them proved nominal and he did not, as Charles had feared at one point, send troops against England. But Charles still lacked help and as spring gave way to the start of a long hot summer, Charles wrote irritably to Madame in May, 'I can only now wish for peace and leave the rest to God.' Worse was to follow. On 1 June commenced that prolonged naval engagement known as the Four Days' Battle, which resulted in a heavy defeat for the English at the hands of the Dutch and French. The English lost six thousand men (many of them burnt to death when their ships caught fire) and, according to the official account, eight ships sank and nine were captured. Against this, the Dutch lost two thousand men and seven ships. By the end of July all sides had had enough and as a result, Charles II, Louis XIV and Johann de Witt were now to be found arguing over terms for peace. And soon a new catastrophe was to descend on the English.

The Great Fire began before dawn on Sunday, 2 September, in Pudding Lane, not far from London Bridge. A persistent east wind then drove the fire along the Thames and across the city. By Monday the flames had gained a front of half a mile and it was only then that the extent of the emergency was grasped, by which time it was very difficult to establish a clear zone to confine the flames. On Tuesday the blaze spread hideously to engulf Blackfriars and the entire parish of St Bride's. Soon the fire 'rushed like a torrent down Ludgate Hill', as an onlooker described it.

Very early on the Tuesday the King and the Duke of York arrived in the City on horseback and stayed there all day, riding from place to place, at times directing their Guards to fight the fire, and at times, accompanied by only a small escort, going to the very limits of the blaze, distributing water.

By the end of the day the King's clothes were soaking, his face black, his whole person muddy and dirty. But there were many testimonials to his bravery and resolution as he stood up to his ankles in the water, joining in the work with a will, wielding a bucket and spade with the rest, and encouraging the courtiers to do likewise. In all, the flames destroyed an oblong-shaped area about one-and-a-half miles long and half a mile deep before, after four days of burning, dead calm came. On Sunday the first rains fell. But there were periodic alarms for weeks after that, and the smouldering amidst the ruins continued, with occasional outbreaks of minor fires, until a vast downpour of rain in October put an end to it altogether.

Opposite: Frances Stewart, by Peter Lely.
Above: Britannia, the image used on British coins for centuries, was made in the likeness of Frances Stewart.

The Monument, the imposing landmark erected to commemorate the ending of the Great Fire in 1666. Its height is 202 feet.

The official report of the Privy Council noted that 'Nothing had been found to argue the Fire in London to have been caused by other than the hand of God, a great wind and a very dry season.' It may seem strange to our ears that when, on 6 September, the King addressed all the homeless Londoners assembled at Moorfields, his first care was to state with all the firmness at his command: there had been no plot. The Fire was due to the hand of God.

He spoke in vain, except to the rational. From the first, the Catholics were prime suspects for firing the City, with the Anabaptists second in line. As fear of revolution was to some (like King Charles), fear of the Catholics was to others: irrational, but a fact of the age. Hidden from outward eyes, the infection festered and waited for the next outbreak of strident anti-Popery.

In his Moorfields speech of 6 September the King had vowed, by the grace of

St Paul's and the City in flames, viewed from across the Thames. The painting is attributed to Wyck.

Wyck's painting captures the hysteria which gripped London as the fire raged.

God, to take particular care of all Londoners. The replanning of London was of course a long-held aim. The King had a strong streak of the town-planner in his nature, be it palaces or parks, streets, squares or gardens. But above all the urgency to re-build a devastated capital coincided with the availability of the genius of Christopher Wren. From the first, King Charles had attempted to employ Wren's manifold talents, and now the work most popularly associated with Wren's name, the rebuilding of London, owed much to the energy of King Charles, and his proclamations. Although not all Wren's visions, which included a straight view from Ludgate Circus to St Paul's, and then on to the Royal Exchange were carried through, the King's prompt and determined action remains something for which later generations should call him blessed.

As the dreadful year 1666 gave way to 1667 the King had yet other worries, above all financial. One effect of the fire was to cripple the yield of the taxes. Then there was the question of the King's debts and those of his father, which Parliament had promised to redeem, though it had not done so. By July 1667 Clifford, who was one of the five Commissioners appointed to act as Lord Treasurer after the death of Southampton, estimated the general debts at £2,500,000 – with one million owing for the Navy. Retrenchment was the order of the day and a committee of the Privy Council was set up with that in mind.

But still the war, the greatest cause of poverty, dragged on. Dutch, French and English were unable to agree on terms. It was against this seemingly dreary background of diplomatic manoeuvre and counter-manoeuvre that the Dutch carried out their daring raid on the Medway in June 1667.

With the aid, it is distressing to relate, of two renegade English pilots, the fort of Sheerness was captured, the boom at Chatham broken and, worst of all, the English fleet ravaged – in Evelyn's words: 'A dreadful spectacle as ever Englishmen saw and a dishonour never to be wiped off!'

The result exceeded De Witt's wildest expectations. There was panic in the capital, ruled over by an uncertain King with an uncertain government. One rumour suggested that the King had abdicated and escaped. Peace was essential. Clarendon wrote, 'Although peace can be bought at too high a price, it would suit us highly in the circumstances and we are not in a position to decline.' Thus the Peace of Breda between the two countries was officially brought about at the end of July. The Dutch were conceded their demands in West Africa, England was confirmed in the tenure of the former Dutch possessions of New York, New Jersey and New Delaware.

It could not be said therefore that the country itself had bought peace at too high a price, but, even so, the price had to be paid – by someone.

June 1667, humiliation for the English as the Dutch sail up the Medway and destroy warships at Chatham and Rochester. 'A dreadful spectacle as ever Englishmen saw', wrote Evelyn.

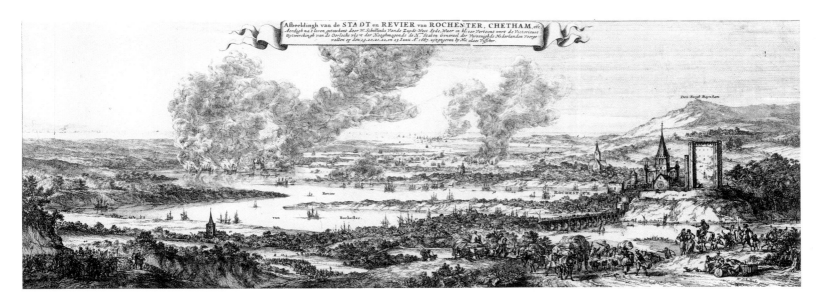

Wren, St Paul's and his City Churches

Above: The interior of St Mary at Hill, re-built by Wren and completed in 1677.

Right: St Bride's in Fleet Street, built 1671-78, viewed from the west.

Below: St Stephen's, Walbrook, 1672-79, showing the classical dome structure characteristic of much of Wren's work.

No name is as associated with Restoration London as that of the great architect Christopher Wren. Yet Wren, born in 1632, began his brilliant career as a scientist and mathematician in Oxford, where he became Professor of Astronomy in 1657. He was thirty before he began

Wren's immortality is visible in his works around us today.

his architectural career, designing the chapel at Pembroke College, Cambridge, and the Sheldonian Theatre, Oxford. It was, of course, the Great Fire which enabled Wren to become part of the nation's history. He rebuilt St Paul's and fifty-two of the City churches. In 1669 he became surveyor-general of the King's Works and extended his work to, for example, Hampton Court, Chelsea Hospital, Whitehall and the Royal Observatory.

The organ in St Paul's. The carving, by Grinling Gibbons, has been called 'the most magnificent wood carving in England'.

St Paul's; the magnificent choir.

Sir Christopher, painted by John Closterman against a background of his most famous achievement. St Paul's was rebuilt between 1675 and 1710.

CHAPTER EIGHT

INTO THE ARMS OF FRANCE

For a long time Charles II's relationship with the Earl of Clarendon had been permeated by resentment. Some of this was personal. It was not pleasant to be treated as a lazy schoolboy, as the King approached his fortieth year. The notes passed between Charles and Clarendon in the Privy Council, despite the humorous exchanges, illustrate how firmly the elder man considered himself in control.

But there was more to the fall of Clarendon from Charles' favour than mere annoyance at an irksome manner. It has already been noted that the King did not favour Clarendon's emphasis on the Privy Council. He had also suffered acutely in recent years from Clarendon's failure to control the House of Commons. As a result, its 'angry pettish' members had in his opinion kept him woefully short of funds. Nor had Clarendon produced the French alliance of his dreams, which would have made the whole Dutch business so much easier to pursue.

Additionally, two marriages were further held against him – the alien Portuguese match to Catharine was laid at his door; while the fact that his own daughter was likely to be Queen, if Charles died without issue, only increased Clarendon's widespread unpopularity, recently exacerbated by the failure of the Dutch War.

Detail from Jean Nocret's painting of Louis XIV, the Sun King, and the French Royal Family, 1670.

Edward Hyde, created Earl of Clarendon. He was the central figure in Charles' reign until his downfall in 1667.

Following the fall of Clarendon, new ministers rose to greater prominence. Five of them are known to history as 'the Cabal', after the initials of Clifford, Arlington, Buckingham, Ashley and Lauderdale. Above: Henry Bennet, Earl of Arlington, a prime intriguer against Clarendon. Above right: George Villiers, Duke of Buckingham. Right: Thomas Clifford, Lord Clifford of Chudleigh who became Charles' able Lord Treasurer. Opposite above: John · Maitland, Earl of Lauderdale who ruled Scotland with an iron hand. Opposite below: Anthony Ashley Cooper, later Earl of Shaftesbury who became the King's most redoubtable opponent.

In the meantime, the King was discovering for himself the advantages of younger, more accommodating servants. Besides Arlington and Thomas Clifford, there was Buckingham's Yorkshire protégé Thomas Osborne, two years younger than the King. The sport of Chancellor-baiting was an easy one for these younger men in the embittered atmosphere of that autumn of 1667. And there was Barbara Castlemaine, who hated Clarendon – the feeling was mutual – who joined with her cousin Buckingham and exerted what influence she could.

The public move against Clarendon came from Arlington and Sir William Coventry combined. Coventry, another of the new men who was roughly the

same age as the King, was an attractive character, possessing both wit and courage. His work at the Admiralty, under the Duke of York, was devoted and intelligent, and in the summer of 1667 he was made a Joint Commissioner of the Treasury. Now Coventry turned to the attack on Clarendon with zest.

Parliament bayed for blood. The Chancellor's windows in Piccadilly were broken. Flight was suggested to avoid the penalties of impeachment. Lady

Clarendon in her anguish was 'given over for dead'. The Chancellor duly went, his departure witnessed by Arlington, amongst others, 'with great gaiety and triumph' from Barbara's windows. Clarendon looked up. 'Pray remember that, if you live, you will grow old,' he said to the radiant favourite.

So the ageing Earl of Clarendon took up his residence at Montpellier, to write, with measured anger but also with sonorous recall, the history of his own times.

'It was impossible for me to live with it,' wrote Charles to Ormonde, 'and do those things with Parliament that must be done or the government will be lost.' In 1667 he saw his problem quite correctly as ruling with Parliament – his policies, their supplies – and this Clarendon had not enabled him to do. The spectacle of a sovereign 'dropping the pilot' – the phrase applied to the dismissal of Bismarck by the Kaiser – is never an attractive one. But from 1660 onwards King Charles II was not in business to charm by his actions. To rule, if possible with the approval of Parliament, struck him as being the first duty of the King.

Who now gained political power? Certainly the Buckingham faction benefited from Clarendon's fall. Osborne became a Joint Treasurer of the Navy. Other supporters of Buckingham were preferred. But it was not simply a case of the rise of the Cabal – that acronym which, as every schoolchild knows (or tries desperately to remember), conveniently covers the names of Clifford, Arlington, Buckingham, Ashley and Lauderdale. For one thing, the Cabal was not nearly as united as the acronym suggests.

The most striking immediate effect of Clarendon's fall was to divide the King and the Duke of York. The closeness which had existed between them earlier in the reign gave way to a 'kind of inward distance', in Pepys' phrase. Indeed Charles' attitude towards James had long been slightly ambiguous. James had grown up to be an interesting character: he was brave, genuinely so, and not unintelligent. But he had a rigidity which sometimes goes with courage. Charles, on the other hand, had decided early on to bend, not break. The same contrast can be discerned in their respective attitudes towards the Catholic religion. Unlike Charles, James had shown a propensity towards it during the later years of exile, as though its certainties appealed to that streak of the martinet in his own nature. At the Restoration he was described as 'a professed friend to the Catholics'. The inclinations of his first wife played their part. Anne Duchess of York died as a Catholic in March 1671, having leant in that direction for several years. The precise date of James' own conversion is not known but it seems that he was officially received into the Catholic Church early in 1672. However, he continued to attend Anglican services until 1676. After that his conversion was an open secret, although, at his brother's request, he never declared it publicly.

With Charles the whole process was very different. It was not that he had any temperamental aversion to changing his religion, but he drew a sharp distinction between a political standpoint and a private faith. Then the notion of his own conversion, leading on to that of England herself, began to serve as a useful card in the tortuous negotiations with the Catholic Louis XIV. Later still, the furore of the Popish Plot made royal Catholicism once again dangerous. All this remained in the domain of politics.

The fact is that Charles never did declare himself to be a Catholic during his active life. As late as 1675 he told the French Ambassador Barrillon that his brother James' Catholicism endangered the thone – which was of course true. Most cogent of all is the testimony of Father Huddleston, the priest who finally received the King. Charles II, in his general confession, declared himself heartily sorry 'for that he had deferr'd his Reconciliation [to the Catholic Church] so long'. That was a strange statement for a man to make on the eve of his death, if it was not true; and a strange statement for Father Huddleston to publish afterwards if it was demonstrably false.

At the same time, Charles the pragmatist was not without a reluctant admiration for James the man of principle, where religion as well as politics were concerned. He never, for example, wished James to suffer for his religious principles, and even, incredibly, did not forbid James' second Catholic marriage – a manifest political disaster. Then there was the whole question of the succession. That too was crucial to the relationship between the two brothers. Like the religion of Charles II, it was not at all a straightforward matter.

James' position as heir presumptive went through several phases during the 1660s, first weakened by the King's marriage, then strengthened by the Queen's apparent infertility. As the years went by, several of the notorious ways of dealing with a barren wife had already been publicly mentioned. At the time of Charles' unrequited romance with Frances Stewart, the notion of his remarriage – perhaps on the Queen's death, perhaps on divorce – had been vaguely mooted in gossip, if nowhere more substantial. By May 1668 the rumours had grown. Meanwhile, the groundswell of suggestion that his illegitimate son by Lucy Walters was actually legitimate, or would be now legitimized, grew. This would of course have constituted a lethal snub to James. But in the event the King did nothing. Catharine remained undivorced, Monmouth unacknowledged. Meanwhile, this temporary ruffle between King and York became gradually smoothed. James' stature as heir presumptive was undiminished.

The King's main preoccupation was to recover some of his prestige lost against the Dutch and, not many months after Breda, he secured a remarkable diplomatic reversal of this degrading position. A Triple Alliance was constructed between England, Holland and Sweden. Newly vulnerable, France immediately concluded the Peace of Aix-la-Chapelle with Spain, and an ostensible tranquillity prevailed across the map of Europe.

It is probably correct to regard this astonishing turnabout as mere shadow-boxing. There is no evidence that Charles II's aversion to the Dutch had abated. But he hoped that the Triple Alliance might prove an efficient way of dealing with his growing domestic problems. These included a bankrupt Treasury and a highly restive House of Commons, many of whose members were beginning to voice anti-French – and anti-Catholic – sentiments. The Triple Alliance had a nice Protestant sound to it; more money might be forthcoming from Parliament as a result.

The Dutch involvement was popular with the English Parliament because it aimed at France. In February 1668 the King spoke eloquently of his renewed need for money: 'I lie under great debts contracted in the last war; but now the posture of our neighbours abroad, and the consequence of the new alliance will oblige me, for our security, to set our considerable fleet to sea this summer.' Retrenchment, again, was the order of the day. Pensions were cut, or stopped, without being cancelled, by the simple expedient of not paying them. Ambassadorial expenses were severely checked and plate, often regarded as a perquisite of office, was demanded back after use.

Nor did the influence of Buckingham introduce any kind of order into the chaos. If Buckingham, and for that matter Osborne, had pursued some constructive policy of their own, their destructive efforts in other directions might not have proved so catastrophic. Examples are Buckingham's engineering of the downfall of the able Coventry at the Admiralty and of the truly great Ormonde in Ireland. In fact the Cabal was anything but united. Clifford was against the Alliance, while between the pro-Dutch sympathies of Arlington, for example, and the pro-French leanings of Buckingham there was an obvious and unbridgeable gulf. In the late 1660s nothing like a homogeneous Court party was in fact at the command of Charles II.

His groans to Madame over his constant financial troubles amply illustrate one side of this, as do his reiterated pleas to Parliament itself on the subject of money. Charles expressed it thus to Parliament, called again in October 1669 after an eighteen months' gap for this precise purpose: 'I desire that you will now take my debts effectually into your consideration.' The House of Commons remained deaf.

The Triple Alliance notwithstanding, at some point late in 1668 King Charles decided formally to pursue an alliance with his cousin Louis XIV by any necessary expedient. His cynicism towards his own Parliament was growing, and his French initiative cannot altogether be separated from it. The secret feelings of such a wary character as Charles II must always be analysed with care; nevertheless, the distinct impression is gained that he saw in the French alliance, from the first, one solution to his domestic insecurity. The character of Louis XIV also exercised a baleful fascination over Charles II – as indeed it did over the whole of Europe. The personality and reputation of Louis XIV represented the living challenge to Charles II, much as that of Oliver Cromwell represented the dead. Religion – or 'the design about R.', as Madame coyly termed it – does not seem to have played any part at all in Charles' calculations at this point. Aiming at greatness abroad, security at home, and having lassoed for the time being the horns of the Dutch, Charles prepared to stalk the bigger game of Louis XIV. He was not ashamed to admit to Madame that the Triple Alliance had its genesis in his disappointment with France. She might be 'a little surprised' by the treaty he had concluded with the Dutch, he wrote airily in January 1668, but she should not be. 'Finding my propositions to France receive so cold an answer, which in effect was as good as a refusal, I thought I had no other way but this to secure myself.'

By the end of 1668 cautious negotiations were proceeding. Madame, appropriately, was the intermediary. She had planned a visit to England in December, postponed owing to her pregnancy, yet the visit had obviously been intended to forward discussions between the two kings.

So the scene was set for Madame's embassy, the zenith of her life. It was also the most vital period so far in the reign of Charles II. For so, surely, the months between the signature of the Triple Alliance and the signature of the Secret Treaty of Dover in May 1670 must be regarded. Madame was given a special cipher for the purpose by her brother, and remained the ambassadress of England rather than of France. Nothing emerges more clearly from Madame's letters to her brother than the continuance of her English sympathies.

Secret but exhilarating negotiations continued throughout the spring and summer of 1669, in part reflecting the growing disillusionment of the King with Parliament. For it is an inescapable fact that in early 1670, at the very moment Charles was negotiating with France, he played on the hatred of the House of Commons for the French by asking for money to fight them. The conclusion of the King's contempt for his Commons is unavoidable.

Henriette-Anne, Charles' beloved sister who died shortly after she had helped to secure the French alliance embodied in the Treaty of Dover. A miniature by Samuel Cooper c. 1665.

What inspired him? It was most emphatically not the vision of an autocratic monarchy; but there was a vision all the same. It was the vision of an England strong abroad and at home, her fleet triumphant, superior to the Dutch, supported and abetted by her natural friend France.

By May 1670 the negotiations with France were sufficiently advanced for Madame to pay her long-deferred, long-desired visit. She arrived off Dover on 16 May. Unbelievably, it was close on ten years since they had met face to face, for Henriette-Anne had last visited England that winter of 1660 before her marriage. Yet the intimacy was as close as ever.

It was true that the girl Charles held in his arms at their ecstatic reunion aboard the flagship was more exquisitely fragile and ominously paler than ever. And the King found in her even greater enchantment. However, when he tried lightly to obtain one little favour – his sister's lady-in-waiting Louise de Kéroüalle, with her 'childish simple and baby face' – Madame firmly refused on the grounds that she was responsible to the young lady's parents in France. The inception of this new royal relationship had to wait for another occasion.

In time came the dreaded hour of Madame's departure for France. Charles and James, overcome with grief, accompanied her on board the ship that would carry her away. Charles in particular could hardly tear himself away. Three times he said goodbye, only to return and embrace her.

Alas for King Charles: Madame, his delight, had only a few days of life left to her on her return to France. On 27 June she wrote a touching letter from Paris to Thomas Clifford in England: 'This is the ferste letter I have ever write in inglis, you will eselay see it bi the stile and the ortografe ... i expose miself to be thought a foulle in looking to make you know how much I am your frind.' The first English letter of this expatriate Stuart princess was to be her last. She fell seriously ill on 29 June and died the next day, after convulsions and other agonizing sufferings which appalled all those who attended her death-bed.

When Charles was brought the desperate news by a courtier coming post-haste from France he collapsed with grief, not emerging from his bedroom for days.

Madame left her brother with more than a broken heart however; she also bequeathed to him the objective of her visit – a treaty of alliance with France. It was as though she had died in giving birth to it: the King, the bereaved survivor, now had to raise the infant.

There were in fact two separate treaties. The first, which was kept secret, was signed by the English, including Clifford and Arlington, on 22 May 1670. Not only was it secret, but it was also a strange and slippery document. King Charles was to support the claims of King Louis to the Spanish monarchical possessions (pursuing his wife's alleged rights), as and when they should be made; in return, England would receive certain South American territories. But a further clause stipulated that King Louis would not break the Treaty of Aix-la-Chapelle recently concluded with Spain, enabling Charles to remain, theoretically at least, faithful to the Triple Alliance. Yet the two kings intended to wage a war against the United Provinces, and the military and naval arrangements for such a war were laid down: this might seem clear enough, albeit aggressive. But this clause was linked to another, often regarded as the crucial text in the so-called Secret Treaty. This described the English King as 'being convinced of the truth of the Catholic religion and resolved to declare it and reconcile himself with the Church of Rome as soon as the welfare of his kingdom will permit'. In order to carry out this declaration (for which no date was given) Charles II was promised money from the French King, half of it in advance, and troops as well, if necessary. The Anglo–French assault on the Dutch was scheduled to follow rather than precede the undated declaration.

The second treaty was signed by the five members of the Cabal – Clifford, Arlington, Buckingham, Ashley and Lauderdale – on 21 December 1670. It was in effect a cover-up. For those ministers not in the know, a phoney treaty with France was worked out, including details of future Anglo–French action against the Dutch. But the 'Catholic' clause of the original Secret Treaty of the summer was not included. Thus no string was attached to the timing of the Anglo–French initiative.

It must be obvious that the strength of this famous – or notorious – Catholic clause was in consequence much diluted. For better or for worse, the way was left open for a combined operation to be mounted against the Dutch, without the King of England declaring himself a Catholic – as indeed happened. There is another significant point to be made about the Catholic clause, for it was not suggested in the Secret Treaty that Charles was going to change the religion of England as a whole – merely his own. Under the circumstances, the equivocal nature of this clause, dependent upon the 'welfare of the kingdom', hardly needs stressing further.

An engraved frontispiece of 1665 shows Charles on a secure throne while the Pope's totters. The climate would change as the implications of a French alliance became clear.

For this treaty Charles II has been harshly judged. He has been condemned for two reasons: first, for the acceptance of French money. Yet this was an age when foreign subsidy was by no means shocking or rare. Nor was it exorbitant. Throughout his reign Charles received a total of some £746,000 (then), not all of it from the Secret Treaty, which amounted to less than one year's income from his ordinary revenue. The second charge, however, is one of treachery – that he intended to subvert England to a Roman Catholicism it had rejected, becoming, in the words of Lord Macaulay, the 'Slave of France'. Given that Charles II was not, by 1670, the convinced Catholic of some imaginings, it must

immediately be granted that a certain mystery surrounds the religious clause of the treaty. What then was its purpose?

The Church of England solid on a rock while St Peter's wobbles on shifting sand, and the non-conformist chapel wallows in the sea. Such confidence at the start of the Restoration had disappeared ten years later.

One possibility would be that the religious clause – the 'design about R.' – was inserted to please Madame. But it is doubtful whether Charles would have allowed himself to go with her wishes had it not suited him in the first place. It is necessary to seek a less charming and more cynical explanation.

The religious clause set the seal, in the King's view, on that security which he expected to enjoy from the support of King Louis XIV. It was not so much a question of Charles II's religious proclivities as those of Louis XIV: the English King, in signing such a clause, which committed him to a personal declaration with no time schedule whatsoever, expected to bind the French King to him further. In politics, it cannot be denied that the end very often does justify the means. By 1670 Charles II had decided to make this truth – regrettable or otherwise – the principle of his actions both at home and abroad.

London:
The Pulse of
the Nation

PIAZZA in Conventgarden.

The Piazza of what was originally known as the Convent Garden after a nunnery which adjoined it.

Charles' statue at the entrance to the Cornhill Exchange. This was the site of the second

Royal Exchange, the first having declined long before it was destroyed by the Fire.

Charles II's London was, to a considerable degree, transformed by the Great Fire of 1666. Vast numbers of medieval wooden dwellings in their narrow alleyways disappeared and even if Wren's visionary plans were not executed, a more spacious and certainly safer capital emerged. London was, inevitably, the focus of national life. Only later, with the Industrial Revolution, would 'second cities' like Manchester develop from the small villages they were in Charles' reign.

An engraving by Hollar of Lincoln's Inn Fields. The public park was largely created in the seventeenth century, its size reputedly that of the base of the Great Pyramid.

The Statue of KING CHARLES II. at the Entrance of Cornhill.

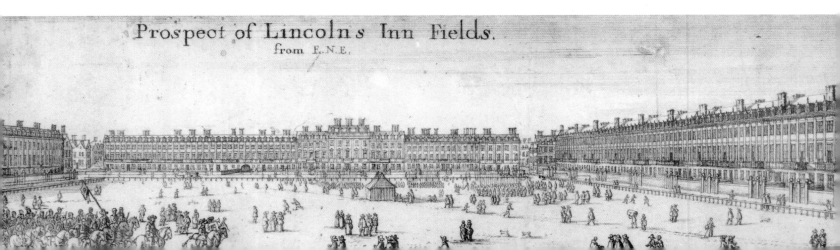

Prospect of Lincolns Inn Fields.
from E.N.E.

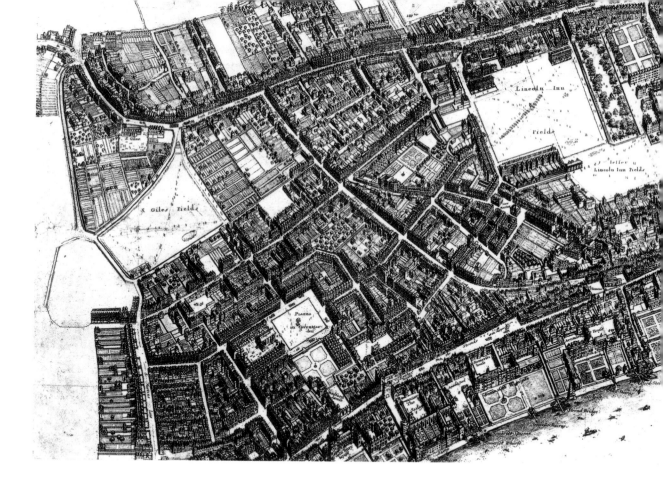

Hollar's superbly detailed plan of 'West Central' London bordered, roughly, by St Martin's Lane to the west and Lincoln's Inn to the east.

A scene outside Inigo Jones's Banqueting House at Whitehall. Whitehall Palace was the focus of court life.

A late seventeenth-century London coffee-house. Coffee houses became centres of gatherings opposed to the King's policies.

The great fire

proved a blessing in

disguise.

IX

PERSONAL PLEASURES

The summer of 1670 – when Charles II reached his fortieth birthday – marked his emergence not only as a fully fledged governor of his own kingdom but also as a mature man set in his ways. On 29 May 1660 the crowds cheering the restored monarch had been greeted by an evidently wary, if affable, man. By 29 May 1670 the reserve had become so deep as to be impenetrable, though as a man of political strength, cunning and purpose, he remained prepared to show himself at all times gracious to his people. As a monarch, Charles II was renowned for his friendliness, the ease of access which he offered to his subjects, to include not only the poorest amongst them but also his critics.

There was, however, one aspect of his public face in which his subjects might feel that ease had gone altogether too far. It was after the fall of Clarendon that the Court of King Charles II began to enjoy that reputation for debauchery which has surrounded it in the popular imagination ever since. Clarendon had been an imposing figurehead, who might not be revered but whose name was certainly never synonymous with debauchery. Buckingham offered a very different image, and of the Cabal not only Buckingham gave offence; the Duke of Lauderdale was in private a gross figure and his wife Bess a legendary amorist. As against that, it should in fairness be pointed out that Clifford's Devonshire-based life was a pattern of domesticity; Arlington's private life was impeccable and Shaftesbury's interests lay in political controversy rather than in private indulgence.

Can it then be argued that this reputation for debauchery in 'Good King Charles' Golden Days' has been much exaggerated? The clue is to concentrate not

John Wilmot, second Earl of Rochester, among the most prominent of the dissolute courtier-poets and wits whose behaviour scandalized many of the King's subjects. After Jacob Huysmans, c. 1665-70.

Peter Lely's painting of the Duke and Duchess of Lauderdale. Although in no sense to be numbered among the witty and amoral courtiers who gave Charles' reign its reputation they were nevertheless loose enough in their private lives to add their share to a general sense of debauchery.

so much on the question of debauchery but on the true keynote of the King's Court after 1667: and that indeed was laxity.

Much of the colourful aura which surrounds the Restoration Court in the popular imagination is derived from the behaviour of 'the Wits', rather than of the more powerful ministers. This little group, which flourished for about fifteen years after 1665, included John Wilmot, the second Earl of Rochester, Henry Jermyn, Lord Buckhurst, John Sheffield, Earl of Mulgrave, Henry Killigrew, Sir Charles Sedley, and the playwrights Wycherley and Etherege, as well as Buckingham (who straddled both circles).

These high-spirited gentlemen – the 'merry gang', as Marvell called them – were in the main younger than the King, grown up in the post-Civil War years. They diverted themselves at times with poetry, plays and literature in general, at times with sardonic comment on everything about them, couched, very often, in scabrous language. Despite this vulgarity, however, it was to the Wits that much of the abundance of Restoration drama was owed, and it did not harm the theatre that play-writing became a fashionable occupation, practised by aristocrats, aspired to by gentlemen.

While the King indulged himself with the company of these boon companions as a form of relaxation, he is definitely not to be identified with them. Far from being a 'Wit' himself, he could even be called their victim – along with anything else remotely established which came within their sights. For this was above all a liberal or, as we should now say, a permissive era. The obvious laxity in high places – coupled with conspicuous extravagance at a time of national financial stress – antagonized, as it generally does, those in low places who were unable to share in it. Yet, pleasure-loving, easy-going as the Court of Charles II was, it was not a bad and certainly not an evil place.

As a matter of fact, where Charles himself is concerned, his personal 'debauchery', as opposed to sheer love of women, does not appear to have been very great. It can even be argued that in the first seven or eight years of his reign Charles was something of a 'one-woman man'. Pepys, in conversation with Evelyn in that period, accepted that the King never kept two mistresses at the same time. Obviously this paradoxical fidelity did not last for ever. The seventies were a different matter.

Louise Duchess of Portsmouth and Nell Gwynn unquestionably shared his official favours in the early years of the decade. There were shorter-lived parallel romances. Not only was there the affair with Moll Davis, but there was also a fling with one of the Queen's Maids of Honour, Winifred Wells; the singer Mrs Knight; Mary Killigrew, the widowed Countess of Falmouth; and Elizabeth Countess of Kildare. Then there were the nocturnal visitors introduced up the Privy Stairs by William Chiffinch, the King's confidential servant, and Page, Keeper of the Privy Closet. Their numbers, like their identities, remain unknown to history.

Nevertheless, Pepys' conversation with Evelyn should not be totally dismissed. For one thing, Pepys was an acute observer of sexual matters in general, because he was so interested in them. Then Evelyn was a reliable source on the subject of the King in particular because he had close contact with him over so many years. Pepys' Diary entry pointed to an important strand in the King's character: Charles was not by conviction promiscuous, whatever the temptations offered to a king in a permissive age.

Frances had declined the honourable post of King's official mistress with what Barbara ungratefully described as 'the new-fashioned chastity of the inhuman Stuart': as a result, Barbara's own star remained artificially in the ascendant until the late 1660s. This was a remarkable achievement when women were said to be 'at their prime at twenty, decayed at four and twenty, old and insupportable at thirty', in the words of Etherege's Dorimant.

Then the appearance of a pert young professional actress named Nell Gwynn signalled that Barbara's era was over. Barbara was asked to remove herself from her

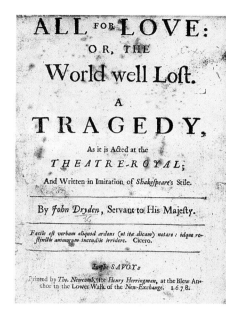

A playbill for *All for Love*. John Dryden was foremost among Restoration dramatists as well as a powerful polemical poet and satirist.

John Evelyn, traveller, translator and author of works ranging in subject from navigation and commerce to medals and salads. Famous above all for his Diary, he recorded the laxness of the Restoration Court.

The last page of Pepys' diary. He described the foibles of the King, as well as his own. His extraordinary code was broken over a century after his death.

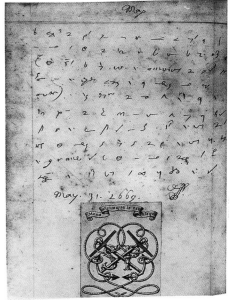

convenient Whitehall apartments. It was true that in August 1670 she was created Duchess of Cleveland, Countess of Southampton and Baroness Nonsuch; all this was however in the nature of a golden handshake.

The King's new mistress was familiarly known as Nelly Gwynn. She was introduced to the King by Buckingham some time before January 1668. She remained on fond terms with the Duke, visiting him in the Tower during one of the periods of his disgrace. Nell was not the only actress to entrance her sovereign. Moll Davis also succeeded in doing so by singing a particular song, 'My lodging is on the Cauld ground …', after which, as John Downes commented, her lodging was in the royal bed. Moll presented the King with a daughter, known as Mary Tudor, but the relationship was not enduring. Whether or not the evil tale is true which has Nell Gwynn lacing Moll's sweetmeats with julap (a purgative) when she was due to sup with the King, Moll fell from favour comparatively soon. She took refuge in another less lucrative passion – for cards and high play.

Nell Gwynn was made of sterner stuff, as was her connection with the King; one way and another, it would only end with his death some seventeen years later. Nell was of Welsh extraction, becoming an orange girl in the theatre, a profession which existed in the exciting, nebulous territory just outside acknowledged prostitution. The first reference to her as an actress in the King's Players occurs in 1664, when she would have been fourteen. By 1670 Nell had achieved that guarantee of an establishment, pregnancy by the monarch; she gave birth to the first of her two sons and was set up in consequence in a little house at the east end of Pall Mall, later closer to Whitehall. Throughout 1670 and most of 1671 she reigned supreme.

Physically, Nell was tiny, with, it was said, the littlest foot in England as well as perfect legs. The King, who had a penchant for good legs, indulged his passion to the extent of paying for some of her theatrical costumes, including some 'Rhinegraves' – short, wide, divided skirts, guaranteed to fly up provocatively as the wearer danced. Nell certainly did not have the classical looks admired at the time: her nose turned up, unlike the aquiline noses of the conventional Stuart beauties. But everything about her was charmingly rounded, including her plump cheeks, where two dimples appeared when she smiled.

Like Charles himself, Nell had natural wit. Her surviving letters, dictated to others as they may be (she could barely manage her own initials), show a sparkle nonetheless. Nell's rivalry with Louise de Kéroüalle, who prided herself of coming of a good French family, was enlivened when Louise went into mourning for the death of some grand relation; Nell proceeded to dress herself in mourning for the Great Cham of Tartary. And Nell is of course famous for her riposte, at the time of the Popish Plot, to the angry crowd who mistook her for the Catholic Louise. Poking her head out of her carriage, Nell cried, 'Good people, this is the Protestant whore!'

But if she justified her reputation in one respect as 'pretty witty Nell' Nell Gwynn was in other ways not quite the golden-hearted prostitute of popular imagination. Or rather, she may have had a heart of gold, but she also liked the stuff for its own sake. The records show that, like all Charles' mistresses, she was extremely

Nell Gwynn with her two sons. Charles, characteristically, never sought to deny paternity where he believed himself the father.

Tennis in some form or another is among the oldest of ball games. Charles was particularly fond of it and a good player.

mercenary and demanding. By the end of 1674 she had acquired at least eight servants, a French coach needing six horses, satin window curtains, sky-blue shoes, other shoes of silver, green, gold and scarlet, all as befitted the grand lady she sought to be. Nell also coveted some kind of rank, to acknowledge her position. But Nell never did carry her democratic point of equality. Just as Nell was about to be created Countess of Greenwich – the other 'ladies' were all made Duchesses – the King died. To commentators, up to the King's last hours, she remained 'Nelly', where Louise was 'Portsmouth' and Barbara 'Cleveland'. And thus she has gone down to history.

It is sometimes overlooked that the private tastes of Charles II ran as much to conventional as to unconventional sports. Viewing his obsession with exercise of all sorts, including tennis, swimming, walking and riding, it is tempting to suggest that his legendary 'amorous complexion' was merely an extension of this natural physical bent. To Clarendon he once referred to his daily tennis game – real tennis as we should term it, played in an indoor court – as his 'usual physic'.

Charles II also adored swimming. On occasion he was found plunging happily into the freezing waters of the Thames while his courtiers shivered on the bank. His swimming too was apt to take place early in the morning. He would rise at five a.m., go boating and swim, often with his brother James at Battersea, Putney or Five Elms.

The life of the Thames, river life in general, appealed to him: he was an enthusiastic fisherman. It was a taste Queen Catharine

– tactfully – came to share. We hear of the King getting up at five a.m. to join her at Hampton Court to go fishing, 'a recreation in which she takes much pleasure'.

Fishing at least was a sedentary occupation, one of the few that the King practised. In general, his extreme physical restlessness was an attribute to which all contemporary observers drew attention. His famous walking, for example, went on at a horrendous pace. It was an activity which dovetailed with the King's passion for dogs. Wherever he went he moved with a little train of spaniels scampering and barking – or yapping as their detractors had it. He did not actually introduce his favourite breed of spaniel but such was King Charles'

The King, c. 1680, taking one of his famous walks in Horseguards Parade which used to wear out his more youthful companions.

A King Charles spaniel, painted by Gysbert van der Kuyl. Charles' affection for the breed gave it its name.

A huntsman with hounds and hare, by Jan Wyck.

A hunting scene of Charles assisting the Duchess of Portsmouth and her attendant.

enthusiasm for them that they have become identified with his name.

Horses had of course been an early love. By the age of ten Charles had been riding 'leaping horses', often controlling those who had managed to throw more experienced horsemen. His subsequent prowess was of infinite satisfaction to his old tutor Newcastle (created a Duke after the Restoration). He wrote: 'No man makes a horse go better than I have seen some go under His Majesty the first time ever he came upon their backs, which is the quintessence of the art.'

Charles II grew up with a taste for hunting, including deer, stag and otter. At the Restoration the parks and forests had to be filled again with deer, poached unmercifully throughout the Commonwealth period. Thus the New Forest and Sherwood Forest were restocked. The King's house at Lyndhurst in Hampshire was

used as a hunting lodge for the New Forest. Charles II spent £4,000 enlarging it and building new stables. An edict of 1662 concerning Sherwood Forest forbade anyone there to kill a deer without a warrant from the King, unless Charles himself or the Master of the Buckhounds was actually present.

As the King grew older, this enthusiasm for hunting gave way to a passionate involvement in racing, concentrating on what has become known appropriately enough as the Sport of Kings. The value of his patronage to British racing can hardly be over-estimated: at the beginning of his reign, race meetings were still suffering from the blight put upon them during the Protectorate, when they were banned as being opportunities for the seditious to meet. By 1685 racing was thoroughly established as an integral part of British social and sporting life.

The King probably first went racing at Epsom Downs in 1661: but it was Newmarket in particular which owed so much to his prolonged personal patronage. There were races at Newmarket by March 1663. In 1666 Charles II paid his first visit to the spring meeting; thereafter he went two or three times a year for visits lasting several weeks. Although tents and pavilions formed part of the royal baggage, the King himself stayed at Audley End with the Earl of Suffolk. Gradually the King found Audley End so convenient for his racing life that in 1669 he bought it for £50,000.

The King watches the races at Datchet, below Windsor Castle. Charles was, famously, indefatigable as a racegoer and was himself an accomplished jockey.

The King's involvement in racing embraced every aspect of this rich and many-sided sport, including, on occasion, dining with the jockeys. He instituted four-mile heats at twelve stone for a Plate 'for ever' – the precursor of all the subsequent Royal plate races at Newmarket. The idea of these heats over such a long distance – by modern standards – was to develop the breeding of 'big stout horses'. What was more, the Plate race had something generally lacking in races at the time, a set of formal rules. Otherwise, informality was so great that the King was sometimes used as an adjudicator. In 1675, when he was in his mid-forties, the King rode in three heats, a course and the Plate, all being 'hard and near run races': he won the Plate by sheer 'good horsemanship'.

Today the Rowley mile at Newmarket still commemorates Charles II in its own fashion: it was named after a famous stallion of the day, sire of a vast progeny. Charles himself was nicknamed Old Rowley in honour of his own similarly prolific powers.

Audley End, the magnificent house purchased by the King because of its convenience for the Newmarket races.

There was another rather different natural extension to the King's love of physical exercise – his addiction to garden and park planning. He reafforested Greenwich. Avenues of Spanish chestnuts were planted and over six thousand elms, as well as small coppices of birch, hawthorn, ash and privet, Greenwich today still being remarkable for its luxuriant hawthorns. At Hampton Court the King planted what Evelyn approvingly described as 'sweet rows of lime trees'. Botany also caught his scientific fancy: a famous picture shows King Charles II, before the façade of Ham House, being shown the first pineapple cultivated in England.

Not every British sovereign has had a genuine love of London, but Charles II had a passion for the city of his birth. St James's Park was his *chef d'oeuvre*. Here he loved to walk on his fast daily round or 'saunter' from the adjacent Palace of Whitehall, accompanied by his dogs. The King threw open the park to the public, who could watch games such as croquet and bowls, both of which the King enjoyed. For the game variously called pêle-mêle or pall-mall, a form of croquet using a wooden ring suspended above the ground, a fine new mall or alley, nearly fifteen hundred feet long, was laid out on the site of the present-day Mall.

The King's new rectangular lake (or canal), for all its formality, was another new source of popular pleasure. Although only the King swam in it, winter was different. That of 1662 was one of the harsh seasons common at the time. The Dutch practice of skating, or 'sliding', as it was known, was quickly introduced. Pepys, much taken with the spectacle of the 'sliders', with their skates, in the park, described it as being 'a very pretty art'.

Danckert's view of Whitehall and Westminster. Building was among Charles' many interests and his surveyor-general Christopher Wren made additional improvements to the Palace of Whitehall.

CHARLES, KING
JAMES, DUKE.
KATHARINE, QUEEN.
MARY DUTCHESS.
ANN, PRINCESSE
GEORGE, PRINCE
HANS IN KELDER

London: Printed by G. Croom, on the ICE, on
the River of Thames, January 31. 168

Top: The Frost Fair on the Thames, held during the winter of 1683-4. Painting by Abraham Hondius. It was not unusual for the Thames to freeze and skating on the ice and attending the fairs was a popular pastime.
Above: a souvenir ticket issued to the King and his family in commemoration of the 1683-4 Fair.

Much as he enjoyed catering to his subjects' tastes – and his own – King Charles' real excitement within the confines of the park consisted in the various species of bird which he introduced, both in his specially built aviary and on the 'Duck Island' in the middle of the lake. It was true that exotic livestock had been seen in St James's Park before: James I, another connoisseur of wildlife, had introduced two young crocodiles as well as duck and pheasants. Charles II was able to make the more picturesque, less predatory addition of a pair of pelicans from Astrakhan, a present from the Russian Ambassador. The King's interest in rare birds is remembered in the name of Birdcage Walk, just beside Buckingham Palace, and Storey's Gate, called after his aviary keeper.

It is necessary to stress the outdoor character of many of the sports and amusements which marked the reign of Charles II since, in contrast to the so-called debauchery of the Court, they united him with, rather than divided him from, his humbler subjects. It is less necessary to stress his well-advertised love of the theatre. It has been mentioned how many of his friends were patrons of playwrights. So, for that matter, were many of his mistresses, including Barbara, Nell Gwynn and Louise. With much encouragement from the highest in the land, the theatres proliferated, as did the theatrical companies. The King's first troop had been formed a year after his own birth – 'Prince Charles' Players'. Only three months after the Restoration he issued patents to Thomas Killigrew and Sir William Davenant to form two licensed theatre companies – the King's Players and the Duke's Players respectively. The King's Players eventually came to rest at the new Theatre Royal, Drury Lane, in May 1663; the Duke's Players' best-known theatre was at Dorset Garden, designed by Wren, which opened in 1671.

This is not the place for a history of the Restoration theatre. Suffice it to note that King Charles II, in his genuine passion for the art, was once again united with, rather than divided from, his subjects. The gentry – and the orange-girls – who saw him at ease at the play did not love him the less for sharing their own pleasures. As for the advancement of at least one former orange-girl – Nell Gwynn – that, like the story of Cinderella or the boss who marries the secretary, gave encouragement to all the rest.

Peter Lely's painting of the actress Peg Hughes, mistress of Prince Rupert. The climate of Restoration England did much to improve the status of actresses though it would be a long time before they achieved 'moral equality' with actors.

An illustration of 'The Empress of Morocco' performed at Dorset Gardens Theatre in 1673. Charles' personal patronage of the theatre was of considerable significance.

Charles II and His Mistresses

'Pretty witty Nell'. Nell
Gwynn, the most famous of
Charles' mistresses, as Diana,
in a painting by Simon Verels.

The Duchess of Mazarin, the
niece of the Great Mazarin,
who briefly won the heart of
the king.

Charles II's reputation as a 'Merry
Monarch' rests, not least, on
his succession of mistresses. The
mistresses were well treated, many
given imposing titles and their
children similarly acknowledged and
ennobled. It can even be argued that
Charles was fundamentally a 'one-
woman man' rather than obsessively
promiscuous so that although the
Duchess of Portsmouth certainly
overlapped with Nell Gwynn, the
main tendency was for one main
mistress to hold sway at any one
time. Perhaps the most remarkable
feature of Charles' relationship with
his mistresses is that they did not
destroy his marriage.

The court was pleasure-loving and easy-going, but it was never an evil place.

Moll Davis, like Nell Gwyn, was an actress, though her reign as favourite mistress was much shorter; the portrait is by Sir Peter Lely.

Barbara Palmer, the mistress who held sway at the time of the Restoration, later elevated to become Duchess of Cleveland; a portrait by Sir Peter Lely.

Louise Duchess of Portsmouth; a painting by Henri Gascars.

CHAPTER TEN

PARLIAMENTS AND CRISES

The position of Charles II in the two years following the Secret Treaty of Dover of 1670 would have struck any cognizant observer as ironical, even humorous. On the one hand, the English King was committed by the treaty to a war against Holland as soon as was convenient – and the French King was committed to participate in the action. For such a war Charles II would need an ample additional 'supply' from his Parliament. On the other hand, the very existence of this treaty was unknown to the English Parliament as a whole: of those ministers who were in the secret, only the most intimate knew the whole truth.

One result of this secrecy was that Members of Parliament remained extremely suspicious about the use the King might make of the supplies they voted. Just as the King feared in the recesses of his mind the return of revolution, Parliament feared the arrival of absolutism. Neither side trusted the other. And there was a good deal to be said for both points of view.

The behaviour of the Parliament called by the King in February 1671 did nothing to smooth the situation. By July the Duke of York was writing, 'Affairs are at present here in such a state as to make one believe that a King and a Parliament can no longer subsist together.' The fractious Parliament was prorogued; it did not meet again till February 1673. The trouble was that the King still needed money to make his promised war, and his finances were in their familiar critical state. By adjourning Parliament, he had forfeited certain valuable revenues not yet voted to him. This was the background to the desperate new remedy proposed – probably by Clifford – known as the Stop of the Exchequer. This measure, in effect a

The Sea Triumphs of Charles II, a painting by Antonio Verrio, 1674. This allegorical vision is more reflective of Charles' love of the sea than the successes of his fleet.

183

By the King.

A PROCLAMATION

For further Proroguing the

PARLIAMENT.

CHARLES R.

Whereas We lately Prorogued Our Parliament from the Sixteenth day of April last, unto the Thirtieth day of October next ensuing; We by advice of Our Council, for divers weighty Reasons Us thereunto especially moving, do hereby Publish and Declare our Royal Will and Pleasure; That the same Parliament shall be again Prorogued from the said Thirtieth day of October, until the Fourth day of February next ensuing. Whereof the Lords Spiritual and Temporal, Knights, Citizens, and Burgesses, and all others whom it may concern, may hereby take notice, and order their Affairs accordingly.

Given at Our Court at Whitehall, the Seventeenth day of September 1672. in the Twenty fourth Year of Our Reign.

God save the King.

In the SAVOY,
Printed by the Assigns of John Bill and Christopher Barker,
Printers to the Kings most Excellent Majesty. 1672.

Parliament prorogued. Ceaseless battles between King and Commons continued until the final years of his reign.

repudiation by the government of its debts and financial obligations, was described by Evelyn as 'an action which not only lost the hearts of his subjects, and ruined many widows and orphans, whose stocks were lent him, but the reputation of his Exchequer forever'. In many quarters the fatal impression was created that it was too dangerous to lend money to the English monarchy.

The unpopularity and distrust incurred over the Stop did not assist the King in the promulgation of his next measure. This was the Declaration of Indulgence, given out by the King on 15 March 1672. Charles II had long wished to do something for both types of religious extremist contained within his kingdom, dissenters and Catholics. It will be remembered that back in 1662 he had issued a declaration granting toleration to both sets of believers.

Then he attempted – in vain – to get the declaration ratified by the authority of Parliament. Now he made no such attempt, using 'that supreme power in ecclesiastical matters which is not only inherent in us, but hath been declared and recognized to be so by several statutes and Acts of Parliament ...' Resting on this power, he proposed to suspend all penal laws against nonconformists and Catholics. Nonconformists should further be allowed public places of worship by licence; the Catholics would be allowed to worship in their own way privately in their homes.

Yet it was by no means generally agreed that the King possessed any such 'supreme power in ecclesiastical matters'. The attempt of Charles II to exercise such a power without seeking Parliamentary ratification, while Parliament was not even in session, and by appearing to favour Catholics (for so it was inevitably interpreted by the anti-Popish lobby), confirmed suspicions already aroused by the rumoured conversion of the Duke of York.

Even so, the King might have succeeded were it not for the demands of the Dutch War, declared on 17 March. There were a series of ostensible excuses for

A satirical 'Justification of this Present War against the United Netherlands' by Henry Stubbs, 1673. It shows the Dutch dogs of war getting short shrift from the sturdy English axe.

making war on Holland. The official line was given by Charles II in March 1672, when he wrote of England, to his brother, as 'having received many wrongs and indignities from the States General of the United Provinces'. On the Dutch side, there was a new and explosive element present. This was their recently appointed General, William of Orange. The Orangists naïvely believed that William's new office would sway his uncle of England in his approach to Holland. The insensitivity which Charles continued to show in his letters to William throughout 1672 is striking in such a normally diplomatic man. In April Charles suggested that although 'our interests seem to be a little differing at this present' – a blithe way of alluding to a state of war between their respective countries – he had still done William a considerable service; for had war not broken out, William would never have become General of the Dutch services!

The Battle of the Texel, 1673, by Willem van de Velde. The combined English and French fleets failed to inflict a decisive defeat on de Ruyter despite numerical superiority.

When war broke out, the total forces of French and English far outnumbered those of the Dutch, both by land and by sea. Only in naval guns did the Dutch approach any kind of equality. But at the first proper battle of the war, neither French nor English – nor, by implication, the English commander the Duke of York – covered themselves with glory. On 7 June, lying in Southwold Bay, off the East Anglian coast between Yarmouth and Lowestoft, the combined squadrons were surprised by the great Dutch Admiral de Ruyter. In the ensuing action both sides endured vast losses. On the English side, the Duke of York had to abandon two successive flagships, the *Prince* and *St Michael*. De Ruyter was now limited by lack of funds to using guerrilla tactics. Yet this he did brilliantly, using his superior knowledge of the shoals and islands off the Dutch coast to pounce and harass, then disappear.

It was on land that the Dutch situation seemed most desperate. How could the unfortunate Dutch hope to hold off the great swoop of the French forces through their southern and eastern provinces? The answer was the dramatic and totally unexpected response of a small nation to the aggression of a great power. The Dutch opened their dykes, flooding the land in the face of the incoming invader. Shortly afterwards William received supreme civilian as well as military command.

In England, in contrast to fierce and fighting Holland, reactions to the war were desultory. By June, many of the English were talking openly of peace. Charles had a growing problem with the Catholicism of the Duke of York, and he was not the only prominent Catholic who had newly swum into the public gaze. The King's latest mistress, that well-born French girl who had caught his eye in his sister's train at Dover, Louise de Kéroüalle, was also a Catholic. Out of this, the Queen's discreetly conducted but acknowledged Catholicism, the conversion of Barbara Duchess of Cleveland, the suspected Catholicism of Clifford and even Arlington, it was possible for the imaginative to weave a positive web of Popery around the King.

Under the circumstances, it cannot be denied that the choice of a new Catholic mistress was unfortunate. It was additionally unfortunate that Louise was French. Thus in her beguiling person she managed to combine the two attributes most likely to worry the English paranoiacs.

Louise arrived at Court a virgin. Such was her mixture of romance, propriety and ambition, she may actually have convinced herself that the King intended to marry her before she allowed him to seduce her. She was nearly twenty-one when she caught the King's eye; it was surprising that such a beautiful girl remained unmarried: 'la Belle Bretonne' she was called at the French Court, where the manners were politer than Nell Gwynn's. The explanation lay in her parents' poverty: Louise had no dowry. As a result, she imported into her role as *maîtresse en titre* a nice sense of the importance of money. It was respectable French Louise who saw to it that her pension was tied to the profitable wine excise, where reckless English Barbara settled for a much less stable source of income.

Tears and hysterics, as well as respectability, were part of Louise's stock-in-trade; it was not for nothing that Nelly chose to call her the 'weeping willow' when bored by 'Squintabella', a nickname quickly chosen by Nelly when she detected a slight cast in her rival's eye. Louise had correctly summed up Charles as a man who would be made uncomfortable, then guilty, by female tears.

Louise's rise was rapid. Her seduction by the King – if one may use the word for an event so obviously planned on both sides – seems to have taken place in October 1671 at Euston Hall, Arlington's splendid new country house near Newmarket. Roughly nine months later she gave birth to her only child; this boy was, incidentally, to be the last of the acknowledged royal bastards. In February 1673 Louise was created Duchess of Portsmouth, Countess of Fareham and Lady Petersfield – while Nelly still languished as a commoner.

Oddly enough, Louise's strongest card with the King appears to have been the aura of charming domesticity which she cast around her. In the end, it was this traditional attribute of a French mistress down the ages which delighted Charles II: the ability to provide agreeable surroundings and good food (Louise was famous for her table) as well as her physical appeal.

Nevertheless, the murmurs against Popery in high places grew from the spring of 1672 onwards. Charles might in fact be immune from petticoat persuasion, indeed he was; but it was too much to expect his raucous popular critics to believe it. For all the private ease it granted, the rise of Louise, coincidental with the conversion of the Duke of York and the disappointing course of the war, increased the problems the King had to face by the autumn of 1672.

To the north, the outlook was not much brighter. Lauderdale had promised his sovereign a citadel in Scotland. But in June 1672 the Scottish Parliament demonstrated that its sympathies lay – perhaps not surprisingly – with the Protestant Dutch, with whom the Scots did a great deal of trade, rather than with the Catholic French. It was as well for Charles II, concentrating on the needs of an 'important, necessary and expensive war', as he would later call it to Parliament, that Ireland was in one of her rare periods of quiescence. The country's condition was ameliorated when the Earl of Essex succeeded as Lord Lieutenant in 1672. The lot of the ordinary Irish as a whole was not enviable; but the harsh choice of the next centuries, emigration or misery at home, had not yet reached them. Catholic laymen, although virtually excluded from Parliament, were able to practise most other professions. Essex's main domestic problem was one he shared with the Irish people as a whole – the failure of law and order (the rise of those brigands known locally as Tories brought the word into the vocabulary of the English people). Essex was much esteemed by his contemporaries for his upright character as well as his love of learning.

If Ireland gave out little hard news, by the end of 1672 there was plenty of news in London. In particular there was the imminent recall of Parliament, for failing to secure victory over or peace with William of Orange left the King with the impossibility of sailing his fleet the following spring without money to hand. The session of February 1673 contained a crucial appeal by the King for money for his 'important, necessary and expensive war', and an equally crucial rejection of that appeal by both Commons and Lords. Instead, the Commons clamoured furiously to have the Declaration of Indulgence of the previous year withdrawn. Only

Parliament, they reiterated, could suspend the penal laws. Finally the King was obliged to withdraw the Declaration in return for an assessment of £70,000 a month for three years. It was a galling defeat.

There was worse to come. Immediately after their triumph the Commons pressed through a Test Act. This measure was as divisive as Charles' Declaration of Indulgence had been potentially healing. Every holder of office had to take public communion in the Church of England. Furthermore, various oaths of allegiance were framed, together forming a test, in the truest sense of the word, which it was impossible for any sincere Catholic to pass. Once again, the King found himself in no position to combat the challenge.

Bowing his head before the storm, a familiar posture, he gave his assent to the Test Act on 29 March. The consequences were felt at once. The Duke of York and Thomas Clifford both failed to take Anglican communion at Easter. The Duke laid down his post as Lord High Admiral in June. Clifford also resigned as Lord Treasurer – to die shortly afterwards. Inevitably, the King prorogued Parliament once more; the long war of attrition between King and Parliament was in fact gathering new momentum.

It was the presumed connection of Catholicism with royal absolutism which dominated the politics of the next few years. Charles seemed unable to grasp the part that the prospect of absolutist government on the French model played in the suspicions of Parliament. And not only did it arouse fears in Parliament, it was also fertile ground for the Protestant lobbying of William of Orange and his ever active agents anxious to detach England from France in their life and death struggle against Louis XIV. Moreover the spotlight was on James, whose character lacked the flexibility of his brother's. James was a zealous Catholic; his formative years had been partly spent in the rigid traditions of the French Army; he had every reason to embrace the Divine Right of Kings and the legitimate, his own, succession to the throne. Absolutism was by no means as foreign to his temperament as it was to that of Charles. Now, since the death of Anne Duchess of York in March 1671 he was looking for a new, Catholic, wife.

In his search for a bride, one of the Duke's aims was to provide himself with a male heir whose claims to the succession would supersede those of his two surviving daughters Mary and Anne, now eleven and eight respectively. But the Duke, who was showing himself almost as convincing a womanizer as his brother, also paid particular attention to his future wife's appearance: as he approached

Opposite: Mary of Modena, by Lely. At a time when anti-Catholic sentiment was violently increasing, the Duke of York's second marriage brought further tensions.

A lampoon of Mary of Modena, James' Catholic wife, gullibly confessing to the Jesuit Father Edward Petre.

forty, his taste ran to young and beautiful girls, despite Charles' witticism that his brother's mistresses were so plain that they must have been imposed on him by his confessors as a penance.

Various candidates were considered. Some were unavailable, or rejected by Charles as too poor, or by James as too plain. When word came of the availability of two Princesses of Modena, the fifteen-year-old Mary Beatrice and her thirty-year-old aunt, James' marital pulse raced – particularly when he learnt that these pious Catholic ladies would be backed up by substantial payments from Louis XIV. For Modena lay within the French interest: Mary Beatrice's mother had been a niece of Cardinal Mazarin. In the end, reports of Mary Beatrice's beauty as well as her tender age, inclined James towards her. The proxy marriage was performed on 20 September with Lord Peterborough acting the part of the groom.

When the news was made public, the uproar was immense. It became the violent concern of Parliament to fend off this marriage with 'the daughter of the Pope', as Mary Beatrice was unkindly termed, before it could actually be consummated. Shaftesbury in particular was vociferous in his opposition. In any case, this strange, warped and talented politician was veering towards more public opposition to the King, and his days as Lord Chancellor were clearly numbered. Admittedly, he had voted for the Declaration of Indulgence, but he had also, like Arlington, voted for the Test Act.

At the same time, the balance of power in the King's inner councils altered. In June 1673 Thomas Osborne was made Lord High Treasurer: he was also created Earl of Danby the next year. The rise of Danby, a firm Anglican, a supporter of the Triple Alliance, and a man obstinately determined to put the King's finances on a better footing, was in fact

CONVERTE ANGLIAM

It is a foolish Sheep that makes the Wolf her Confessor

the most hopeful thing which had happened to Charles II, domestically, for several years, although its full effects would not be felt immediately.

The angry chaos provoked by the news of the Duke of York's match remained. London was already awash with ugly rumours. More talk was heard on the subject of the King's favourite son, the Protestant Duke of Monmouth. Shaftesbury suggested in Council that the King should divorce Catharine and marry a Protestant. It was a nerve-racking time for the King. Parliament, when it met in the autumn of 1673, proved itself horribly vociferous on the subject of Popery, royal absolutism and royal money. The King saw no other course but to prorogue it once more till after Christmas. In November the King finally got rid of Shaftesbury. Although he continued to sit on one council, that of Trade and Plantations, till the following March, he was dismissed as Chancellor. When Mary Beatrice finally arrived at Dover towards the end of the month, the atmosphere was still so strained that hardly anyone dared ride out to meet her. Yet Charles II had in the end demonstrably preferred the interests of his brother's marriage to those of Parliament. The politicians, including Shaftesbury, who would stir up the powerful movement to exclude James from the succession five years later, should perhaps have remembered the fact.

January 1674 inexorably brought another session of Parliament. Its inception, as usual, was due to the acute royal need for money, and in an effort to secure it, Charles now found it in him to give Parliament a personal assurance: 'There is no other treaty with France, either before or since, not already printed, which shall not be made known.' It is true that he fumbled with his notes as he spoke: but that was probably due to nervousness, not shame. The straight lie did not however save him. Both Houses of Parliament voted for a separate peace with the Dutch – a culmination, amongst other things, of the secret intrigues of William of Orange.

Once more Charles II took cover. Abandoning the policy which had secretly obsessed him for the last five years, he gave Parliament another assurance on 11 February: he hoped for 'a speedy, honourable and, I hope, lasting peace with the Dutch'. And his ally, Louis XIV, still bent on securing those lowland dominions on which he had set his heart? Charles, that redoubtable diplomat, who had concluded the Triple Alliance while secretly negotiating with France, was equal to the task. He convinced Louis XIV that he was obliged to adopt this course by lack of money. A year later he would be able to form another secret alliance with Louis XIV, seamed together by further French subsidies.

At home, the King speedily prorogued Parliament once more, but, before this, Parliament witnessed the final disintegration of the Cabal. Buckingham overreached himself in his criticism of the royal policies and was stripped of his offices. With Shaftesbury and Buckingham out of the way, only Lauderdale and Arlington remained of the original five, and Arlington's star had been eclipsed by that of Danby.

In the economic sphere at least, Danby scored an early success. He raised the royal revenues considerably, an increase which joined with a natural upswing in trade in the early seventies to provide new affluence. Danby also introduced some kind of austerity once more into the conduct of the royal household and finances.

The trouble was that it was impossible to divorce the economics of the period from the politics – and the Court intrigues. Unquestionably the King's expenditure on his mistresses had moved into a more lavish sphere, and it would expand still further as the decade wore on. Where women were concerned, the King was weak, not only in the bed-chamber, at the sight of their tears, but in the counting-house. Louise Duchess of Portsmouth regarded a large income as one of the unalterable perquisites of a royal mistress; Nelly Gwynn was equally mercenary, if not equally successful; Barbara Duchess of Cleveland – mother of five children by the King – was still on his payroll; Hortense Duchesse de Mazarin would prove

Thomas Osborne, Earl of Danby. The brilliant administrator and chief minister of Charles' later years.

another expensive luxury. It is surely impossible to acquit the King altogether of extravagance, or rather weakness, where his mistresses were concerned, certainly in the last ten years of his reign.

In the short term – but only in the short term – the political methods of Danby looked like being as successful as his economic policies. Stoutly Protestant himself, Danby aimed at a political alliance in Parliament which would comprise Anglicans, and other confirmed Royalists, against those whom he conceived of as being the King's enemies. These were the Catholics, the nonconformists, and the opponents of the royal prerogative. It was also Danby's policy to strengthen ties with the Dutch. It was essential to this particular policy that the King should secure sufficient supplies from Parliament to uphold his beloved Navy. Otherwise it was easy to see that the King would have little motive to wrench himself from the lucrative embrace of Louis XIV. When Parliament met again in April 1675 for Danby to secure supplies, the King was all honey to its members. He told them that he wanted 'to know what you think may yet be wanting to the securing of religion and property'.

It was all the more important that Danby should succeed in managing Parliament to good financial effect, since his policy of promoting positive Anglicanism by curbing the Catholics went against the King's natural inclinations as well. On 1 May the King signed a declaration expelling Jesuits and other 'Roman priests' from the realm. Already in February, an Order in Council had been made for the strict enforcement of the penal laws against the Catholics, and for the restricting of Catholic chapels to those of the Queen and the ambassadors.

But this session of Parliament proved to be a contest between two equally handicapped opponents. The Commons continued to cry out against the French involvement, and were intractable over the supplies the King wanted for the Navy. There was even a move to impeach Danby, as the King's minister, for his pro-French attitudes – which would have been a wry turn of events, considering Danby's own attitude to France. On 9 June the King saw no alternative but wearily to prorogue Parliament. He spoke bitterly of 'the ill designs of our enemies [that] have been too prevalent against those good ones I had proposed to myself in behalf of my people'.

When Parliament met again in the autumn, Danby returned with new vigour to the task of carrying through the government's policies. Nor had he wasted his time in the intervening months. Over a hundred MPs had been lobbied by the Secretaries of State, to ensure their attendance. Yet Danby found himself quite unable to secure the King's financial needs, while the demand for the dissolution of Parliament grew.

The irony of this demand – and irony is never far away from the politics of this period – was that Charles II himself was more or less committed to dissolving Parliament, but in secret. In his latest negotiations with Louis XIV, it was proposed that Charles should dissolve Parliament if its attitude towards France grew too aggressive, or if it failed to vote the King the supplies he needed. In return, Louis XIV would give Charles II a yearly subsidy of something like £100,000. Did Danby know of the bargain? It seems that he did. Even so, he still pressed on, doggedly trying to secure money for the King via Parliament, for much more than £100,000 was needed to float the Navy.

A political cartoon shows Charles riding high while a flustered Louis XIV begs for money. Reality, for much of the 1670s, was closer to the reverse.

When Danby failed, it was still open to Charles to dissolve Parliament and call on the French subsidy. But Danby, by pulling out all the stops of his own organization, managed to defeat the motion for a dissolution in the House of Lords so Charles deftly but determinedly proceeded to prorogue Parliament yet again.

What was more, by taking advantage of France's military involvement, he managed to secure the French subsidy all the same. The newest secret treaty with Louis XIV, that of February 1676, provided for an annual subsidy, payable in quarters. In vain Danby begged his master to commit himself to the Dutch – the old principle of the Triple Alliance. Charles II once more pursued his own bent, albeit secretly, and signed on with France again for a three-year period.

Oddly enough, for a brief period between the latest prorogation of Parliament and its reconvening in 1677, it seemed possible that Charles might achieve some form of peace at home without a struggle. It was true that a 'Country' – as opposed to 'Court' – opposition was being developed by the coalition of Shaftesbury and Buckingham. Increasingly this group had to be reckoned with. The Green Ribbon Club was in existence by 1676, and provided an important rallying point for those discontented with the government – particularly when Parliament was not sitting. It linked the various disparate elements – former Puritans, merchants, lawyers and so forth – which would go to make the future 'Whig' party.

All the same, the appearance of peace was maintained. And the upswing in the royal and the national finances increased the illusion. As late as June 1677 the King told the French Ambassador that England enjoyed 'a profound tranquillity'. She successfully enriched herself, while other nations were drained or ruined by war. The English would one day thank him, he observed, for having kept them by prudence in 'so happy a state and so advantageous for their commerce'.

In fact the trade boom broke early in 1676. And as the seventies wore on, the image of a liberal and healing King was being succeeded by something rather different. It is true that towards individuals the King had lost none of his humorous affability. But while the King retained his popular touch with individuals, many of his policies – such as the Stop of the Exchequer – presented him in a much less attractive light. Then there was the question of his honour. Naturally the full extent of the deceit which he had employed in foreign policy was known to very few. But a feeling that the King's word, like the King's financial bond, was to be regarded with caution, began to pervade Court and political circles. The sardonic epigram ascribed to Lord Rochester on his master comes to mind:

> We have a pritty witty King
>
> Whose word no man relies on,
>
> Who never said a foolish thing
>
> Nor ever did a wise one.

Even more fatally, Charles II ignored the force of popular prejudice with regard to Catholicism, France and their hated bedfellow, arbitrary government. He would shortly receive a terrible lesson, but before that happened, Charles II was subjected to an assault of a rather pleasanter nature: from a beautiful woman, Hortense Mancini, Duchesse de Mazarin. The affair would be Charles' last very public throw in that direction. But Hortense, unlike Louise, was not of the material of which successful mistresses are made.

Hortense's ostensible reason for arriving in England in the winter of 1675 was her cousinship to Mary Beatrice, Duchess of York. But her conquest of the King was rapid. By the summer of 1676 it was being said that the only time Hortense was not at the King's side was when he was bathing. By August Louise was in floods of tears – and Hortense was in Barbara's old apartments. By the following summer, however, the eternal Eve in the self-destructive Hortense had reasserted itself. She indulged in a prolonged and public flirtation with the Prince de Monaco. Hortense was dismissed. Louise dried her tears. The King settled back with a shrug into her waiting arms. Since Hortense had not presented the King with a child, alone among his mistresses-in-chief to fail to do so, the main residue of her reign was the unfortunate political impression she created. Marvell expressed the general indignation:

> That the King should send for another French whore
>
> When one already hath made him so poor.

Charles had not sent for Hortense. But the smear remained.

A new French connection was untimely, to say the least, in view of developments overseas. Protestant pro-Dutch factions were alarmed when the spring of 1677 brought a wave of victories for Louis XIV, and in the United Provinces, William girded himself for another span of heroic defence. When Parliament re-assembled early in the year, Charles found himself faced not only by the predictable 'opposition' but by Danby who was strongly advocating alliance with the Dutch.

But the King declined to declare war, either at the instance of Danby or of the House of Commons. On 23 May the Commons asked in plain terms for an offensive and defensive alliance with Holland. Public interference with foreign policy undeniably invaded the royal prerogative and the King said so sharply. To mark his displeasure and his determination to preserve his prerogative, he prorogued Parliament until 16 July.

There was an uncomfortable feeling of stalemate by the summer of 1677. Parliament would not vote all the money needed for a war until the King declared that war. The King naturally would not declare war without money. As a result Charles II signed his third secret agreement with Louis XIV, by which Charles was to hold off his anti-French Parliament until the following May, and in return Louis was as usual to pay up. At the same time Danby was making progress in negotiations which would have profound consequences for the future – the marriage of the Duke of York's eldest daughter Mary to William of Orange.

Danby enjoyed a great success with the Dutch marriage project. Indeed, the only unhappy principal in the whole affair was the fifteen-year-old Princess. She wept 'grievously' when she heard the news. She saw herself being exiled for political reasons to an unappealing country, on the arm of an equally unappealing bridegroom: William was several inches shorter than she – to her hysterical eye, virtually a dwarf. The odd thing was that the marriage of this Mary, begun in tears, was to turn out the most successful of them. Moreover, in time, not only would she occupy the throne of England, but her marriage of convenience turned into a genuine love affair on her side.

It may seem surprising that Charles II should accept a marriage so calculated to outrage Louis XIV. It is true that Danby pressed the match with great firmness, so that in a sense Charles was able with perfect accuracy to plead political pressure. But Charles could see another advantage to it. Mary was the heiress presumptive to the throne and the King hoped that the Protestant match would distract attention from the furore surrounding the Catholic elements at Court.

All that Charles II actually did at the ceremony in November 1677 was to play the part of a jolly, slightly bawdy uncle, as he urged on the prim William on his wedding night, 'Hey nephew, to your work! Hey, St George for England!' It was left to Louis XIV to protest and, more to the point, stop payment of the latest subsidy to Charles II.

Charles II retaliated by summoning Parliament. By this time he had already entered into a defensive alliance with the Dutch on 10 January. Yet the Dutch never ratified the treaty, and the English never went to war as promised; this treaty should be seen as yet another manoeuvre, in the hope that Louis would now negotiate a peace along lines acceptable to Charles and his nephew William.

But Louis did not make peace with the Dutch, and the fall of Ghent to his army on 27 February made the possibility of a compromise peace more remote. At the same time it increased the demands for a positive Dutch alliance in Parliament. All the same, neither side had devised a way out of the familiar stalemate – If No War, Then No Money on Parliament's side; If No Money, Then No War on the King's. Charles II made an equally familiar move on 25 March when he wrote privately to Louis XIV. He suggested that in return for a subsidy of six million livres annually for the next three years, he would secure a proper peace in Europe, along conciliatory lines. But his winning streak had not left King Louis in the mood for territorial compromise: for the time being, he rejected both terms and subsidy.

Even so, Charles was beginning to find the absolute monarch, Louis XIV, easier to cope with than his own elected Parliament. Protracted diplomacy eventually succeeded, and the way was finally cleared for the Peace of Nymegen on 10 August. By this, France was left with a good deal of the conquered Flemish territory, if not all she had desired; she also secured a workable boundary with the Spanish Netherlands.

The Dutch got the respite that they, rather than William, wanted. William had been reluctant to see his 'mortal enemy' confirmed in so much new ground; nevertheless, he too was able to use the temporary lull of the next few years to build up himself and his country against the final assault. Sir William Temple, the English Ambassador at The Hague, hailed the role of Charles II in all of this grandiloquently: the King, he declared, was once more 'at the head of the affairs of Christendom'.

The same happy claim could not be made for the King's affairs at home. So ragged had relations between Parliament and King become by the summer of 1678 that it has been suggested that Danby at least was contemplating the use of the army to maintain the King's authority. There was no truth in this rumour, or the prospect that the King would have countenanced it. But it was indicative of the continual stalemate existing between King and Parliament. It was necessary to prorogue Parliament yet again, for all the financial and political crises these failed Parliaments implied. Charles II's so-called Long Parliament was thus adjourned on 15 July. But only a wild optimist could imagine that peace in Europe would now be matched by the return of 'tranquillity' at home.

The Decorative Arts

I f there were few crucial developments or innovations during the reign of Charles II, the continued extension of the various decorative arts as applied to furniture, ornaments, instruments, carving, embroidery and so on reflects the widening base of the nation's wealth. One particular feature does stand out, however: the fine detail of needle-work and weaving and therefore the very distinctive tapestries and coverings from the period.

A Charles II polychrome beadwork basket.

A coronation mug of Charles II, the first coronation to be commemorated in this way.

A cylindrical gold counter case pierced and engraved with entwined flowers.

A political pincushion. 'God bless Prince Charles and down with the Rump' is the message.

A Mortlake tapestry by Francis Poyntz, who held the post of Yeoman Arras Worker at the Great Wardrobe from the Restoration until his death in 1684.

A finely worked coconut cup, 7$\frac{1}{2}$ inches high. The cup has carved portraits of Charles II, the Duke of York and the deceased Charles I and Duke of Gloucester.

An age of fine ornamental and decorative achievement.

A London Delft pill-slab of the 1660s showing the arms of the Society of Apothecaries.

Silvergilt knife, fork and spoon, dating from *c* 1670.

Lead-glass serving bottle from one of George Ravenscroft's two glass-houses, *c.* 1677-80.

This casket, with rising lid and two doors, stands 7 inches high. Stitched in silk it dates from *c.* 1665.

Goddard Dunning's 'Self-Portrait with Still Life', 1678.

A looking-glass with a stumpwork frame dating from the third quarter of the century.

An embroidered night case, owned by Charles II.

Red earthenware dish with slip decoration, made in Staffordshire c. 1675

Dating from the middle of the century, this is an excellent example of the needlework of the period.

A Charles II silver tankard.

A True Narrative of the Horrid Hellish Popish-Plot.

To the Tune of PACKINGTON'S POUND. The Second Part.

I do imagine some will say here never was such another strange Ballad, with marginal Notes and Quotations. But I answer, there never was such another Plot, and I am afraid, that if I did not cite very good Authors, and bring Witnesses of untainted Reputation, the next Generation might be so far deluded by Popish Shams, as not to believe it.

Authors Quoted.

(1) As it appears in the several Tryals.
(2) Ireland's Tryal, p. 23.
(3) Hill's Tryal, p. 32.
(4) See his Speech in Ireland's Tryal, p. 81.
(5) The same Tryal, p. 50.
(6) Jesuits Tryal, p. 33.
(7) The same, p. 29.
(8) Oate's Narrat. all along.
(9) See Coleman's Try. p. 23.
(10) The same, page 40.
(11) The same again, p. 21.
(12) The same, p. 24.
(13) The same again, p. 41.
(14) Ireland's Tryal, p. 24.
(15) The same, p. 25.
(16) The same again, p. 24.
(17) See Jesuits Tryal, p. 13.
(18) Ireland's Tryal, p. 24.
(19) Wakeman's Tryal, p. 73.
(20) Jesuits Tryal, p. 91.
(21) Wakeman's Tryal, p. 30, & 35. As also Coleman's Tryal, p. 30.
(22) The same again.
(23) Wakeman's Tryal, p. 40.
(24) That Oats and Bedloe sell him in Langhorn's Tryal.
(25) Mr. Prance.
(26) Mr. Dugdale.
(27) Jesuits Tryal all along.
(28) viz. To prove that Ireland was not in Town Aug. 19. See Wakeman's Try. p. 22.
(29) Mr. Jenison.

The Contents of the Second PART.

Of Arms under-ground for Horse and for Foot;
The KING almost Kill'd, for which Pick'ring is whipt. All of them swear
To be true to the PLOT; yet Oats, not for Fear
Nor Revenge, (though turn'd away, and well bang'd)
Discovers them all; The Jesuits are Hang'd.

I.

The PLOT being thus subtly contriv'd as you hear,
To God knows how many this (1) Secret th'impart,
Some famous for Cheats, yet their Faith they don't fear,
To tye a Knave fast they had found a new Art.
    They (2) swore on a Book,
    And (3) Sacrament took;
But you'l find, if into their grave Authors you look,
Forswearing's no Sin, (as 4) Recorder well notes)
Nor Treason, Rebellion, nor Cutting of Throats.
    The truth of my Story if any man doubt,
    W' have Witnesses ready to Swear it all out.

II.

Still blinded with Zeal, and inveigl'd by Hope,
Store of Arms they provide for Fight and Defence,
Three Lords must command, as Vice-Roys of the Pope,
And all over England they raise (5) Peter-pence.
    Their Letters they send
    By (6) Bedlow their Friend,
Or else by the (7) Post, to shew the intend,
Some hundreds (8) Oats saw, which the Jesuits did write,
'Tis a wonder not One of them e're came to light.
    The Truth of my Story, &c.

III.

Pounds Two hundred thousand and to (9) Ireland they sent;
Fifteen thousand to (10) Wakeman for Potions and Pills,
Forty thousand in Five works we guess that they spent;
And, Item, Ten thousand to pay for Black-Bills;
    Fifteen hundred more
    (11) Grove should have they swore;
Four Gentlemen Ruffians deserved (12) Fourscore!
Pious Pickering they knew was of Atass's more fond,
And for (13) Thirty thousand they gave him a Bond.
    The truth of my Story, &c.

IV.

These two, to Kill the King by fair promises won,
Had watch'd now some (14) years in St. James's Park;
And Pick'ring, who never yet (15) shot off a Gun,
Was about to take aim, for he had a fair Mark:
    Just going to begin'r,
    He (16) missed his Flint,
And looking in Pan, there was (17) no Powder in't;
For which he their Pardon does humbly beseech,
Yet had (18) thirty good lashes upon his bare Breech.
    The truth of my Story, &c.

V.

But a sadder mischance to their PLOT did befall,
For Oats, their main Engine, fail'd when it came to't;
No marvail indeed if he cuzen'd 'em all,
Who turn'd him a (19) begging, and (20) beat him to boot:
    He wheeling about,
    Th' whole Party did rout,
And from lurking holes did so ferret 'em out;
Till running himself blind, he none of them (21) knew,
And fainting at (22) Council, he cou'd not swear true.
    The truth of my Story, &c.

VI.

To comfort our Doctor, brave Bedloe's brought in,
A more Credible Witness was not above ground;
He vows and protests, though a Rogue he had been,
He wou'd now not swear false for Five hundred pounds;
    And why shou'd we fear
    They falsly wou'd swear,
To damn their own (23) Souls, and to lose by it here.
Poor Oats, who before had no Peny in Purse,
Discov'ring the PLOT, was Seven hundred pound (24) worse.
    The truth of my Story, &c.

VII.

Two Witnesses more were let loose from the Jayl,
Though (25) One 'tis confest did run back from his word,
(In danger of Life a good man may be frail)
And th' (26) Other they slander for Cheating his Lord.
    T'every one of these men
    The Jesuits brought (27) Ten,
To disprove 'em in Time and in Place; but what then?
One Circumstance lately was sworn most clear
By a (28) Man who in hopes has Five hundred a year.
    The truth of my Story, &c.

VIII.

And then we are told, We must always suppose,
To murder the King a Great PLOT there has been;
And who to contrive it so likely as those
Who Murder and Treason do hold for no Sin.
    Things being thus plain,
    To plead was in vain;
The Jury (instructed again and again)
Did find them all Guilty, and to shew 'twas well done,
The People gave a Shout for Victory won.
    The truth of my Story if any man doubt,
    W' have Witnesses ready to Swear it all out.

IX.

'Tis strange how these Jesuits, so subtle and wise,
Shou'd all by the Pope be so basely trepan'd,
To Hang with much comfort when he shall advise,
And go to the Devil too at his command.
    He may give them leave,
    To Lye and Dece ve;
But what when the Rope do's of Life them bereave?
Can his Holiness, think you, dispense with that pain,
Or by his Indulgences raise them again?
    The truth of my Story if any man doubt,
    W' have Witnesses ready to Swear it all out.

X.

Yet (like Madmen) of Life a Contemp: they express,
And of their own happiness careless appear,
For Life and for Money not one would confess;
Th' had rather be Damn'd, than be Rich and live here.
    But surely they rav'd,
    When God they out-brav'd,
And thought to renounce him the way to be sav'd;
With Lyes in their mouths go to Heaven in a string;
So prosper all Traytors, and GOD save the KING.
    The truth of my Story if any man doubt,
    W' have Witnesses ready to Swear it all out.

Concordat cum Recordo. Cl. Par.

FINIS.

See th' Authors I quote, there's Witnesses plenty,
Approv'd by a —— Nemine Contradicente.
Yet Juries (for tender Conscience so famous)
To save a True-Protestant, write Ignoramus.

Some Notes on the Pillars to prevent Popish Cavils.

I. I'e not scandaliz'd at a word or two of Latine, 'Tis only to shew the folly of the Papists, who pray in an unknown Tongue.

K. This is not meant of any Oath against the Papists, but of their wicked Oath of Secrecy; which though the Doctor often took, yet we may charitably believe he never did intend to keep it; since he positively affures us he did but counterfeit: He only seemed to be a Papist, but was all the while a True-Protestant in his Heart. See L. Staf. Tryal p. 123.

L. Arms for 5 or 600 Men were hid in his Parlour; yet by Art Magick were invisible to the Gentlemen of the Country, who often dined with him in the same Room. See his Tryal.

M. Sir H.T's Vault was search'd for Arms, and Coffins opened; but all the Arms they had hidden there were turn'd to Bones.

N. Sir R.T's. Sink was searched for Arms and Gunpowder, yet not so much as one Black-Bill could ever be found there, nor in any other place.

O. See Wakeman's Tryal, p. 78.

P. Grove, that he might be sure to give an Incurable Wound, did traiterously and maliciously champ a Silver Bullet with his poysonous Teeth. See his Tryal, p. 24, & 81.

Q. Either another man in such a Coat, or else (as some believe) the Devil in his likeness, went often to Court, and occasion'd this unlucky mistake, which was the cause of his being beaten. See the Jesuits Tryal p. 16, 17.

Many may perhaps wonder, that the crafty Jesuits would suffer him to be in such a miserable beggerly Condition, and much more, that they would bear and abuse one, whom they had trusted with Secrets of so high a nature. But we can easily answer this, and an hundred other seeming Improbabilities, only by saying, They were infatuated.

R. See Coleman's Tryal, p. 30.
S. Wakeman's Try. p. 51, & 52.
T. Langhorn's Memoirs, p. 6.

CHAPTER ELEVEN
NO POPERY!

The August of 1678 was fiercely hot: a surprise which even the English summer can sometimes spring. One morning, just as the King was entering St James's Park for his habitual saunter, a man named Christopher Kirkby warned him about a plot against his life. Kirkby was known to the King because he shared his interest in chemical experiments. The story he told was subsequently supported by one Israel Tonge, a slightly dotty Anglican clergyman who had allegedly uncovered the plot.

The plot's substance was quite incredible: it involved the Catholics in England, notably the Jesuits, and Louis XIV ganging up together to kill the King; then they would all take up arms together to prevent the accession of the Duke of York; the end result would be the conquest of England for France. The assassination complex of the time had taken Charles as far as listening to Kirkby and Tonge – at his leisure – but it could take him no further, given the ludicrous nature of their revelations. It was therefore probably because the accused Catholics included a member of the Queen's household, Sir George Wakeman, that Charles handed the matter over to Danby. Then he went as planned to his favourite retreat at Windsor.

In Danby, Tonge found a more susceptible audience. Danby did not love France, to put it mildly, and had a prejudiced Anglican view of the Papists. Besides, it was Danby's duty to ensure the safety of the King. Tonge produced papers which Danby found sufficiently convincing to proceed to a further examination. It was in this way that another character was summoned onto the stage, one whose sheer roguery should, if there had been any justice, have shown the drama up at once and for ever

One of the innumerable pieces of propaganda literature which flooded from the presses in the wake of the Popish Plot, the *cause célèbre* of the age.

TITUS OATES.
Anagramma
TESTIS OVAT.

Titus Oates, the adventurer whose 'revelations' lay at the core of a scandal which convulsed the capital and virtually paralyzed the government.

Opposite: Catharine of Braganza, painted by Jacob Huysmans as St Catharine. Nothing is more remarkable than the way this once reviled lady remained relatively untouched by the anti-Catholic mood of the people. Charles' support for her was unswerving.

for what it was. This was a man named Titus Oates.

Contemporary descriptions of Titus Oates are almost universally unfavourable. His low forehead, little nose, tiny deep-set eyes, fat cheeks and vast wobbling chin make him sound more like a pig than a man. First examined by the Council, at Tonge's suggestion, on 28 September, Oates produced a fusillade of fantastic accusations. Some of his rounds were fired across the water at the Catholic Archbishop of Dublin, Peter Talbot. Most of his charges constituted a tarradiddle of lies, easily contradicted. It was only when Oates pointed his weapon wildly but enthusiastically in the direction of the personal servants of the royal family that he met with a piece of undeserved luck. Oates named Sir George Wakeman, Queen Catharine's physician, and Edward Coleman, secretary to the Duchess of York. Using Wakeman's medical expertise, they were supposed to have plotted the death of the King by poison. And very soon the Council did bring to light some highly unwise correspondence between Coleman and the confessor to Louis XIV.

Coleman's indiscreet and of course treacherous correspondence had consequences beyond its own intrinsic importance. For, using guilt by association, it enabled a finger to be pointed at the Queen's household. The relationship of Charles II and Catharine of Braganza had changed since those rather pathetic days when Catharine first came to England. The King, with his ready sense of guilt and tenderness where the fair sex was concerned, now felt quite different emotions towards the woman who had been at his side longer than any of his mistresses – except Barbara, now dismissed.

Besides, the Queen herself had changed. Like many good women, she had gained support from her virtue over a long period and had emerged as a character of remarkable fortitude. It was not only a case of the King's esteem and that of the Court. Where the English public were concerned, Catharine's dignity and goodness were just the sort of qualities to appeal to them in their Queen. Yet in

1678 Charles II could not take it for granted that his wife's virtue would protect her. Supposing Wakeman as well as Coleman had been indiscreet, who knew what might be charged against her, however unfairly?

Even without the investigations of the Council, the autumn of 1678 bid fair to be a time of unusual tension. A new session of Parliament had been promised by the King, which prospect enchanted no one but excited not a few. Then in early October an event took place which transformed the whole situation from one of measured enquiry into strident panic. This was the death of a Protestant magistrate, named Sir Edmund Berry Godfrey, which took place some time between the evening of 12 October, when he left his house to go out to dinner, and 17 October, when his battered corpse was discovered on Primrose Hill.

A strip cartoon version of the plot, printed in 1679. The dedication to Shaftesbury tells its own story.

The death of Sir Edmund Berry Godfrey has still not been satisfactorily explained three hundred years later. When Godfrey's bruised body was discovered, he had been dead for some days. Murder was the obvious explanation, but the injuries on Godfrey's body were mysterious; although he seemed at first sight to have been killed by his own sword, the autopsy showed that this wound had actually been inflicted after death. In any event the true explanation of Godfrey's death is of secondary importance compared to the furore its discovery caused at the time. It was most unfortunate, with the nerves of London society already on edge, that Godfrey had recently taken Oates' deposition on oath and was reputed to have given Coleman an informal warning. Popular imagination suffered no difficulty in unravelling the cause of Godfrey's death, and at once. It was quite clearly 'the wicked Jesuits' at work. Godfrey had been killed because he knew too much. On 21 October, only a few days after the discovery of Godfrey's corpse, Parliament was recalled. The King still hoped that this assembly could be held to the purpose for which it was intended: to reimburse him for the cost of the army still in Flanders.

But in London the chase was on. The capital was in ferment. Such was the atmosphere that fashionable ladies took to going about with precautionary pistols in their muffs. But the search for weapons, supposedly concealed by rabid Catholics in preparation for their insurrection, produced a singularly unheroic armoury – 'from the Widow Platt, one old gun', and so on.

Shortly after the recall of Parliament, Oates had some further resounding revelations to make. He charged five Catholic peers – Lords Arundell of Wardour, Powis, Petre, Stafford and Belasye – with plotting to kill the King. These were honourable men and there was not a shred of evidence against them. On 2 November Shaftesbury judged the time ripe to demand the exclusion of the Duke of York from the Privy Council. A Bill was introduced into both Houses to debar Catholics from sitting – a far stronger measure than the Test Act of 1673, which had only been concerned with the actual office-holders. The royal householders were also attacked, but the servants of the Queen were once more excepted – a great tribute to her prudence. The King appeared to bow. He persuaded the Duke of York that it would be unwise to attend the Privy Council, and, as to the Catholics, he told both Houses that 'he was ready to join with them in all the ways and means that might establish a firm security for the Protestant religion'.

Although the measure was passed, Danby fought a brilliant rearguard action: it was to prove the last triumph of the Parliamentary organization he had sought so hard to establish. James was excluded from the Act. The measure had thus netted the mice but lost the lion, since one Catholic heir presumptive, still legally at liberty to sit, was worth a clutch of Catholic MPs and peers excluded. Nor was the King himself quite so meek as he pretended, and refused to allow his old friend Father Huddleston to be included in the general proclamations against the Catholic priests.

November was ever a notorious season for anti-Popish demonstration. There was a new venom in the celebration of Guy Fawkes Day in 1678. Pope-burnings had been on the increase recently, and in 1678 there were several effigies to be seen. On 24 November, at the second of his two meetings with Oates during that month, the King listened to accusations coupling Queen Catharine with Wakeman in trying to poison him.

Not for one instant could the King credit that his wife had conspired to poison him. Throughout the examination of Oates, the King represented the voice of common-sense. When Oates in his testimony mentioned the Queen's apartments where the plotting was supposed to have taken place (he could not even describe them), the King reacted swiftly. He clapped Oates into prison; there the perjurer remained briefly until the House of Commons had him released.

At the end of November, Coleman, a less innocent figure, was tried for high treason. The presiding judge, William Scroggs, spoke of him as being condemned 'by his own papers', which had been seized; it was thus for the treason contained in his papers, not for the fabricated plot, that Coleman was condemned to death and executed on 3 December. Oates was rewarded with an allowance of £1,200 a year.

At the end of November the House of Commons presented the King with a Bill for placing the Militia under the control of Parliament. This, the very measure which had precipitated the Civil War, was a sign of hostility to the prerogatives of the Crown which Charles II was hardly likely to miss. For the first time in his reign the King employed his veto to put an end to the Bill. But the King had an Achilles heel in politics as well as in private life. This was the position of Danby. Danby was a marked man where the opposition was concerned and when an opportunity came to hunt him down it was

The King's proclamation, shortly after the 'discovery' of the plot. It offers a reward of £200 for information and a pardon should the informers themselves be part of the conspiracy.

seized with alacrity. This opportunity was provided by yet another unsavoury character, Ralph Montagu, the English Ambassador to the Court of France. Montagu made an enemy of no less a figure than Barbara Duchess of Cleveland by making amorous overtures to her daughter Anne. In revenge, Barbara revealed some of Montagu's intrigues with Danby. Montagu returned to England to defend himself, and to create havoc. He stood for Parliament – nor could Danby's much-vaunted organization prevent him from being elected. Montagu's intention was to gain immunity for his attack on Danby.

In vain Danby tried to seize Montagu's papers. Two crucial letters eluded the snatch. Montagu revealed their contents to the House of Commons. They were lethal. Here was Danby undeniably proposing to Louis XIV that England would settle the war in return for a substantial whack of cash. It would have taken much less than that to bring the gleeful cry of 'Impeachment!' to the eager lips of the members of the House of Commons. To protect his minister, Charles, at Danby's suggestion, wrote, 'I approve of this letter C.R.' on the drafts of Danby's letters produced in Parliament. And to protect himself he then got rid of Parliament on 30 December by dissolving it. So ended the life of the 'Cavalier' Parliament.

The General Election of February 1679 was the first to be held for eighteen years. Not only was the experience therefore novel to the country as a whole, but that country was also in a continuing state of ferment, attendant on the 'Popish' revelations of the previous autumn. In such a climate it is hardly surprising that Shaftesbury and the Whigs would look to Parliament to carry the one measure which would ensure a Protestant succession, the exclusion of the Duke of York from his right to inherit the throne. On the surface, the King appeared to be pliant in the face of necessity, as so often before. In February he told the Duke of York that he must leave England for the time being. But the crucial observation was that made by the King to Parliament at the end of April. As the new session was ending, he volunteered to accept any law whatsoever that the House of Commons could devise 'that may preserve your Religion' – provided that there was no interference with 'the Descent of the Crown in the right Line' – that is, the legitimate succession. There is no clearer statement of the conviction Charles II had reached with regard to the future of the monarchy. In his view interference with the succession held present, not just future, dangers – the top of the slippery slope leading downwards all the way, via political strife in Parliament to the dreaded abyss of civil war and revolution.

William of Orange, who became William III. As one of the possible successors he was of course a significant – if off-stage – figure in the various twists of the Exclusion Crisis.

The Duke of York, accompanied by Mary Beatrice, sailed for the Netherlands on 3 March. The ostensible reason for his journey was to visit his son-in-law and daughter, William and Mary of Orange. He left behind him a political scene unpleasantly transformed by the recent General Election. This, which has been described as the first English General Election fought along 'distinctively party lines', resulted in a happy triumph for that Country group increasingly identified as the Whigs over those of the Court supporters nicknamed Tories.

The men who now mustered in the Commons at Westminster immediately requested Danby's arrest and the Lords agreed. This of course posed a threat to Danby's actual safety as well as his ministerial position. Danby, reluctantly, offered his resignation. On 25 March the King, after assuring the House of Lords that he had authorized the Montagu letters, accepted it. Afterwards Danby blamed the King's decision on a new man in his counsels: Robert Spencer, Earl of Sunderland. Originally designated as Montagu's successor in Paris, Sunderland belonged to the rising generation (he was in his thirties) which would increasingly dominate political events in the last years of the King's reign. But Sunderland was merely echoing the general feeling of the Court party that Danby had to go. Besides, Charles himself could propose no better solution to save Danby than to pardon him for all the offences he had committed up till 27 February. The pardon infuriated the Commons. The King insisted. In the end, Danby was imprisoned in the Tower.

The introduction of the First Exclusion Bill was in the King's opinion a further assault on his own position. For the time being however the Exclusionists were weakened by their own internal disagreements. Exclusion was a comparatively new concept. Essentially it was personal to James, but what then? If James were debarred from succeeding, the main contenders for the throne were his two daughters: Mary, married to William of Orange, and Anne, as yet unmarried (she was just thirteen). Then there was 'the Protestant Duke' – James Duke of Monmouth, still the crowd's darling, still unlegitimized. All sorts of combinations of these figures would be suggested in the months to come.

Yet even without unity on the part of the Exclusionists, the situation was quite ugly enough for the King. In Parliament he was being pressed on all sides, not simply for or against his brother's cause. In Scotland, his faithful servant Lauderdale was being attacked. In Ireland, Archbishop Talbot died in prison in Dublin late in 1678, and about the same time Oliver Plunkett, Archbishop of Armagh, was arrested. Plunkett was a man of the greatest probity, yet a charge of

high treason was later fabricated against him. Since it proved impossible to find an Irish jury to convict him, two years later this particular witch-hunt was destined to move to England – the land of more amenable jurymen, where a Catholic prelate was concerned – with scandalous results.

Meanwhile, in England the summer of 1679 seemed a protracted nightmare. Danby was gone, leaving no obvious successor. The trial of Sir George Wakeman, with possible injury to the Queen, was pending. Parliament was sitting and about to debate the Exclusion Bill. The King as usual lacked money. Popular prejudice had, if anything, heightened since the previous autumn. Titus Oates still rode high, proclaiming that the Great Rebellion and the death of Charles I were due to the Jesuits, and that the Duke of York had started the Great Fire! It was an atmosphere in which rational decision was almost impossible. No one knew what the next day would bring, whether they were a Catholic fearing slaughter, or a righteous Englishman fearing the assassination of the ruler, followed by armed insurrection. The predatory Shaftesbury, blowing his hunting-horn to encourage the Whigs, added both to the excitement and to the confusion. Through it all Charles II maintained his balance by firm adherence to twin principles – for the Queen and against Exclusion.

During that unacknowledged deadlock which existed between Charles and his Parliament after the fall of Danby, the King instituted a new type of Council. It consisted of thirty members, half of whom were to be ministers and half without office. It was an intelligent move. Such a choice had the desirable effect – from the King's point of view – of promoting discord between those who were selected and those who were not. At the same time, it was the intention of this Council to transform poachers, such as Shaftesbury and the increasingly influential Halifax, into gamekeepers. Halifax, endowed with great brilliance of intellect, had been made a Privy Councillor in 1672; he had opposed the Test Act. Where James was concerned he did not take a hard line. Halifax stood more for the limitation of James' powers than for his total Exclusion.

The other members of this Council, trainee gamekeepers, included Sunderland and Laurence Hyde – 'Lory'. Like Sunderland, he was in his thirty-ninth year, eleven years younger than his master. He had inherited from his father a great loyalty towards the monarchy, and was against Exclusion. Then there was Sidney Godolphin, in his early thirties, who had close Dutch contacts and disliked the Duke of York. The junior member of the group was the Earl of Mulgrave, barely thirty, who preferred the Duke of York to Monmouth.

BABEL and BETHEL: or, The POPE in his Colours.

WITH

The Church of *ENGLAND's* Supplication to his Majesty, our gracious Soveraign, the true Defender of the Faith;

To protect her from all the Machinations of *Rome*, and its bloody Emissaries.

Rome's *Scarlet* whore doth here in *Tryumph Ride*,
And, Spurns off Soveraign Crowns in Height of Pride
Poor *Christians* and brave Citties too shee Burns
And Stabbs and Poisons daily serve her Turns.

Behold our Church (like *Esther* here doth tender
Her Supplication to the Faiths Defender
In vain Rome Plots, whilst Charles & Scepter Sways
May Sled and Gibbet end all Traitors Days.

From their youth, these men were to be known as 'the Chits'. A mark of this generation in 1679 was a capacity to remain on friendly terms with Shaftesbury and his associates, as well as with the Court, where their natural interests lay, unless there was some specific and dangerous issue. Indeed, there is a fluidity about the stance of men like Sunderland and Godolphin which echoes the generally confused political alliances of this period.

Despite such expedients, smooth government was becoming virtually impossible. On 29 April, as an effort against Exclusion, the King agreed to considerable limitations on the powers of any 'Popish' successors, but Shaftesbury and his clique continued to demand the sacrifice of James. Thus the Exclusion Bill was given its first reading and carried. On 21 May it was also carried on the second of its three necessary readings. On 27 May the King prorogued Parliament until 14 August.

A typical propaganda sheet contrasts the machinations of the Pope with the faithful diligence of Charles II in combatting them.

Parliament was not the only front where the royal authority was directly threatened. In Scotland, the murder of the anti-Covenant Archbishop Sharp on 13 May led to a dramatic change in the position of Monmouth, who was despatched north to command the loyal militia as Captain General. His triumph at Bothwell Brig on 22 June brought him a kudos which his actions at the English Court had not.

With Parliament prorogued, the King was under no illusion that Exclusion was a dead issue. Having gained a breathing-space, he cast his thoughts, as before, towards a means of ruling without this tiresome assembly.

Renewed negotiation – or intrigue – with France was one answer. Charles II had never yet turned to Louis XIV totally in vain. The reopening of discussions on the subject of a French subsidy was planned in the summer. Throughout the autumn these deliberations with the French Ambassador, Barrillon, would continue.

On 10 July, the King dissolved Parliament against the wishes of the majority of the Council, which effectively terminated the constitutional experiment. A further week later, on 18 July, Wakeman, the Queen's physician, was acquitted by a jury presided over by the Lord Chief Justice William Scroggs. At the time it was widely believed that Scroggs had been got at, but there is in fact no evidence that he was influenced. The Popish issue was not yet dead – the trial of the Catholic lords was to come – but at least some progress had been made in killing it off.

The acquittal of Wakeman on the one hand, and the possibility of renewed Anglo–French manoeuvres on the other, meant that by August 1679 the King could at last hope for the ease which had been denied to him during the last twelve months. It had been, indeed, an *annus horribilis*. Virtually everything he held dear, both of a private and a public nature, had been under attack. But the essential sea wall had not yet been breached. It was at this point, by one of those strange flukes of personal misadventure from which the course of history is never wholly free, that the King fell violently ill.

This dramatic twist to events – occurring at a moment of maximum uncertainty concerning the succession – was all the more startling because it was so unexpected. The King was famous for his superb health. Now, on 22 August at Windsor, he was struck down with an acute fever. If the King were to die, what was to be done about the Duke of York, lurking in unofficial exile in Brussels? James' legal position as heir presumptive was quite unaltered, and councillors could foresee an ugly situation arising. Suppose the Duke of York took over the throne, but they had somehow neglected to acknowledge his right to do so. On the other hand, it was equally possible that the Duke of York, being absent, would fail to secure the throne: Monmouth, dominated by Shaftesbury and bolstered by his position as Captain General, might grab it.

On 24 August Sunderland, faced with this dilemma, sent word to James that the King was ill. On 2 September the Duke arrived back in England. It was a decisive moment. Admittedly, by this date the King himself was recovering, but all the same, it was a decisive moment because James made it so. The situation brought out the best in the military-trained Duke, accustomed to a lifetime of decision and command in the field and at sea. Suddenly his stalwart figure appeared as a reassurance against the possibility of civil strife.

The Duke of York went back to the Continent three weeks later, but not before he had been assured that, had the King died, the Lord Mayor of London would have proclaimed James as his successor. Thus the whole episode secured an ascendancy for the established candidate, in which the pretender Monmouth was the inevitable loser. Monmouth still had much to prove, and he did not help matters by his own behaviour.

In vain had Monmouth attempted to prevent the return of the Duke of York. Now it was he who was deprived of his general's commission and, like the Duke of York, was asked by the King to absent himself from the felicity of the royal circle for a while. Monmouth, unconvinced, lingered for a time disconsolately. Then he headed for The Hague, where he managed to cause the King even more annoyance by striking up an unholy alliance with William of Orange.

The ascendancy of the Duke of York was not achieved without sacrifice. In return for the dismissal of Monmouth as Captain General, James was obliged to agree to leave the centre of things himself. He was appointed to the post in Scotland left tacitly vacant by Lauderdale and on 27 October 1679 James and his family, whom he had collected from Brussels, set off north. It was significant that it became something in the nature of a royal progress. Gentlemen took care to greet the heir presumptive to the throne on his way. It was an expression of that law put poetically by the great Queen Elizabeth: 'Men ever seek to worship the rising sun ...'

Meanwhile Charles II was obliged to cope with the trail of damage left by his illness and the behaviour of his brother and son. Moreover the General Election of the summer had given him another House of Commons, while the bitterness of the anti-Popish mood of the capital persisted. The popular celebrations in November reached a new pitch not only of hysterical malevolence, but also of organization.

In such an atmosphere, it was hardly surprising that when a new Plot was put forward for popular inspection by one Thomas Dangerfield, it was not found wanting. This new farrago was nicknamed the Meal Tub Plot, after the hiding-place where a Catholic midwife was supposed to have concealed incriminating papers. The King, commenting that 'he loved to discover Plots, but not to create any', made it clear that he regarded it all as dangerous nonsense. Under the circumstances, encouraged also by the renewal of the French negotiations, the King decided not to meet his new Parliament.

At this point, Shaftesbury went too far for the second time. Just as he had infuriated the King in the autumn of 1673 by his open attack on the Duke of York, he now called a meeting of the Privy Council to discuss James' projected departure for Scotland. The King dismissed Shaftesbury instantly, and the next day drove the message home by telling the Council that he did not propose to allow Parliament to meet until the following January. On 10 December the King let it be known that he had thought better of that date too, and, still further buoyed up by the progress of matters with France, indicated that Parliament would not actually meet again until November 1680. By December 1679 the irrepressible Monmouth had still further blotted his copybook by returning from the Netherlands against the King's specific orders. In the absence of a Parliamentary session, an angry war of pamphleteering concerning the claims of the rival dukes broke out in the late summer of 1680.

In particular, the legend of the King's marriage to Monmouth's mother, watered by the hopes of the opposition, grew apace. All kinds of rumours proliferated and at last, driven beyond endurance on the subject, the King decided to put an end to these once and for all. The *London Gazette* of 8 June, the official government organ, gave the authorized version: 'We cannot but take notice of the great Industry and

Jan Wyck's painting of the Duke of Monmouth, Charles' illegitimate son who became a Protestant candidate for the throne out of the turbulence of the Plot and Exclusion.

Malice wherewith some men of a Seditious and Restless Spirit, do spread abroad a most false and scandalous Report of a Marriage or Contract of Marriage ...'

But the false report persisted simply because it suited men's purposes at the time. It would haunt the first year of James II's reign for the same reason, and bring the wretched Monmouth to his death.

The King, in fact, was fighting back. In May, for example, the judges (now far more the King's men than before, thanks to the new policy towards judicial appointments) gave a unanimous opinion to the Council that the King might prohibit all unlicensed news-books and pamphlets in the interests of good order. The King had another asset in the crucial royal warrant by which municipal corporations were granted their charters, in essence a question of control over the composition of the House of Commons. Four-fifths of the Commons at that time were city or borough members, and, by controlling the governing body of the corporations in charge of their election – or in fact selection – attractive results could in theory be gained.

By 1680 there was no question of the King avoiding a clash with the House of Commons: as he saw it, the Whigs were snapping at his privileges. Moreover, his dissolutions of Parliament had been disastrous: he found himself with a more Whiggish body each time. By calling in the charters, he might provide a more satisfactory selection of Parliamentary candidates. Once again he saw himself combating a trend; others might view the situation differently.

A new Parliament met in October. For the King its purpose was the defence of Tangier, the Queen's dowry, an outpost in danger, beset by the Moors. Charles II therefore opened Parliament in October strongly on the theme of Tangier and its desperate plight. The answer of the House of Commons was to introduce the Second Exclusion Bill.

The meetings of the Commons also took place against a dramatic background of movement on the part of the rival claimants. The Duke of York, who had returned from Scotland in February, was despatched there again by the King in October. Monmouth, who had still not learnt his lesson about the limits of the King's indulgence, set off on a series of progresses around the country which aroused a satisfying loyal chorus of support from those who witnessed them. It is possible that Monmouth was encouraged in this unlicensed display of strength by Shaftesbury. If so, Shaftesbury also had not yet understood the King's capacity for sharp action when tried too far; the lesson would shortly be rammed home to him.

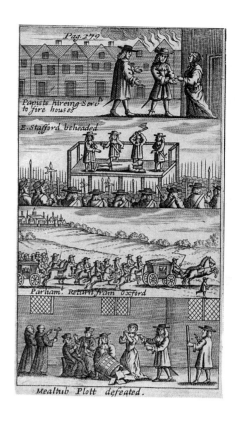

The Commons ignored the King's repeated offers to limit the authority of his successor and proceeded with the Bill's various readings. It passed its third, and was sent on to the Lords. There, the key speech came from Halifax. Only details of Halifax's superb and successful effort remain: but from these it is clear that he dwelt firmly on the possibilities of revolution – or at least an armed rising under James – which the passing of the Bill might offer. The Catholic succession, if it occurred, could be dealt with by other means, such as limitations. To throw out the Duke of York's claim by means of a Bill was to provoke exactly the kind of trouble they all wished to avoid.

It is clear from the reports of contemporaries that Halifax's decision to oppose Exclusion proved crucial. Only Halifax had the trenchant style necessary to cut down Shaftesbury, capable of demonic leadership in such a cause. During the ten-hour debate Shaftesbury never got up to speak without Halifax answering him. The final verdict was that Halifax's rapier was 'too hard' for Shaftesbury.

At the end of the day the Second Exclusion Bill was defeated by sixty-three votes to thirty. And so the issue of the succession was, unexpectedly to many, disastrously to not a few, settled for the time being in favour of the Catholic Duke, who represented the old order as well as descent in the right line.

Below: 17 November 1679, a mock Popish procession. The 17th, the date of accession of Elizabeth I, was for long a public holiday and a natural focus in the seventeenth century for anti-Catholic demonstrations.

Progress in Science

The second half of the seventeenth century saw the sciences flourish. It was the age of the discoverer of the circulation of the

Science was a personal interest of the King's throughout his reign.

blood, William Harvey; of the astronomer Flamsteed; of Robert Boyle and Robert Hooke; of the foundation of the Royal Society and the Royal Observatory; above all it was the age of Newton.

Charles II, the founder of The Royal Mathematical Society by Marceullus Laroon, 1684. His concern with the detail of applied science – whether to naval matters, astronomical measurements or the manufacture of clocks – was a life-long characteristic.

The Royal Observatory at Greenwich. The building was designed by Wren, and the foundation stone laid by Flamsteed on 10 August 1675.

Isaac Newton was a fellow of the Royal Society in Charles' reign and later President.

This frontispiece of an early history of the Royal Society illustrates the King as founder being crowned by Fame.

John Flamsteed, the first astronomer royal who measured the movements of the solar system with unprecedented accuracy.

An astrological map of 1660 by Andreas Cellarius dedicated to Charles II. In fact, Charles, unusually for his time, had a healthy scepticism about astrological predictions.

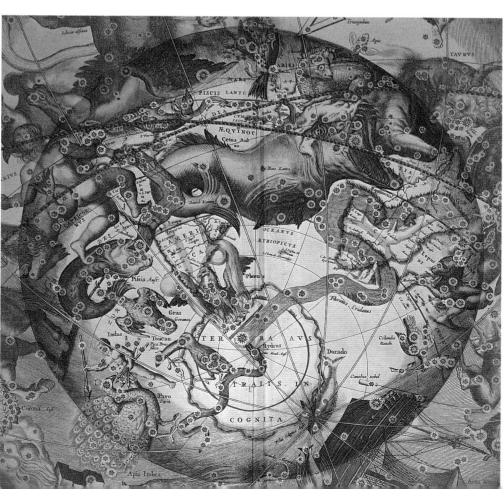

CHAPTER TWELVE
ANOTHER WAY OF RULING

With the defeat of the Second Exclusion Bill, it might appear that Charles II, that expert on the subject of survival, had survived yet again. But in January 1681 the House of Commons moved against Lord Stafford. The five Catholic Lords were still languishing in the Tower of London, to which they had been committed two years before. Now perjured witnesses happily swore that Lord Stafford had bribed them to kill the King, that Oates had delivered to him a commission to act as Paymaster-General for the Pope's Army, and so on and so forth. The condemnation of this decent and harmless old man was a blot on the age in which he lived. He was executed on 29 December.

His fellow lords remained in prison for the next five years, with the exception of Lord Petre, who was released earlier by death. But there were no cheers from the crowd when Lord Stafford's head was held up by his executioner. The public mood was at last beginning to change. Charles II made his anger and disgust at those peers who had voted guilty clear. But he did not reprieve Stafford, as he would later fail to reprieve Oliver Plunkett.

Then, suddenly, on 18 January, the King dissolved Parliament and announced that the next Parliament would meet in March – and in Oxford.

It was an audacious move. It indicated that the King was at last prepared to take the initiative. Here was no London mob, hostile to so many of the King's entourage; and the removal of Parliament from the seething capital also took advantage of the very wide powers remaining with the King. A man who could choose the venue of Parliament without contradiction was still in a very strong

Robert Streeter's ceiling of the Sheldonian Theatre, Oxford. This building was among the first designs of Sir Christopher Wren and the setting for the final meeting of the House of Commons in the King's reign.

Restoration Oxford, staunchly Royalist and the place chosen by Charles II for his *coup* against the Whigs.

position. There was much aggressive talk in the capital in February, but the Commons could not deny the King his choice. To Oxford, then, reluctantly but without the ability to resist, came the Whig leaders.

When the Court reached Oxford, the scene was a curious mixture of the significant and the profane. Both the Duchess of Portsmouth and Nell Gwynn were in attendance, as was the Queen; and there was of course that concomitant of courtly pleasure, the theatre. And troops of soldiers as well as actors were present. It seems that their total did not exceed five hundred. Yet since they lined the roads on the way to Oxford, and lounged in the streets of the city itself, the impression of a trial of strength was there. The Whigs arrived at Oxford marked out by the blue bows of satin in their hats, but, like the King, they were also armed with something more serious than bows. They too had brought their own troops with them.

The King's opening speech to his new Parliament on 21 March was placatory rather than defiant. On the subject of religion and the succession, the King went out of his way to emphasize that he wanted 'to remove all reasonable fears that may arise from the possibility of a Popish successor's coming to the Crown'. Shaftesbury, in the makeshift House of Lords sited in the Oxford Geometry School, wasted no time. He demanded the consideration of a Bill, already passed by both Houses, which would give relief to nonconformists but not to Catholics.

The House of Commons, in cramped quarters which gave rise to complaint, reverted to their favourite subject of Exclusion. Fatally – from their own point of view – the Commons felt no particular urgency. The debate was postponed until the following Saturday, 26 March.

During the next few days the King, brilliantly, paid out the rope for the Whigs. Shaftesbury, for example, was encouraged to come right out with his own solution. This was the legitimation of Monmouth by a Parliamentary Bill. But of course this had the effect of dividing the opposition. Many Whigs quite sensibly preferred Mary of Orange (who was generally understood to represent rule by William) to Monmouth.

This debate in the Commons duly took place on the Saturday. Taking advantage of the Commons' complaints of their uncomfortable accommodation, the King pleasantly suggested that they should meet the following Monday in the Sheldonian Theatre.

The Sunday was passed by the King in secret conference at Merton College.

On Monday the King took his place in the House of Lords, now set in the Hall of Christ Church. There was nothing out of the ordinary about his costume. Very few present were aware that the King's robes and crown, those trappings essential to a dismissal of Parliament, had been secretly smuggled into the building.

The King proceeded to send for the House of Commons, who were engaged in discussing the various precedents over Exclusions from the throne. So off the Commons trooped, not so much disconsolately as eagerly, expecting some new offer or concession.

Elias Ashmole, painted by John Riley. A life-long Oxford Royalist who served on the King's side in the Civil War and was patronized by Charles II after the Restoration. He was an avid collector and founded the Ashmolean Museum in Oxford.

The entrance to the Hall was narrow, down a little flight of steps. There was a crush as the Commons pressed through it. The sight which met their eyes – the monarch attired in full robes and crown – was both unexpected and for one moment inexplicable. Then the King in a single sentence ordered the Lord Chancellor to dissolve Parliament: 'All the world may see to what a point we are come, that we are not like to have a good end when the divisions at the beginning are such.'

Charles promptly left the Hall. He had wasted neither time nor breath. These, the last words he would ever speak in Parliament, were brusque to the point of incivility. They came from a man otherwise famed for the graciousness of his manner. They represented the end of a downhill road and a long-declining relationship.

The confidence, and courage, that Charles II needed to organize his abrupt dissolution came from France, for a new agreement had been reached, including, of course, a subsidy. Charles II would now receive from Louis XIV something over £300,000 spread over the next four years, which would enable him to jog along comfortably without Parliament for the time being. It was not only a question of money though. Once more, as in the 1660s, Charles II drew strength from the notion that Louis XIV was on his side and would help him, if need be, to uphold his 'legitimate authority'.

The summer of 1681 bore a very different air from that of the previous year. On 2 July, Shaftesbury was arrested. The King's move was not unexpected. Shaftesbury had wagered his strength against the King's in a series of provocative actions, including attacks on Louise and James as a prostitute and recusant, as well as sallies at Oxford. Shaftesbury was also on excellent terms with those the King considered his enemies, such as the arch-informer Titus Oates, still at large, if not quite the popular hero of yester-year.

The charge against Shaftesbury was frankly weak, as weak as some of the charges against the Catholic priests who had died. The truth was that Shaftesbury's arrest was an aggressive action which Charles II now felt himself strong enough to make. He was also animated by a strong personal dislike. In fact it would have been wiser to have let Shaftesbury depart for the Carolinas, where he had business interests, as he himself wished. Instead, on 24 November a Grand Jury composed of resolute Whigs returned a verdict of Ignoramus and Shaftesbury went free.

Shaftesbury's acquittal was a blow, but there were compensations. The personal life of Charles II during the last years of his life were extremely happy, even serene. Queen Catharine, comforted by his championship, had settled into a role which suited her and did not conflict with the King's other pleasures. By now, the King's mistresses resembled the great ships he also loved, floating grandly on the tide of the royal favour, their hulls weighed down with jewels and other riches. While Nell Gwynn retained what Aphra Behn called her 'eternal sweetness', the solace of the King's later years was Louise. Relaxation, not religion, was what Louise offered. Just as the King's accord with his wife and her own popularity were the subject of

A medallion struck to commemorate Shaftesbury's acquittal, but the momentum of the Whig cause was already dead.

Opposite: The Duchess of Portsmouth, painted by Pierre Mignard in 1682. By this date she had become the focus of the King's now domestically tranquil life.

comment, the domestic ascendancy of Louise was also remarked. She had grown plumper, more 'fubbsy' than ever (in the King's affectionate phrase), as her later portraits show; it only increased her air of luxurious cosiness. In effect King Charles, Queen Catharine and Duchess Louise created a master triangle in which all parties, for the first time in their lives, were roughly content with the status quo.

The King had an extensive, if illegitimate, family of children to look after. As Buckingham brightly observed, a King is supposed to be the Father of his People, and Charles II was certainly the father of a good many of them. The twelve known bastards were born from seven women: Lucy Walter, Elizabeth Killigrew, Catharine Pegge, Barbara Villiers, Nell Gwynn, Moll Davis and Louise de Kéroüalle. The King honoured his genuine paternal obligations with a mixture of love and liberality. In fact, six of the King's sons received nine dukedoms: Monmouth and Buccleuch for Lucy Walter's son; Southampton, Northumberland and Grafton and Cleveland, on her death, for Barbara's three boys; St Albans for Nelly's surviving son; Richmond and Lennox (joined together) for Louise's only child. Monmouth's marriage to Anne Duchess of Buccleuch in her own right, led to the pair being created Duke and Duchess of Buccleuch in England jointly. After his death, Duchess Anne was allowed to retain her own Scottish Buccleuch title, although that of Monmouth was swallowed up in her husband's disgrace.

But Charles' daughters were not forgotten. Some were married off to lordlings, who were then further ennobled. Mary Tudor was granted the rank and precedence of a Duke's daughter at the same time as her step-brothers gained their coveted dukedoms.

Taken all in all, they were an agreeable bunch, with no real black sheep amongst them – unless one counts Monmouth. Out of a dozen children, that was not a bad record. Deservedly or not, in private the King's life was marked by new contentment as he grew older, and, in terms of good relations with his growing children, he led a life of richness which many men of his age might have envied.

In the winter of 1684 Sir John Reresby was informed that there was no question of a Parliament, since those near the King had 'advised him to another way of ruling the Kingdom'. It was relevant that England enjoyed a trade boom in the early 1680s. This boom, which has been traced in the customs figures, happily transformed the royal receipts from this source.

Unaware of the blessings about to flow, Charles II took a firm line about his own finances. The French subsidies could be counted on to settle outstanding military needs. Where Court and personal expenditure was concerned, the value of economy – an unpleasant prospect, but anything to avoid having to call a Parliament – was recognized.

The extent to which the King himself took an active interest in extending his own powers is more difficult to assess. It is certainly possible to make a case for the Duke of York as the master-mind of this absolutist trend. But the case is not proved. The fact was that James' ideas and policies were now convenient to the King. James, for example, approved in his memoirs that campaign for calling in corporations' charters begun in 1680 and shortly to be stepped up.

The attempt to secure a friendly judiciary was an essential part of 'another way of ruling'. For all the indignation of the Whigs, the calibre of the new men was not low. What they did share however, and share with the Crown, was the view that their tenure sprang from that Crown and depended upon it.

In fact the last years of the reign saw a transformation in the King's fortunes, from the increase in his customs revenue to the growing influence in judicial and ecclesiastical appointments. There was greater control of the press. Perhaps as crucial as anything was the systematic exploitation of town charters, and their country equivalents, enabling the government – through clauses in the renewals – to ensure the return of Tory sheriffs and offices. In this way control even of the City of London was won. By continental standards it was not absolutism, but it was through a combination of luck and planning that a very powerful monarchy was indeed emerging.

The first real effects of these policies were felt in the King's handling of the so-called Rye House Plot of the spring of 1683. The bones of this muddled and confusing plot seem to have been to 'lop' both King and Duke of York to or from Newmarket and install Monmouth as King. It went wrong by accident; a fire caused the royal brothers to leave Newmarket early. The alleged plot, having been put off, was then betrayed.

The importance of the Rye House Plot lay not in itself but in the involvement, or assumed involvement, of the Whig leaders. Nothing more accurately reflects the changing climate of the time than the plot's aftermath, so different from the turmoil which followed the Popish Plot. This time the plot's discovery found the Whigs in full retreat. Shaftesbury, a sick man, had already fled to Holland where he died in January 1683. The Earl of Essex committed suicide in his cell; Lord Russell and Algernon Sidney, prominent among the Exclusionists, were executed. There is no evidence that any of them were direct plotters. They were condemned for their general opposition; guilt by association, and the same went for Monmouth himself.

Overleaf: Playing cards with scenes from the Rye House Plot, which effectively ended Lord Shaftesbury's political influence.

Lord Shaftsbury going
for Holland.
Ferguson taking leave

Walcot coming from
Ireland.

The Counsell of Six
sitting

Colliford Standing
in the Pillory

Walcot & other Conspirators
ready to charge ye K. Guards

The designe of Shooting
the K. Postilian

The designe of Shooting
into the K. Coach

The places mentioned for
Killing ye King

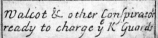

Keeling troubled
in mind.

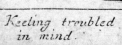

Rumsey Examined by
the King and Councell.

Lord Grey making
his Escape.

The Lord Shaftsbury

The Kings Decleration read in Churches 9th of Septbr

Conspirators veiwing the Citty and deviding it into 20 prts

Ld Russell beheaded in Lincolne Inn Feilds

Hone & Rouse going to be Executed

Rumbolds House

Conspirators waiting for ye K. coming by Rumbold House

Thompson one of ye Conspirators taken at Hamersmith

E. of Essex cutting his throat in ye Tower

The fire at New-Markett

Ld Howard writing an account of the Plot

Lord Russell Tryed at the Old Bayly

West bying of Armes

The magnificent but unexecuted scheme by Christopher Wren for the King's 'new house' at Winchester. Its progress occupied Charles during the last days of his life.

John Webb's design for a bedchamber for Charles II at Greenwich Palace, 1665. It remained only a plan but indicates the King's ? for improvements to his residences.

In July 1683 a Grand Jury found against him and a reward was offered for his capture. Nothing too energetic was done about this, and indeed the King attempted a reconciliation. Monmouth wrote two penitent letters, but then demanded that his recantation should not be made public. Exasperated, the King – though always a loving father in his heart – could tolerate no more. Monmouth flounced off to the Continent, where William of Orange took this opportunity to stir the pot – and stir up family trouble, by entertaining him.

In the closing phase of his life the King found time for activities other than international, domestic and family disputes. What would now be termed the life-style of Louis XIV continued to impress Charles II, as it impressed all Europe. Now, on 23 March 1683, the foundation stone of a new royal palace, to be built in the French manner, was laid at Winchester. The dwelling, designed by Sir Christopher Wren, was to be surrounded by a park and connected to the town's historic cathedral by a 'stately street'. It would lie east and west. There were to be 160 rooms, surmounted by a lofty cupola which would be visible from the sea. As for the park, here a thirty-foot cascade was proposed; the King hoped to repeat his success with ornamental water in St James's Park. A river through the park was intended to be navigable by small

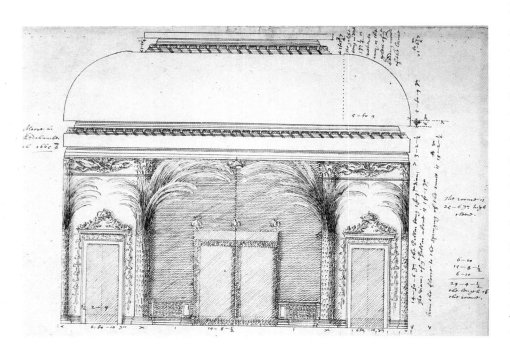

vessels. The park itself, an eight-mile circuit, would open into the forest, suitable for stag-hunting. It was a wonderful project – never to be seen.

The true memorial to Winchester Palace lies in the eager conversation of Charles II with Lord Bruce on one of the last evenings of his life. The King spoke with enthusiasm of the 'favourite castle' he was building, and how he would arrange for Bruce to be in waiting there. 'I shall be so happy this week as to have my house covered with lead,' he exclaimed. As the King's body was wrapped in its lead coffin within the week, it was a prophecy – of the ambiguous sort beloved of the Greek oracle – that came grimly true.

Charles' restless mind did not cease to turn over new schemes, explore new horizons. He founded the Royal Hospital, Chelsea, though it was not opened until 1692.

The Royal Hospital, Chelsea, with Grinling Gibbons' statue of its founder Charles II in the foreground.

Much further afield, he had other interests. In general the reign of Charles II saw a remarkable accession of distant lands to the English flag. The great Hudson's Bay Company was founded in 1670. Not only in North America, but in the West Indies, West Africa and India, this was an age of territorial expansion and, above all, commercial energy. In April 1681 Charles II granted a vast tract of land, now Pennsylvania, to William Penn the Quaker. He liked to hear of the Carolinas, where busy colonists were enjoying a more fruitful kind of exile than he had known.

At home in July 1683 there took place a royal event which might even, had Providence decreed, have granted one final satisfaction: a peaceful future for the monarchy. This was the marriage of James' daughter Anne to Prince George of Denmark. George was widely rated to be a French-inspired choice, because the King of Denmark fell within the diplomatic network controlled by Louis XIV. Very soon this amiable Protestant pair did produce a child. Little significance was attached to the fact that this first baby died: it was merely one of the commonplace griefs of the time. The important point was that Princess Anne had proved herself fertile. No one could foresee that the unfortunate woman would be condemned to bear seventeen children, not one of whom survived childhood.

As the last year of the life of King Charles II dawned, from the point of view of the monarchy there was no longer any reason to fear and much reason to hope.

Architecture of Substance and Symmetry

The word 'architect' only came into use in the second half of the sixteenth century; before that the medieval 'Master' was the common term. The architectural style of Charles II's reign was essentially classical, handsome and symmetrical without the complexities of a Gothic period or the elaborate ornamentation of Rococo. Of course domestic architecture reflected wealth, and men of substance built substantial houses. The need for 'fortified dwellings' with fortress-type features had long since disappeared, and looking at the best examples of seventeenth-century architecture the confidence of the age is clear.

Above: Belton House, Lincolnshire, 1684-7

Right: The great staircase of Sudbury Hall, Derbyshire. The house was built during the 1670s. Plaster work by Bradbury and Pettifer.

Below: Denham Place, Buckinghamshire, painted c. 1672.

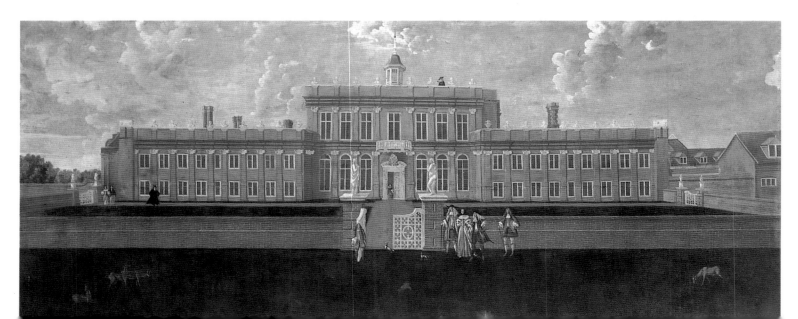

Buildings reflected

the confidence

of the age.

The Custom House at King's Lynn, Norfolk, by Henry Bell, 1683. A rare example of a local commercial building of architectural distinction.

Below: Willen Church, Buckinghamshire, by scientist and inventor Robert Hooke, one of the few parish churches belonging in its entirety to the reign.

Above: Mompesson House, Salisbury, 1680.

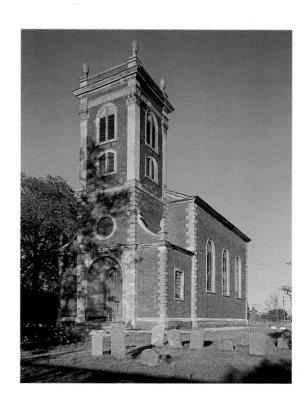

Above: Ashdown House,
Berkshire, *c.* 1650.

Right: Coleshill, Berkshire, by
Sir John Pratt, begun 1650.

Above: Tythrop House, 1680,
near the Buckinghamshire–
Oxfordshire border.

Wisbech Castle,
Cambridgeshire, c. 1658-9.

XIII

'WITH ALL MY HEART'

The last year of the King's life was outwardly a tranquil one. His country was at peace and he took care that it should remain so. The French subsidy, which had been phased over three years, came to an end but the King remained openly, even gaily pro-French. He sent a message of congratulation to Louis XIV on his acquisition of Luxembourg. The Truce of Ratisbon in the summer of 1684 confirmed the French monarch not only in that precious possession but also Strasbourg. Without English help, there was no way that the United Provinces could play an aggressive part in keeping the French wolf at bay: the checking of this all-conquering animal would have to wait for another day, another reign.

Two matters could, however, have plagued the King, had he allowed them to do so. One was the continued incarceration of Danby in the Tower of London, five years after he had been consigned there (without a formal trial). The other was the return of Parliament, which had now been dissolved for over three years; this was a significant period. Although the Triennial Act of 1664 left it conveniently to the King to decide to call Parliament, there was no machinery to compel him to do so.

The King succeeded in freeing Danby; the supposition is that the King had a private word in the judges' ears. Danby would, it seems, have formed part of a new administration in 1685 had it not been for the King's death.

The question of Parliament was equally resolved, but negatively. Within the King's own councils, Halifax at least believed that the spirit of the Triennial Act should be respected. But the King had 'no thought' of summoning a Parliament.

The famous portrait of the King in his last years, attributed to Thomas Hawker, c. 1680-85.

In May 1684 the Duke of York took his place in the Privy Council once more. It was the final step in his restoration. At about the same time Titus Oates was arrested at a coffee-house in London on a charge of calling the Duke a traitor. Tried briefly by Jeffreys, he was consigned to prison.

James, triumphant, was restored to his former post as Lord High Admiral in all but name: the King continued to sign documents since the provisions of the Test Act were still officially in force, but the moving spirit was that of James. Where the succession was concerned, neither Monmouth nor William of Orange had now the muscle to bar the smooth ascent of the Duke of York towards his legitimate goal.

There was a wistful notion entertained by Monmouth's admirers after the King's death – still occasionally resurrected even now – that some time during the last autumn Monmouth was actually promised the succession. Monmouth himself spoke wildly on the subject after his father's death, when there was no one to contradict him. It is true that the forbidden favourite did slip into England from Holland at the end of November. There was probably some kind of limited reconciliation, although it is unlikely that this amounted to more than the mere prospect of Monmouth returning to England. Had the reconciliation genuinely produced a violent change in the King's feelings he would hardly have kept his mouth shut on the subject.

So far as we can tell, the inward man was tranquil too. And his energy continued to startle and confound even those who had known it to their cost for years. It is true that he was having trouble with a sore on his leg as well as painful gout; the long walks were reluctantly cut down. His keenness was now channelled into his laboratory, where he would devote himself to his experiments for hours at a time in the same obsessional manner. Besides, the King believed the delay in the walks was only temporary. Soon he would be striding out once more, outdistancing courtiers and subjects alike, pausing only for the demands of the ducks. In the last winter of his life, he was described by Bishop Burnet as looking 'better than he had done for many years'.

The final drama began quite suddenly on a Sunday night. It was 1 February 1685. The day itself had passed placidly enough. The King's leg still bothered him. He could not take his favourite constitutional; instead, he went for a drive with his attendant Thomas Lord Bruce. It is thus to Bruce that we owe many of the most affecting details of his master's last days, still vivid in his memory when he wrote his memoirs many years later. At supper the King ate his customary hearty meal and then, as usual, loped off to the apartments of Louise to see who might have been supping with her. Barbara was there, as was Hortense, returned to England and restored to favour. Not one of the three could be remotely considered young and between them one way and another they could number nearly fifty years in the King's service. The evening was therefore marked as much by the King's fidelity to old friends as to profligacy.

Afterwards there were plenty of people to bear witness that they had never seen the King in a better mood. Bruce duly conducted his master to bed.

That night the vast, sprawling Palace of Whitehall was restless. There were the endless striking clocks, none of which kept time with each other, chiming through the small hours. There was the flickering, shooting light of the Scotch coal in the enormous grate, lighting up rich tapestries and dusty corners. There were the King's indulged dogs, a whole pack of them in the very bedroom and even in the bed. Bruce, the Lord-in-waiting, could not sleep. None of these sounds, however disturbing, was unusual. Besides, Bruce was going off duty the next day – he could sleep then.

What was both unusual and disquieting was the fact that the King himself tossed and turned. Normally he was a very heavy sleeper. When the King did awake, he looked quite different. His normally olive complexion was 'pale as ashes'. He went immediately, still wearing only his nightgown, into his Privy Closet just off the bedroom. When Howard, a groom, went to join him, he found the King completely silent.

In the meantime, the royal doctors were actually waiting in the ante-chamber to the bedroom to dress the tiresome sore on his leg. As time passed, the worried Bruce searched for William Chiffinch, the King's Keeper of the Closet (and confidant), for etiquette forbade anyone else to enter the closet unbidden. In the end it was Chiffinch, who had carried out so many more cheerful errands in the past, who conducted the King out of the closet back into the bedroom.

The King's speech was obviously by this time seriously impaired. But because no one dared to take it upon themselves to interrupt his routine – although it must have been obvious that he was dangerously sick – his barber Follier now proceeded to shave his master as usual.

The King was sitting as was his wont, with his knees against the window, and Follier was just fixing the linen round his neck, when the King gave vent to the most extraordinary and piercing noise. Afterwards described by one as 'the dreadfullest shriek' and by another as an 'exclamation as one that dies suddenly', it was clearly audible outside the chamber. Then the King sank back into Bruce's arms, unconscious. It was exactly eight o'clock in the morning.

The responsibility for making the first decision about treatment fell upon Bruce, the senior gentleman present. By this time one of the doctors, Sir Edmund King, had arrived in the bed-chamber and had witnessed the incident. Bleeding was the obvious remedy of the time. And bleed the King this doctor now proceeded to do in style, while a panic-stricken message was sent off to the Duke of York and the rest of the Privy Council were summoned as hastily as possible. By the time a Privy Council of sorts had gathered together in the outer room at midday, Charles had had sixteen ounces of blood removed via a vein in his arm, a task for which the doctor was afterwards paid £1,000.

Soon other doctors came flocking in as the news of the King's collapse reached them. A series of remedies were frantically applied. The King's head was shorn. Cantharides was used as a blistering agent. A further eight ounces of blood was removed. And as a result of these steps – or despite them – the King did actually recover. Two hours later his speech had come back.

He found the Duke of York beside him. The Duke was once more in command of the situation, as he had been in 1679, but it was a token of the general disarray that he had forgotten to put on both his shoes and was still wearing one slipper. One of the first things the King did, when his speech returned, was to ask for the Queen.

All round the relief was incredible. The official newsletter of the day, referring to 'the fit' which had seized the King, was also able to pronounce him out of danger.

In the general relief, the doctors at least did not let up on the application of their remedies. It was actually in the presence of his physicians – twelve of them by this time – that next morning, Tuesday, 3 February, the King was seized with another 'fit' or convulsion. Immediately and with renewed frenzy the remedies were stepped up and new ones were imposed.

The King's poor body was purged and bled, cauterized, clystered and blistered. Red-hot irons were put to his shaven skull and his naked feet. His urine became scalding through the lavish use of cantharides. Cupping-glasses and all the many weird resources of medicine at the time were applied. They all had one thing in common: they were extremely painful to the patient.

In the crisis, the ladies of the Court reacted entirely according to type. Louise, the ready weeper, swooned and had to be carried out for air. Nelly 'roared to a disturbance and was led out and lay roaring behind the door'. The Queen was overcome with pure grief and had to be carried back to her apartments in a state of collapse.

In truth, one of the main features of the death-bed of King Charles II was its total lack of privacy. When the room came to be cleared on Thursday, it contained seventy-five assorted lords and Privy Councillors, surgeons and servants. By this time the company also included no fewer than five bishops.

Thomas Ken, the King's former chaplain, now Bishop of Bath and Wells, was the first of these to arrive. He appeared on the Wednesday morning, when the King was thought to be rallying. He was present on the Wednesday afternoon, when the King suffered another major convulsion and the hopes aroused by each small recovery were finally dashed. Ken had last administered Communion to the King at Christmas. He now pressed the King to receive it again. Charles however steadfastly refused to do so, giving two contradictory reasons: first, there was no particular hurry, and secondly, he was too feeble to receive it. He was silent too when Ken asked him to declare himself a member of the Church of England, either because his voice was weak or because some deeper emotion was already stirring within his failing body.

Towards the end of Wednesday the King's condition worsened. He broke out in a cold sweat. He also suffered from intermittent bouts of fever.

Exactly what was wrong with the King? At four o'clock on Thursday afternoon, in the language of the doctors, there was 'some exacerbation or paroxysmal increase'. In other words, the convulsions were mounting. Great bouts of fever were shaking his body. Ironically enough, the same doctors who were so busy at the cure were still very much in the dark as to what they were curing. Their energies were great; but then so was their ignorance.

After the King's death the official verdict was apoplexy. It would be translated today more familiarly as a stroke. It is easy to believe that the King, like many middle-aged men, was suffering from high blood-pressure, followed by a stroke, brain damage and finally cardiac arrest. However, that verdict presents certain difficulties.

If the King had a stroke, then it is remarkable that he was never paralysed – paralysis down one side would have been expected. He also recovered his speech totally, while he never lost his reason. This point is not a purely academic one: for if the King had had a stroke, it could be argued that he was incapable of making a positive decision in favour of the Catholic faith. Yet it is evident from the account of Father Huddleston and others that his mind was quite clear, if his body was weak.

At the present time the theory of Raymond Crawfurd, elaborately set out in 1909, still seems the most plausible: the King was suffering from chronic glandular kidney disease (a form of Bright's disease) with uraemic convulsions. During the winter he had been plagued by gout. The fatal use of cantharides, to promote blistering on the first night of his illness, must have done much to rob the King's kidneys of their vestige of functional activity. It would nevertheless not be fair to describe King Charles, as Macaulay did, as the victim of his doctors. The physicians did substantially alleviate his sufferings, while failing to alleviate the cause. But they did not kill him. The disease would have done so in any case.

In the meantime, a dangerous and different drama was being played out behind the scenes. It is not clear who made the original suggestion that the King should receive a Catholic priest. One obvious candidate was the Queen. As early as Monday Catharine had said to the Catholic Duchess of York: 'Sister, I beg you to tell the Duke that he, who knows as well as I do the King's convictions about the Catholic religion, should do what he can to take advantage of any opportunity that offers.' Mary Beatrice went to her husband. The Duke of York replied, 'I know, and I am thinking of nothing else.' But he took no action.

The Duke's cautious attitude illustrates the extreme delicacy of the situation. The fact was that the King could well recover (and indeed subsequently did so, albeit temporarily). Then, although the Queen referred to the King's 'convictions' about the Catholic religion, a sentiment echoed by Louise, who described him as a Catholic 'at the bottom of his heart', neither lady pretended that these convictions had as yet been given public expression. Indeed, the nervousness of the King's intimate circle is yet another argument against the proposition that the King was already an established Catholic. This whole death-bed episode, attested by so many witnesses, makes little sense if such a conversion had already taken place.

The fateful move to introduce a Catholic priest was only made when the King was clearly dying. It was made when Louise received a visit from the French Ambassador Barrillon in her apartments. He found her, in the midst of her grief, extremely agitated on the subject of the King's religion. She bewailed the fact that he was surrounded by Protestant bishops since, in her limited observation, 'at the bottom of his heart the King is a Catholic'. Was there any possibility of a priest being introduced? She herself could no longer enter his room 'with any decency' since the Queen was nearly always present. Barrillon, with his usual freedom of movement, could go to the Duke of York and did so. James was said to have responded immediately, 'I would rather risk everything than not do my duty on this occasion.'

The King's consent still had to be gained. Only the Duke of York had the opportunity to do so. As discreetly as possible he bent down and whispered in his brother's ear. The King answered. From time to time James had to repeat his words, so low did he speak. The King himself was barely audible, except to those closest to him, who

Father Huddleston, who saved the King after defeat at Worcester and received him into the Catholic Church on his death-bed.

Charles' loyalty to his rescuer after Worcester proclaims an indemnity for Father Huddleston while proscribing the activities of all other Jesuits.

included Barrillon. But the King's basic answer remained the same: 'Yes, with all my heart.'

On Barrillon now devolved the duty of actually finding a priest. And the one found in the Queen's apartments, by a merciful dispensation, was Father Huddleston.

It had been a long road from Worcester for both parties. Disguised in a wig and a cassock, Father Huddleston was led from the Queen's suite of rooms to a closet just off the King's chamber which had a private communicating door. Here he waited. In the meantime, the Duke of York cleared the King's room in soldierly fashion by simply announcing in a loud voice, 'Gentlemen, the King wishes everybody to retire except the Earls of Bath and Feversham.' The former, a fervent Royalist, was the Groom of the Stole; the latter, a Frenchman naturalized English, the Queen's chamberlain. But both gentlemen were Protestants, which served to pacify the Bishops. Their continued attendance, which was contrary to the King's own wishes, was also due to James' concern that his dying brother's conversion should be seen to be voluntary; he did not want to be the sole witness to such a momentous event. When the room was ready, Chiffinch, who had brought so many clandestine night visitors to his master in the past, brought in one more, a man of God.

By the King.
A **PROCLAMATION**
For the Discovery and Apprehending all Popish Priests and Jesuits.
CHARLES R.

Charles II cried out with pleasure at the sight of Huddleston. The various accounts of the conversion scene vary in detail, but the King's general reaction to Huddleston was clear: 'You that saved my body are now come to save my soul.'

Father Huddleston put a series of questions to the King. Did he wish to die in the Faith and the Communion of the Holy Roman Catholic Church? Did he wish to make a full confession of all his sins? To all these questions, Charles answered firmly, in a low but distinct voice. His resolution was clear. Then he made his general confession. Amongst the things for which he declared himself 'most heartily sorry' was the fact that 'he had deferr'd his Reconciliation so long' – these words on the lips of a dying man, reported by Father Huddleston without contradiction, being yet another proof, if proof were needed, that the King was not already a secret Catholic. The King's confession ended in an act of contrition: 'Into Thy Hands, Sweet Jesus, I commend my soul. Mercy, Sweet Jesus, Mercy.' The priest gave him absolution.

Huddleston's last question concerned the Blessed Sacrament: 'Will you receive it?'

The King replied, 'If I were worthy of it, Amen.'

So the King received the Catholic Communion and afterwards Huddleston sat quietly by him, reading the Catholic prayers for the dying in a low voice. It was Charles' own request that Huddleston recited once again the Act of Contrition, ending 'Mercy, Sweet Jesus, Mercy'. Then the priest put a crucifix into the King's hands, saying that it only remained for him to meditate on the death and passion of 'Our dear Saviour Jesus Christ'. Father Huddleston recited more prayers as the King held the crucifix, then left as he had come, through the secret door. The whole momentous episode had lasted three-quarters of an hour.

The King's progress out of the transitory world, although sure, was slow. The King himself summed it up with his ineffable politeness: he told the gentlemen surrounding his bed that he was sorry to trouble them by taking so long a-dying, and he asked their pardon.

Throughout the long night of Thursday, 5 February, Charles remained conscious. The physicians set to work with their remedies again with even greater energy. At one point the King referred to his continuing ordeal. He told his attendants, 'I have suffered very much and more than any of you can imagine.' Once, listening to those innumerable palace clocks striking, he asked the time. They told him and he said, 'My business will shortly be done.' But his stoicism continued to excite the admiration of all about him. It was an exemplary death-bed, as might have been expected of one who had learnt early to confront the unknown with courage and hope.

There were a series of farewells. Catharine came. Charles greeted her lovingly. But her distress, both at the King's tenderness and at his suffering, was too great. Tears overcame her. She was carried back to her own apartments, half-fainting. She sent back a message to her husband to beg his pardon if she had ever offended him.

'Alas! poor woman,' said the King. 'She beg my pardon! I beg hers with all my heart.'

To James, too, linked to him by every shared memory of boyhood and now at last by Faith, the King showed much tenderness. James, kneeling, could not hold back his own tears. Charles begged his pardon too, for the hardships which he had inflicted upon him from time to time. At some point in the long midnight hours he handed him the keys of his cabinet and begged God to give him a prosperous reign. The Duchess of York remained openly weeping at her husband's side.

The King also spoke of his children. He recommended his little family most touchingly to his brother, naming each one meticulously.

But the King did not name Monmouth. And James, repeating the list back to him, did not mention the forbidden name either.

A miniature of James, the illegitimate son in exile at the time of his father's death.

The ladies, those other members of his extended family circle, were not forgotten. In a phrase sometimes supposed to be apocryphal but in fact attested by three sources, the King adjured the Duke of York 'to be well to Portsmouth' and 'not let poor Nelly starve' – even in his last hours the vital social distinction between the two ladies was preserved.

One by one his children came and knelt down by the King's bed and received his blessing. At which the throng of people once more surrounding the royal bed, and crowding into the chamber, cried out that the King was their common father. So all present in fact knelt down for his blessing. It was of course an Anglican blessing. But when Bishop Ken repeatedly urged the King to take the Sacrament, Charles declined it. He would only say that he had thought of his approaching end, and hoped that he had made his peace with God. Ken was unaware what this characteristically courteous evasion meant.

At six o'clock in the morning the King asked for the curtains to be drawn back. He wanted, he said, to watch the dawn for the last time. He

Charles Earl of Plymouth, the King's son by Catharine Pegge.

Opposite: Charlotte Fitzroy, later Countess of Lichfield. She was the King's daughter by Barbara Palmer. Painting by Peter Lely.

was still conscious enough to ask that the eight-day clock in his room should be wound up, because it was the appointed day. An hour later he became breathless and struggled to sit up. Once again the doctors bled him, taking twelve ounces, and gave him heart tonics. At half past eight his speech began to fail once more. This time it did not return. By ten o'clock he was in a coma.

The rising sun over the Thames was probably the last sight he took in. It was an appropriate one for this man who had so loved the early morning on its misty waters.

King Charles II died at noon. It was now high water on the riverand the time of the full moon. The day was Friday, 6 February 1685, and he was in his fifty-fifth year.

Henry Duke of Grafton,
painted by Thomas Hawker.
He was the King's son by
Barbara Palmer who became
Duchess of Cleveland.

Opposite: Henri Gascar's
portrait of Charles Lennox,
Duke of Richmond, the King's
son by Louise Duchess of
Portsmouth.

EPILOGUE

After the death of King Charles II the ordinary people walked about 'like ghosts'. They felt that they had lost a father, that feeling spontaneously expressed at the King's death-bed when all present, not only his children, had knelt for his paternal blessing.

The King's body lay in state in the Painted Chamber at Whitehall for several days. As was the custom of the time, his wax effigy, standing upright over the catafalque, dominated the scene. It was dressed in robes of crimson velvet trimmed with ermine, and surmounted with an imperial crown of tin gilt, all specially ordered for the occasion by the Lord Chamberlain. Such effigies, taken from the death-mask, often have a haunted look: the lines on the face of Charles II are deep, the face is slightly twisted, the expression very sad. Still to be seen exhibited in the precincts of Westminster Abbey, it commemorates the cruel sufferings of his death-bed.

The funeral itself took place on the night of 14 February. The King's body was enclosed in a lead coffin – that 'house of lead' which had been prophesied. Then the body of Charles II was laid to rest in a vault beneath the Henry VII Chapel in Westminster Abbey. There it remains to this day.

Careful provision was made for discreet display – banners of black taffeta with strings and tassels of black silk – and appropriate sad sounds – black-coated trumpeters, kettle-drummers, and a fife.

So, in a mellow atmosphere of regret the King was buried. It seemed that the peace which he so much desired for his country had fallen upon it, even as he himself was laid to peace in his grave.

It was not to be. Only a few months later those characters dismissed from the stage by the final curtain of one play, found themselves engaged in quite a different

James II, who succeeded his brother in 1685. Charles supported the 'legitimate line' against all opposition, but his successor was to forfeit his throne just three years later.

The effigy of Charles II in the crypt of Westminster Abbey.

drama. There was to be no happy ending to the reign of King James II.

Monmouth died at the executioner's axe after his foolish and bloody rebellion, only a few months after his father's death. Three years later James himself was fighting off the political onslaught of William of Orange and his own daughter Mary; the birth of the long-dreaded Catholic Prince to Mary Beatrice in June 1688 had brought disaster in its wake. By 1689 Titus Oates, savagely whipped after trial for perjury in May 1685, was being received by William, now King of England: Oates remained a weather-vane for the direction of the English political wind. As a counterpoise it is good to relate that Father Huddleston lived on to the ripe old age of ninety – protected in the household of Queen Catharine at Somerset House.

Another mercurial figure, whose story had been even more closely entwined with that of Charles II, did not survive to see the new Protestant reign. Buckingham died two years after his master and childhood friend; but it was somehow characteristic of the man that his burial at least – like that of Charles himself in the Henry VII Chapel at Westminster Abbey – was a most splendid affair. As for the younger politicians, Sunderland, Rochester, Godolphin and the like, for the most part they stepped willingly onto the new stage to act out all the intricate if not heroic dramas of politics in the ages of William and Mary, and Anne.

The mistresses did not fare so well. Nell Gwynn died – of a stroke – two years after her royal Charles. She was only thirty-five. Barbara Duchess of Cleveland was made of more lasting stuff. She may have lived to regret her own durability. For at the age of sixty-five she married a much younger man, a notorious rake known as Beau Fielding, who treated her abominably. As for Louise, she survived (in France) to the then remarkable age of eighty-five. She died, wrote Saint-Simon, 'very old, very penitent and very poor'. The Louise who held luxurious court at Whitehall would have deplored all three states, but particularly the last.

Catharine of Braganza survived too, until the end of 1705, twenty years after the husband she had loved, served, and in all but one vital respect over which she had no control, satisfied. In her case a magnificent state funeral in Portugal testified to the general esteem in which this practical and pious lady was held.

King Charles II had inherited a country war-torn and poor, divided, restless and suspicious. He left behind him a country outwardly at harmony. He was personally beloved from his early days, when the crowds saluted their Black Boy come again, to those last years, when he still basked in national affection. When Evelyn wrote of his sovereign as having 'many Virtues and many great Imperfections' he did not specify the contents of either category. The balance of the character of Charles II, where vice and virtue are concerned, was in fact a very human one which could not fail to appeal to many of his subjects and fellow-sinners. Here was a man who knew all about Sloth and Lust, but was singularly free from Pride, Greed, Avarice, Anger and Envy. As for the Virtues, he was touched in some measure by them all, from Charity downwards, including Temperance while in exile, and Prudence at home.

The admonition of Halifax at the very end of his *Character of King Charles II* (written some time after 1688) expresses the final mood of that time:

> Let his royal ashes then lie soft upon him, and cover him from
> harsh and unkind censures; which though they should not be
> unjust can never clear themselves of being indecent.

The author and publishers would like to thank the following individuals, museums, photographers and photographic archives for permission to reproduce their material.

1 Christie's, London; 3 By courtesy of the Board of Trustees of the Victoria & Albert Museum, London; 6 Manor House, Stanton Harcourt, Oxford (The Bridgeman Art Library); 8 Scottish National Portrait Gallery, Edinburgh; 10 above Museum of London, London; below Fitzwilliam Museum, Cambridge; 11 Royal Collection © 1993. Her Majesty the Queen; 12 National Portrait Gallery, London; 13 Royal Collection © 1993. Her Majesty the Queen; 15 above left Private Collection; above right British Library, London; below Private Collection; 16 Petworth House, Sussex (The National Trust Photographic Library); 17 Museum of London, London; 18 Rijksmuseum, Amsterdam; 19 above Wilton House, Wiltshire (The Bridgeman Art Library); below Private Collection; 20 Royal Armouries, H.M. Tower of London, London; 21 British Museum, London; 22 above British Museum, London; below British Museum, London (E.T. Archive); 23 British Museum, London; 26 above Christie's, London; below National Portrait Gallery, London; 27 left By courtesy of the Marquess of Salisbury, Hatfield House; above right British Museum, London; below right The Tate Gallery, London; 28 National Portrait Gallery, London; 29 Private Collection; 30 Royal Collection © 1993. Her Majesty the Queen; 31 Musée de Versailles, Versailles (Réunion des Musées Nationaux); 32 above, below, centre Scottish National Portrait Gallery, Edinburgh; 35 Alnwick Castle, Northumberland (The Bridgeman Art Library); 36 Sotheby's, London; 37 Private Collection; 38 British Museum, London; 40 British Museum, London; 41 Antony House, Cornwall (The National Trust Photographic Library) 42 above British Museum, London; 42-3 By courtesy of The Earl of Rosebery. On loan to the Scottish National Portrait Gallery, Edinburgh; 44 By courtesy of the Board of Trustees of the Victoria & Albert Museum, London; 45 British Museum, London; 46 above Private Collection; below Yale Center for British Art, Paul Mellon Collection, U.S.A.; 47 above Sotheby's, London; centre British Architectural Library, R.I.B.A. Drawings Collection, London; below British Museum, London (The Bridgeman Art Library); 48 British Museum, London; 49 National Portrait Gallery; 50 British Museum, London; 51 left University of Oxford for the Bodleian Library, Oxford; right Private Collection; 52 Private Collection; 53 National Library of Scotland, Edinburgh (The Bridgeman Art Library); 56 British Museum, London; 57 British Museum, London; 58-9 Smith Art Gallery and Museum, Stirling (The Bridgeman Art Library); 62 above left National Portrait Gallery, London; below left The Master and Fellows, Trinity College, Cambridge; below right The Master and Fellows, Trinity College, Cambridge; 63 above Fitzwilliam Museum, Cambridge; below Dyrham Park, Avon (The National Trust Photographic Library); 64 Holburne Museum, Bath (The Bridgeman Art Library); 66-7 Royal Collection © 1993. Her Majesty the Queen; 68 Boscobel House, Shropshire (English Heritage Photographic Library); 69 The National Trust Photographic Library, London (Jeremy Whitaker); 71 National Portrait Gallery, London; 72 British Museum, London; 76 above Christie's, London; below Victoria & Albert Museum, London (The Bridgeman Art Library); 77 above Private Collection (Angelo Hornak Library); below left Christie's, London; below right Ham House, Surrey (The National Trust Photographic Library); 78 The National Trust Photographic Library (John Bethell); 79 left, centre, right Christie's, London; 80 Private Collection; 82 Royal Collection © 1993. Her Majesty the Queen; 83 Private Collection; 84 British Museum, London; 85 York City Art Gallery, York (The Bridgeman Art Library); 86 Scottish National Portrait Gallery, Edinburgh; 88 Christie's, London (The Bridgeman Art Library); 90 National Portrait Gallery, London; 94 Christie's, London (The Bridgeman Art Library); 95 Private Collection; 97 Private Collection; 98 Cromwell Museum, Huntingdon; 100 left above, below The Master and Fellows, Magdalene College, Cambridge; right National Portrait Gallery, London; 103 Private Collection; 104 Private Collection; 105 above Private Collection; below Christie's, London (The Bridgeman Art Library); 106 Christie's, London (The Bridgeman Art Library); centre Ashmolean Museum, Oxford; below Sotheby's, London; 107 above Norfolk Museums Service/Norwich Castle Museum, Norwich; below left Museum of London, London; below right The Royal College of Music, London (The Bridgeman Art Library); 108 Royal Collection © 1993. Her Majesty the Queen; 110 By courtesy of the Director, National Army Museum, London; 111 National Portrait Gallery, London; 113 Private Collection; 119 British Architectural Library, R.I.B.A. Drawings Collection, London; 120-1 above, below left, below right Museum of London, London; 123 Royal Collection © 1993. Her Majesty the Queen; 124 above British Museum, London; below Exeter Cathedral Library, Exeter; 125 above Private Collection; below Cyril Humphris; 126 National Portrait Gallery; 127 Christie's, London; 129 British Architectural Library, R.I.B.A. Drawings Collection, London; 130 above Ashmolean Museum, Oxford; below By kind permission of the Right Honourable The Baron Harlech (Angelo Hornak Library); 131 above By

courtesy of the Board and Trustees of the Victoria & Albert Museum, London; below Welsh Folk Museum, St Fagan's; 132 above, below Yale Center for British Art, Paul Mellon Collection, U.S.A.; 133 left British Library, London; right above Belvoir Castle, Leicestershire (The Bridgeman Art Library); right below National Portrait Gallery, London; 134 National Maritime Museum, London; 140 National Maritime Museum, London; 141 National Maritime Museum, London; 142 left, right, below Museum of London, London; 144 Royal Collection ©1993. Her Majesty the Queen; 145 above British Museum, London; below Hulton-Deutsch Picture Library, London; 146-7 Sotheby's, London; 148 Museum of London, London; 149 Museum of London, London; 150 above Angelo Hornak Library, London; below left and right A.F.Kersting, London; 151 above left Angelo Hornak Library; below left A.F.Kersting; right Royal Society, London; 152 Musée de Versailles, Versailles (Giraudon-Bridgeman Art Library); 153 National Portrait Gallery, London; 154 left, right, below National Portrait Gallery, London; 155 above National Portrait Gallery, London; below Sotheby's, London; 160 Victoria & Albert Museum , London (The Bridgeman Art Library); 162 British Museum, London; 163 British Museum, London; 164 above Museum of London, London; centre O'Shea Gallery, London (The Bridgeman Art Library); below Private Collection; 165 above Museum of London, London; centre Private Collection; below British Museum, London (The Bridgeman Art Library); 166 National Portrait Gallery, London; 168 Ham House, Surrey (The National Trust Photographic Library); 169 British Museum, London; 170 left The Master and Fellows, Magdalene College, Cambridge; right Roy Miles Gallery, London (The Bridgeman Art Library); 172 above and below Private Collection; 173 above By courtesy of His Grace the Duke of Roxburgh, Floors Castle (The Pilgrim Press Ltd.); below Marble Hill House, Middlesex (English Heritage Photographic Library); 174 above Sotheby's, London; below Royal Collection © 1993. Her Majesty the Queen; 175 British Museum, London; 176 Audley End, Essex (English Heritage Photographic Library); 176-7 Museum of London, London; 178 above and below Museum of London, London; 179 left The Tate Gallery, London; right By courtesy of the Board of Trustees of the Victoria & Albert Museum, London; 180 above Sotheby's, London; below By courtesy the Board of Trustees of the Victoria & Albert Museum, London; 181 above By courtesy of the Earl of Bradford; 181 below left and below right Sotheby's, London; 182 Royal Collection © 1993. Her Majesty the Queen; 184 British Museum, London; 185 British Museum, London; 186 Felbrigg Hall, Norfolk (The National Trust Photographic Library); 190 British Museum, London; 191 Ranger's House, London (English Heritage Photographic Library); 193 National Portrait Gallery, London; 195 British Museum, London; 200 above left Christie's, London; above right Christie's, London (The Bridgeman Art Libary); below left and below right Museum of London, London; 201 above left Victoria & Albert Museum, London (The Bridgeman Art Library); above right Private Collection; below Christie's, London; 202 above left British Museum, London (The Bridgeman Art Library); above right By courtesy of the Board of Trustees of the Victoria & Albert Museum, London; centre Lady Lever Art Gallery, Port Sunlight (The Bridgeman Art Library); below Blickling Hall, Norfolk (The National Trust Photographic Library); 203 above left and centre right By courtesy of the Board of Trustees of the Victoria & Albert Museum, London; above right Private Collection; below left and right Christie's, London; 204 British Museum, London; 206 National Portrait Gallery, London; 207 Royal Collection © 1993. Her Majesty the Queen; 208 British Museum, London; 210 British Museum, London; 213 Sotheby's, London; 215 British Museum, London; 218-19 National Portrait Gallery, London; 221 above and below British Museum, London; 222 above By courtesy of The Governors of Christ's Hospital, Sussex; below Hulton-Deutsch Collection, London; 223 above left and below left Private Collection; above right Hulton-Deutsch Collection, London; below right British Library, London (The Bridgeman Art Library); 224 Thomas-Photos, Oxford; 226 Private Collection; 227 Ashmolean Museum, Oxford; 228 Cyril Humphris; 229 National Portrait Gallery, London; 232-3 British Museum, London; 234 above Private Collection; below British Architectural Library, R.I.B.A. Drawings Collection, London; 235 A.F.Kersting, London; 236 above Belton House, Lincolnshire (The National Trust Photographic Library); centre John Bethell, Hertfordshire; below Sotheby's, London; 237 above, below left, below right A.F.Kersting, London; 238 above Angelo Hornak Library, London; below Eric de Maré, Gloucestershire; 239 above Buckinghamshire County Museum, Aylesbury; below Peckover House, Wisbech (The National Trust Photographic Library); 240 National Portrait Gallery, London; 247 above and below Ampleforth Abbey Trustees © 1993, Yorkshire; 249 Royal Collection © 1993. Her Majesty the Queen; 250 Private Collection; 251 York City Art Gallery, York (The Bridgeman Art Library); 252 Private Collection; 253 Private Collection; 254 National Portrait Gallery, London; 256 Westminster Abbey, London By courtesy of the Dean and Chapter of Westminster.